T0247836

Advance Praise for *The CEO Playbook for Strategic Transformation*

"This book is a practical guide that will help any leader improve their chances of driving transformative change in their organization. Scott A. Snell distills the essence of successful transformations into four factors and provides enduring principles and frameworks that make success less of a mystery for leaders pursuing transformation efforts. With the pace of technology-driven change, I wish this book was available a decade ago!"
—Nilanjan Adhya, Chief Digital Officer, BlackRock

"A must-read for CEOs and business leaders whose ecosystems are evolving at record pace, *The CEO Playbook for Strategic Transformation* provides proven tools to set strategic direction and drive the organizational alignment required for successful transformations."
—Melissa Anderson, EVP and Chief People Officer, Albemarle Corporation

"Helpful read on the overall challenge of transformation and filled with practical insights to incorporate into your own transformation journey."
—Michael D'Ambrose, EVP and Chief Human Resource Officer, The Boeing Company

"Every transformation, like every sporting match, is unique. Scott A. Snell's playbook provides an array of effective tools to help leaders develop their transformation gameplan and plays to run based on the specific situation."
—William Phelan, Chief Financial Officer, The American Bar Association

*THE CEO PLAYBOOK FOR STRATEGIC TRANSFORMATION*

# THE CEO PLAYBOOK FOR STRATEGIC TRANSFORMATION

*Four Factors That Will Make
or Break Your Organization*

## Scott A. Snell

**STANFORD BUSINESS BOOKS**
An Imprint of Stanford University Press  ·  Stanford, California

Stanford University Press
Stanford, California

Special discounts for bulk quantities of Stanford Business Books are available to corporations, professional associations, and other organizations. For details and discount information, contact the special sales department of Stanford University Press by emailing sales@www.sup.org.

Printed in the United States of America on acid-free, archival-quality paper

Library of Congress Cataloging-in-Publication Data

Names: Snell, Scott, author.

Title: The CEO playbook for strategic transformation : four factors that will make or break your organization / Scott A. Snell.

Description: Stanford, California : Stanford Business Books, an imprint of Stanford University Press, 2024. | Includes bibliographical references and index.

Identifiers: LCCN 2023045729 (print) | LCCN 2023045730 (ebook) | ISBN 9781503634558 (cloth) | ISBN 9781503639195 (ebook)

Subjects: LCSH: Organizational change. | Strategic planning.

Classification: LCC HD58.8 .S6435 2024 (print) | LCC HD58.8 (ebook) | DDC 658.4/06—dc23/eng/20231206

LC record available at https://lccn.loc.gov/2023045729

LC ebook record available at https://lccn.loc.gov/2023045730

Cover design: Will Brown

Typeset by Newgen in Minion Pro 11/15

*Dedicated to Marybeth, my wife, who has led us on a thirty-six-year transformational journey together.*

A ship in harbor is safe, but that is not what ships are built for.

—John Shedd

# TABLE OF CONTENTS

## ACKNOWLEDGMENTS

While writing this book, I was continually reminded of the many quiet collaborators I have had in the process. Many of them don't realize just how influential they are in shaping my thinking and inspiring my work.

First, there is my family: Marybeth, Emily, Jack, Sara, Frank, little Hayes, and Jane. As I witness their lives and careers, I am inspired by what is possible and why challenges are worth the undertaking. I'm so proud of them and truly count my blessings.

There's a slew of business executives who have provided counsel and perspective over the years. Our transformation work together has been especially meaningful, and I'm grateful for their insights and experience, and for their encouragement during this project. Much of their wisdom is contained in these pages. They include Melissa Anderson (Albemarle), Ken Carrig (FutureSolve), Jim Clark (BGCA), Mike D'Ambrose (Boeing), Simon King (Daiichi Sankyo), Scott Price (DFI), Johnny C. Taylor (SHRM), and Betty Thompson (Booz Allen), to name but a few.

My academic colleagues have always been my intellectual heroes. I'm indebted to Tim Baldwin (UI), Shad Morris (BYU), Chuck Snow (PSU), Juani Swart (Bath, UK), Patrick Wright (USC), and others who have challenged and stimulated my thinking through their own thought leadership.

My colleagues at the Darden Business School, especially the strategy faculty, Mike Lenox and Jared Harris; the team in Executive Education, Jennifer Hicks and Ty Scheiber; and the pros at Darden Business Publishing, Jane Haxby, Steve Momper, and others. My initial framing and writing of this material were road tested on these folks, and they brought much more coherence to the text.

I'm honored that Stanford University Press wanted to publish this book. And I'm thankful for the editorial team of Cindy Lim, Richard Narramore, Kate Wahl, and especially Steve Catalano, who was the original champion of this project.

Finally, to wonderful friends and family who impatiently cajoled me with some version of the question "Is your book done yet?" Well, yes, it is now. (A copy is on the way.)

Thank you for the opportunity to share what I've learned from these people and many others. My hope is that this book helps shape your learning as well.

*THE CEO PLAYBOOK FOR*
*STRATEGIC TRANSFORMATION*

# 1 THE CEO'S BIGGEST CHALLENGE: THE PROMISE AND PERIL OF STRATEGIC TRANSFORMATION

ONE OF MY first jobs was at IBM in its Strategic Studies unit. It was the mid-1980s—a glorious era for IBM. The company's market cap made it the most valuable firm on the planet, and it dominated in virtually all its markets. Rivals used to lament, "IBM is not the competition, it's the environment." Its competitive advantage seemed unassailable. The company had incredible talent, including Nobel prize–winning scientists, and a continuous flow of technology advancements and innovative products.

But IBM stumbled badly when it missed the industry shift from mainframes to PCs. Many today are still unaware of just how dire the situation became and how close the company was to going under. (More about the underlying reasons for decline in chapter 6.) By the time Lou Gerstner was hired as CEO to replace retiring John Akers, IBM was losing more money than any company ever had up to that point in U.S. history—it reported an $8.10 billion loss in 1992 alone.[1]

What did Gerstner do? Well, he didn't have experience in the computer industry, but he had a record of transforming companies. He had turned around RJR Nabisco, and before that, he had rebuilt American Express. At IBM, Gerstner wasted no time launching what he called Operation Bear Hug, an initiative to reconnect IBM's senior leaders with customers and encourage them to listen more intently. Bear Hug revealed that customers wanted a new value proposition from IBM, one focused on integrated solutions (i.e., one-stop shopping for all things computing). The industry was changing rapidly, and the possibilities in computing were exploding. Customers needed someone to stand between them and that overwhelming confusion of opportunity. IBM promised that it would.

To make good on this promise, Gerstner restructured the company to get rid of bloat, selling off any part of the business that was non-core and assiduously eliminating excesses. But he did more than just slash costs. His reengineering initiative focused on improving process efficiencies, quality, and speed to market. The company began building new capabilities in hardware, software, supply chain, customer relationship management, and global services—the aspects most critical to IBM's promise of integrated solutions. Gerstner also made some difficult decisions to transform the venerated IBM culture to focus more on teamwork, execution, and winning business.

From its near-death experience, IBM emerged transformed. With a new strategy and a new market position, it was a new organization with new capabilities, wrapped in a new culture. Within two years, Gerstner's strategic transformation made IBM competitive again, with revenues in excess of $78 billion and a stock price that had quadrupled. By the time Gerstner retired in 2003, IBM's stock price had increased by 800 percent, and the company had regained its position as a technology leader. In truth, the company is not as dominant as it once was, but the story of Gerstner's transformation is still one of the classic lessons in strategic leadership.

On a personal level, my experience with IBM was life-changing, and it set me on a new course professionally to understand the phenomenon. I confess that in those early years my assumption was that great companies were enduring, and I had an implicit checklist of what made for a great company. You know the list—profitability, market share, brand, leading products, great talent, strong culture, and so on. IBM had all of that, but its rapid decline nullified that checklist. Great companies can falter quickly, and no one is immune. Since that time, my professional focus—and the reason for this book—has been to figure out how organizations can build opportunities for breakthrough performance, and to delineate the role of leadership in bringing that about.

## THE NATURE OF TRANSFORMATION: DIGITAL AND MORE

A CEO has no task more significant than undertaking strategic transformation. Why? Because large-scale strategic change involves major decisions about how to engage the external world and equally big decisions about how to organize internal operations. It truly requires a "total enterprise" perspective. The stakes are high, the prospects offer risk and reward obvious to all, and the chosen strategy sets the organization on a new path for the future. It is exciting.

And it typically doesn't go well.

IBM's experience illustrates that both inside and outside the organization, there are powerful forces reshaping businesses and industries—forces that compel leaders to dramatically rethink their enterprise. The impact is game-changing. For example, organizations today spend over $4 trillion a year on technology upgrades as part of the "digital revolution." Technological innovation is disrupting industries, creating new industries and new competitors, and changing the nature of competition.[2]

But while digital is part of the equation, there is more to strategic transformation than technology. Strategic transformation means altering the organization's strategy, structure, technology, and culture to meet the shifting demands of the environment. This is not middling change at the margin.

Some of the best companies have done this very well: think Amazon or Apple. Others have struggled: think Sears, Kodak, Blockbuster (the list goes on...). The truth is that change is difficult. And *strategic change* is especially difficult.

Here are a few sobering facts:

- Since the year 2000, more than half the Fortune 500 firms have declared bankruptcy, been acquired by another company, or simply ceased to operate because of industry disruption.[3]

- An IBM study of more than 1,500 executives showed that enterprise transformation ranked among their top concerns. The surveyed CEOs said their need to lead change is growing, but their ability to do so is shrinking.
- McKinsey found that over 70 percent of strategic change initiatives fail to achieve their objectives.
- Research by Willis Towers Watson showed that even when change initiatives are successful, the gains are sustained only 25 percent of the time.[4]

Take a moment to reflect on these data. The pattern is startling. Industries are being upended. Perennially, top firms are faltering and failing. CEOs see transformation as essential, but they're playing catch-up. Unfortunately, the vast majority of their change efforts prove unsuccessful or are short-lived.

## The Promise of Strategic Transformation

But the news isn't all bad. Some market leaders use strategic transformation to propel themselves forward, accelerating their lead and building competitive advantage. They get out in front of change, creating disruption for others.

A study by Boston Consulting Group (BCG) found that nearly 25 percent of companies undergoing transformation were top performers before the transformation as well as after. Strategic transformation can galvanize the organization around a promising future and align everyone in the firm toward the shared goals of enhanced value, innovation, and world-class capability.[5]

Why don't more organizations embrace this enlightened perspective?

The problem is that we often hold on to outdated assumptions about the process of change. Conventional wisdom used to be that transformation was undertaken only as a last-chance "Hail Mary" to save a company that was underperforming and out of options. This thinking was premised on the idea that successful organizations build a strong foundation that endures in the face of disruption and challenge. Even the phrase *sustainable competitive advantage* that we use in the world of strategy implies that change reveals a loss of advantage.

As a result, many CEOs are reluctant to engage in transformation unless there is a "burning platform" and the company is in crisis. In such cases, change is probably not strategic, but merely reactive, and the journey will be more difficult—and painful—for the CEO and everyone associated with the company.[6]

Fortunately, this way of thinking is increasingly archaic. In the BCG study, fewer than half the organizations undergoing transformation were chronic underperformers. Some were approaching change with a real sense of urgency, and some did so as part of an ongoing adaptive process. Either way, the transformation represented a new trajectory—and an opportunity for greater success.

But transformation is challenging. And its track record across companies is not great. There are three fundamental reasons why companies struggle with this.

### Complexity Is Confounding

First, enterprise transformation is difficult because it has a lot of moving parts. When teeing this up with management teams, I almost always begin by asking, "What is the most significant organizational change you have been through? What made it difficult?" Executives frequently say that the biggest challenge of change is making sure all the elements—structures, processes, technologies, talent, and culture—are synchronized with each other and the competitive world outside.

Organizations are complex. And there remains a significant gap between the intuitive idea of "change" and the realities of many elements that are interlinked and mutually dependent. When transformation efforts fail, it is most often because these elements are *not* synchronized: Some are stuck in the past, while the others forge the future. The system binds up, coherence is lost, and performance suffers. You've undoubtedly seen this.

The trouble is that while many managers recognize the complexities, they often don't truly *understand* them. In my experience, very few see the big picture of the entire enterprise. And if they do get a sense of this, they often see it only from their vantage point. In some ways, this is to be expected, given the way organizations are structured, departmentalized, and specialized. But if managers don't comprehend the complexity in its entirety, or if they get mixed messages from different corners, they will misread some of the key interdependencies needed for transformation. Worse, they might misdiagnose the problem and make changes in unnecessary or harmful ways, unleashing a barrage of unintended consequences that reverberate negatively through the organization.

So, as a starting point, if strategic transformation is to succeed, your approach must help managers see the complexity of the organization, understand how one element depends on another, act to build connections and complementarities, and minimize conflicts to achieve your collective goal. Strategic transformation requires system-level thinking and action. In that sense, it is a design puzzle.

### Disruption Is Unrelenting

The second reason transformation is difficult is because (ironically) change is constant. Globalization, digital revolution, geopolitics, economic shifts, regulations, disease, social issues, demographics: All these and more create unrelenting disruption.

Change is no longer an exception; it is the new normal. Some change we refer to as "continuing," like the steady path of progress in mature technologies of manufacturing. Continuous improvement strategies and optimization models impart a modicum of continuity even during periods of change. But much change is *discontinuous*, meaning it is abrupt, unexpected, and ill-structured. It is jolting upheaval after a period of calm. Discontinuous change can have great impact, and then recede—but with enduring consequences. Think of the COVID-19 pandemic and its profound global effect.[7]

Disruption is unrelenting because these discontinuous change events are layered upon one another, creating uncertainty and disorder, altering the calculus of economic, technological, political, and social environments in which organizations operate. It makes predicting the future more difficult, if not impossible.

Because of this volatility, strategy today is less about achieving stable competitive advantage and more about developing adaptive capabilities and energizing innovation in dynamic environments. Traditional strategies based on stable market positions, scale, or legacy advantages are increasingly ineffectual. Established business models run the risk of rapid obsolescence. The demise of organizations creates churn in industries, as dominant players are overtaken by new, agile rivals, leading to even more volatility.

What's the upshot of all this for leading strategic transformation? Well, at a minimum, we can conclude that traditional assumptions about change as episodic, linear, or sequential ("unfreeze-change-refreeze") are quickly becoming antiquated. Strategic change is not a "once and done." In today's environment, strategy is dynamic, agile, and nimble, and it requires flexible resource deployment. Unfortunately, most organizations aren't built for change. They're designed for stability and repetition, and changes are designed to solve yesterday's problems. Powerful forces lock these firms in place. I would argue that these organizations need not only to update their profiles, but also to upgrade their dynamic capabilities. Transformation is no longer an event; it is a strategic capability.

Think of unrelenting disruption as analogous to "permanent whitewater." If the outdated image of a successful company is a rowing crew sculling on a placid lake, perfectly synchronized, where only the coxswain faces forward and everyone else has their backs to the future, today's successful company is ready for permanent whitewater. The brittle shell of a rowboat would splinter in the rapids of, say, the Colorado River. A flexible rubber raft that can bounce through the rapids and off the rocks is needed instead. Given the urgency, every member of the team must turn around, face forward, throw one leg over the edge, and dig in. Teamwork is dynamic, requiring constant adjustment. The ride is thrilling.[8]

If strategic transformation is going to succeed in an environment of unrelenting disruption and permanent whitewater, your approach needs to build flexibility into the organization membrane to help it adjust and respond. It needs to support everyone as they deal with inevitable uncertainty, and it must help them work collaboratively to focus on what matters most: adapting to the waves of change.

## Change Is Risky

The third reason transformation is difficult is simply that change is risky. At a personal level and an organizational level, change incurs costs. You can think of risk as a function of those costs; that is, how much is at stake multiplied by the degree of uncertainty. Individuals are often reluctant to give up old routines or practices that have become comfortable, proved successful, or been reinforced by legacy reward systems. Personal risk may be the number one cause of resistance to change.

But change is risky at the organizational level too. Altering the strategy, structures, processes, systems, and culture in an organization risks endangering the firm's position in the market, relationships with key stakeholders, resource and information flows, decision processes, and expectations, throwing the organization into disarray and jeopardizing performance.

Because of this risk aversion, leaders often view transformative change as unadvisable. The paradox of execution is that many executives focus on the urgency of performance improvement, trying to get the organization to do better, when what they really need is to do is bite the bullet and do things differently (or do different things). Delaying transformation—perpetuating the status quo—has its own set of risks. Doing nothing in the face of disruption may be the riskiest proposition of all.

Don't get me wrong. Risk assessment and mitigation are vital to any transformation. If strategic transformation is to succeed, it must uncover the underlying sources of personal and organizational risk, and then address the causes of risk aversion. Doing so leads to better engagement and more informed decisions. Managing an acceptable level of risk is inherent to any strategic transformation.

So, if we put this all together, we can conclude a few things. On the one hand, strategic transformation is important because it can set the organization on a new path to higher value and better market performance, enhancing the organization's capabilities and competitive position. On the other hand, transformation is challenging because organizations—and environments—are complex, with many interdependent elements that are difficult to fully ascertain and even more difficult to manage as a system. When change is unending and volatility leads to increased risk, the organization could lag when it needs to lead, or pause when it needs to push forward. In this context, change may be hard to energize and sustain, as many in your organization experience change fatigue just when the transformation needs to accelerate.

Warren Bennis and Burt Nanus coined the acronym "VUCA" to describe this environment: volatility, uncertainty, complexity, and ambiguity profoundly influence the nature of decision-making, problem-solving, organizational response, risk, and change.[9]

In this sense, VUCA makes strategic transformation both more important and more difficult than ever. The increasing prevalence of organizations undertaking strategic transformation—and the increasing priority they place on it—is a direct result of these VUCA elements. The unfortunate failure rate, noted earlier, among those efforts is also a function of VUCA elements. It's not easy to bring order out of chaos. For these reasons, management guru Peter Drucker observed,

> One cannot manage change. One can only be ahead of it. In a period of upheaval, such as the one we are living in, change is the norm. To be sure, it is painful and risky, and above all it requires a great deal of very hard work. But unless it is seen as the task of the organization to lead change, the organization will not survive.[10]

In Drucker's view, if you're trying to "manage" change, you've already lost. He advised instead approaching transformation as a process of building an organization that perpetually manifests change, one that orchestrates agility from disruption as a source of advantage. That's a main theme for this book.

## BUILD A PLAYBOOK

With these points in mind, my goal for this book is to focus on contemporary challenges of strategic transformation, the promise it affords, and the perils and pitfalls it entails. Notice again the title, *The CEO Playbook*. I intentionally use the word *playbook* rather than *handbook* or *rulebook* for good reason. A playbook is not an instruction manual. It is not a lockstep sequence of formalized and codified steps, as though

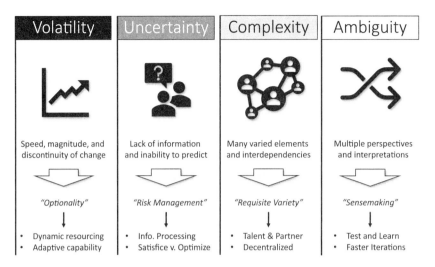

| Volatility | Uncertainty | Complexity | Ambiguity |
|---|---|---|---|
| Speed, magnitude, and discontinuity of change | Lack of information and inability to predict | Many varied elements and interdependencies | Multiple perspectives and interpretations |
| "Optionality" | "Risk Management" | "Requisite Variety" | "Sensemaking" |
| • Dynamic resourcing<br>• Adaptive capability | • Info. Processing<br>• Satisfice v. Optimize | • Talent & Partner<br>• Decentralized | • Test and Learn<br>• Faster Iterations |

FIGURE 1.1. Strategic Transformation in a VUCA World

the world were certain, programmed, and locked in. Instead, a playbook provides a set of tools for interpreting what's happening and highlighting the most promising sequences to guide coordinated action and performance. It is a collection of tested options to use as points of intervention to achieve your goals.

Most people associate a playbook with sports, but the logic extends beyond that. For example, musicians often use what is called a jazz playbook. In contrast to a libretto, which includes all the details in a set musical composition, a jazz playbook gives the essential chord progressions that provide the foundation for improvisation. A jazz musician listens and watches the other members in a group and plays off their contributions, adjusting accordingly. Having internalized the playbook, together they play in the shared foundational structure of melody and harmony to jointly create an outcome.

That's a pretty good analogy for the process of strategic transformation. In my experience, the application of "playbook logic" is useful because it helps you refine and adapt your approach to transformation *as the situation changes*. That frames transformation capability as a learning process—not just an implementation process. What follows is an elaboration of my approach, the logic that guides each of the chapters, the framework that ties the pieces together, and some practical tools for application in your organization.

## An Integrative Approach

First, my approach is integrative. Organizations are complex and transformation is multifaceted, but most books on leading change are limited to the social psychology of teams and the interpersonal aspects of change (and resistance to change), emphasizing the role of leaders in addressing these challenges. That's perfectly appropriate but provides only a partial picture. Strategic transformation extends beyond behavioral science and involves a more expansive approach, one with an enterprise perspective, where senior leaders integrate the broader cross-functional challenges of competitive strategy, innovation, economics, investment in organizational infrastructure, technology, and human resources.[11]

The multidimensional and dynamic nature of transformation makes the process elusive. This requires an integrative approach. Instead of adopting a psychological perspective, I frame the organization as an entire ecosystem of strategic change. That includes issues of business model transformation, technology disruption, stakeholder engagement, organizational orchestration, agile resourcing, culture, and the like. Strategic transformation requires that these all be aligned and mutually reinforcing.

After I published *Strategic Execution: Driving Breakthrough Performance in Business* (with Ken Carrig), executives I spoke with about their experiences suggested that I follow up with a new book on strategic transformation. In their view, guidelines for execution are helpful for improving performance using a firm's current strategy, but business transformation, which many were facing, requires new strategies, technologies, processes, skills, and cultures. In other words, they didn't just need to do things better, they needed to do things *differently*.

## Questions and Answers: Scenarios and Options

Second, my approach is designed to help you sort out the questions you should be asking about transformation, not just providing you with a blanket set of answers. Assistant Secretary of the Navy Elliott Branch often noted that "good leaders don't provide answers, they ask good questions." In other words, they make you think so that you can devise answers on your own.

Consequently, as we go through this book, I won't simply offer lists of the attributes of "best practice" companies that you should mimic. There is a strong temptation to do that, and in fact, many executive teams initially ask for that. But every organization is somewhat different. My approach is to provide guidance about the "zones of efficacy," places where effort and energy make the most impact on successful transformation.

To be sure, I'll give company examples to show how different organizations approach large-scale change. I'll provide scenarios that illustrate different options. The examples are instructive as much for the way executives frame the strategic questions as for the solutions they implement. None of these companies' leaders believe they have figured everything out or reached a threshold of best practice (even if they have). Their reluctance to claim victory is not false modesty. Instead, they explain where they have made progress, and they share the lessons they have learned along the way. But they are the first to note that what they did and what has worked for them in the past may not work for others. And it may not even work for them in the future. The nature of change itself is changing, and in the long run, understanding how to approach the challenge may be the most important thing.

## Multilateral Goals: Accurate, Generalizable, and Simple

Third, my approach is intended to achieve the same goals of simplicity, accuracy, and generalizability that I aimed for in my prior book, *Strategic Execution*. In science, these three are referred to as parsimony, internal validity, and external validity, and it is impossible to include more than two of these in any one experiment—or strategic business intervention. My work is grounded in research, and I focus on ensuring the accuracy and internal validity of my observations. These are reinforced by the practical experiences and case studies of exemplary firms. This book includes a variety of firms and industries to improve the generalizable inferences and external validity. And perhaps most importantly, I have kept you—the reader—foremost in mind. The value of my work is inherently dependent on its parsimony and usability.[12]

## FROM PRINCIPLES TO PRACTICE: REAL-WORLD CASES

My colleague Mark Haskins recently quipped, "In school, students learn the lessons and then they take the test. In life, you are tested first and then you learn the lessons." As you read this book, you'll note that I use several company case studies to show how they were tested and the lessons they learned. The examples help ground the key ideas and illustrate the challenges of strategic transformation. The short case vignettes are woven throughout the book and across chapters, enabling you to follow the journeys of these companies.

These case examples are intended to do three things. First, they demonstrate the experiences of companies and leaders: how they tackled the challenges of transformation, put their ideas into action, and moved from principle to practice. Second, the company examples illustrate what went right, what went wrong, and the nature of the journey. Every case study is a bit different, but they share some common features that I'll reinforce throughout the book. The trick for any organization is to determine how best to approach transformation, given its unique circumstances and goals. The variety of these circumstances and approaches will hopefully enrich your understanding of the phenomenon. Third, by threading the stories throughout the book, you can perhaps better see the continuity of action and learn how their efforts evolved and built on one another.

One word of caution. Case studies are a stimulus for thinking. These organizations are different from yours, and part of the value of example is sorting out what is similar to, and what is different from, your situation. The cases bring the transformation principles to life and reveal how these organizations converted ideas into action. But it is the principles, not the individual practices, that are the key takeaways.

The companies that illustrate these principles are as follows:

## Mayo Clinic

Mayo Clinic is a global leader in health care, medical innovation, and patient care. Based in Rochester, Minnesota, the clinic employs a staff of 76,000, including more than 4,500 physicians and scientists, in an integrated business model that combines clinical practice, education, and research. Offering treatment for complex cases requiring specialized care, Mayo Clinic cares for about 1.4 million patients, from all 50 states and 130 countries, each year.[13]

Mayo Clinic originated in 1864 from the medical practice of William Worrall Mayo, MD. His sons, William James Mayo and Charles Horace Mayo, went into practice with their father by 1888, and soon other partners joined, creating what would become the world's first "integrated group practice."[14] Mayo's philosophy was that the field of medicine was growing so quickly that no one person could acquire or absorb all the knowledge. Doctors needed collaboration for sharing expertise and providing specialized care.

**Mayo Clinic's Transformation Challenge:** Given today's advances in medical science, technological innovation, global demographic shifts, and changes in the regulatory environment, Mayo Clinic has made a commitment to be on the forefront of transformation in the industry. As it looks to the future, Mayo is exploring new business models and delivery modes in an effort to reach more people in more places, improving health and well-being around the world.

## Microsoft

Microsoft is the world's largest software company. Its Windows operating system and Office suite of products defined the market standard for PC software. The company was founded in 1975 by Bill Gates and Paul Allen, and owing to its partnership with IBM during the 1980s, it grew to a virtual market monopoly for decades. Today, Microsoft has approximately 221,000 employees, revenues of $200 billion, and a market cap of nearly $2 trillion.

Satya Nadella was promoted to CEO in 2016. During the preceding decade, while Steve Ballmer was CEO, Microsoft was very profitable, but its share price remained essentially flat. Why? In short, investors didn't see long-term growth prospects or future cash flows because Microsoft was not keeping up with industry trends.

**Microsoft's Transformation Challenge:** Nadella's transformation challenge was to help Microsoft pivot from its nearly exclusive focus on desktop computing to a "mobile-first, cloud-first" strategy. To achieve that, he needed to deal with entrenched interests in the firm's legacy products and reinvigorate the culture to encourage a "One Microsoft" approach to innovation.

## Chalhoub Group

Chalhoub Group is the largest luxury retailer in the Middle East. Based in Dubai, the company was founded in 1955 by husband-and-wife team Michel and Widad Chalhoub, and today it is run by their son Patrick Chalhoub, who serves as CEO. From its inception, Chalhoub Group developed a reputation for excellence, mastering the art of selecting retail partners, working with high-end luxury brands, and nurturing critical relationships. Capitalizing on the expanding business network in the Middle East and Africa, Chalhoub leveraged its knowledge of the region and its expertise in distribution and marketing to build out a network of 750 stores in 16 countries, including more than 125 joint ventures, affiliates, and firms. The Group's partnerships include brands such as Puig, L'Occitane, Estée Lauder, Christian Dior, Louis Vuitton, Tory Burch, Swarovski, Lacoste, and more.

**Chalhoub Group's Transformation Challenge:** The transformation challenge for Chalhoub is to complete the shift to e-commerce and omnichannel retailing. The internet profoundly disrupted the retail landscape, giving consumers a greater range of fashion items, localized collections, rapid delivery models, and competitive prices. Chalhoub needed to reconceive its value proposition and business model to address the new calculus in luxury retail. Business as usual—even executed well—would not be sufficient.

## Unilever

Unilever is a multinational consumer goods company operating in 190 countries. Its most venerable brands include Ben & Jerry's, Dove, Lifebuoy, Lipton, Hellmann's, and others. Lever Brothers was founded in 1885 by brothers William and James Lever, who built a successful soap-making business (Unilever is still the world's largest soap producer). Through a series of mergers and acquisitions, the company became Unilever in 1929.

Today, the company has 148,000 employees, organized into three main divisions: Foods and Refreshments, Home Care, and Beauty & Personal Care. It conducts research and development in China, India, the Netherlands, the United Kingdom, and the United States.[15] Sales exceed $60 billion, and Unilever's market cap is approximately $125 billion.

Unilever has an enviable legacy of successful businesses, but it was particularly buffeted by the economic downturn following the financial crisis of 2008. Paul Polman, then the CFO of Nestlé, was hired as Unilever's CEO in 2009 to revitalize the company.

**Unilever's Transformation Challenge:** Polman's challenge was to sort out the complexity of Unilever's businesses, reconcile competing interests among category managers and operating companies, boost employee morale, reassure stockholders by reducing costs and improving profitability, reengage customers, and build market share. Polman realized that doing all this would not be possible without dramatic change. He needed to lead a bold transformation to deliver growth and serve customers, while at the same time improving the environmental footprint and sustainability of the organization.[16]

## New York Police Department

Established in 1845, the New York City Police Department (NYPD) is one of the oldest police forces in the United States. Today, with a staff of over 55,000, including more than 35,000 officers, NYPD is also one of the largest municipal police departments in the country. It has a fiscal budget more than $10 billion, and it operates 20 bureaus, including Patrol, Transportation, Investigation, and Counterterrorism. NYPD has led innovation in policing, notably with its 1994 introduction of Comp-Stat, a computer-based crime data tracking system, now utilized by other police departments in the United States and Canada.

NYPD has had successes and setbacks. Bill Bratton was appointed police commissioner in 1994, and he served two terms (1994–96, 2014–16), having previously served as the police commissioner in Boston (1993–94) and Los Angeles (2002–9). When he first arrived at the NYPD, the city was in the midst of a decades-long crime wave caused by an epidemic of crack cocaine. The city incurred over a half a million felonies per year, and many constituencies were resigned to the idea that the battle could not be won. NYPD had become reactive, merely responding to crimes after they had been committed. Prevention seemed unachievable. The police force was underpaid, underfunded, and hard to control; it had devolved into a set of turf battles.[17]

**NYPD's Transformation Challenge:** Bratton's transformation challenge was to revitalize the NYPD, upgrade the force, instill pride, bolster collaboration and accountability, build new capabilities, reduce political gamesmanship, instill confidence among constituencies, and eradicate crime in the city. Ultimately, Bratton needed to make New Yorkers feel safe again.

## Airbnb

Airbnb has revolutionized the hospitality industry, rewriting the rules of lodging and tourism. Founded in 2008 by Brian Chesky, Nathan Blecharczyk, and Joe Gebbia, Airbnb's business model is built around the platform concept: Airbnb serves as a "home-sharing" broker connecting customers with property owners. Airbnb does not own the properties but charges a commission for each booking. The company grew quickly, and by 2019, it had more than 6 million rental listings on its platform in over 100,000 cities across 200 countries.

Then the COVID-19 pandemic hit. As the coronavirus tore across the world, reservations plummeted 72 percent in April of 2020, from about 31 million a year before.

**Airbnb's Transformation Challenge:** As CEO, Brian Chesky's challenge was to respond quickly to the pandemic, reframe the company's value proposition, focus on its core business, and reconcile the sometimes-competing interests of various stakeholders, including customers, property owners, shareholders, and employees. Without agile transformation, Airbnb's entire business was in jeopardy.

## THE CEO AND MANY OTHERS

Do you see parallels between these companies and your organization? My guess is that, based on their disparate experiences with change, you will draw some insight into the keys to transformation. And that may help you understand your organization's journey and your role in it. There are many audiences for this book: senior-level executives, middle-level managers, consultants, students, and some academics. Each has a different need, a different viewpoint, and a different set of experiences.

CEOs and other senior-level executives may find most useful the enterprise perspective offered by those at the top of their firms and the playbook logic that guides their approach. The case studies and examples in this book are framed by this perspective and the roles of CEOs and their teams, and they help to set the agenda.

Middle-level managers are often the most directly affected by transformation challenges, as they must put into practice the strategic imperatives. They make the change happen—and they have responsibility and accountability to drive change through others. Many of my executive MBA students and clients are in this cohort, and they often tell me this material stretches their thinking, helping them develop an enterprise perspective more encompassing than their current role. This proves to be developmental in ways that prepare them for the future.

Any reader may value the accessibility of this book's framework in that it captures the key priorities for addressing the transformation challenge. There is much complexity underlying the simplicity of the model, but the framework is designed to capture the essential lessons in a way that emphasizes usability.

This book may also be useful to academic audiences, faculty, and students. It is based on my research and consulting and has been "road-tested" in courses at the University of Virginia's Darden School of Business and elsewhere. It is applicable to both MBA and Executive MBA classrooms. As I often say to my students and clients, some of you may be responsible for formulating the transformation strategy, but *all* of you are responsible for executing it.

I'll also introduce a set of self-assessments and diagnostics to help leaders and others calibrate where they stand on key elements of transformation. This helps them begin to think about priorities for action. When I use these tools with management teams, they spark robust conversation and debate, and help these leaders focus on the most important levers for change. Where they disagree, they confront the realities of those differences. Where they agree, they can begin to devise a plan for implementation. To that end, I also provide a set of application guidelines to ground the ideas, as well as a playbook for developing a game plan for practical action.[18]

My goal in writing this book is to help you better understand the challenges of strategic transformation, enabling you to develop a straightforward, practical approach to engage others to achieve breakthrough performance. If you're in a position to make a difference, this book distills the complexity and insights of managerial experience into a usable framework for action. And it provides a set of tools for translating your strategic ambition into the practical realities of your organization.

Your journey to understand strategic transformation will reveal myriad things to consider. To be sure, I do not claim to have all the right answers, or that these answers are right all the time. However, based on my experience and lessons learned from senior executives, I provide a succinct set of insights, practices, and interventions that you can apply to your organization.

# 2  FOUR FACTORS OF SUCCESSFUL TRANSFORMATION

ALTHOUGH LARGE-SCALE TRANSFORMATION involves many elements, leaders need to prioritize and focus on the things that matter most: those make-or-break factors that determine success versus failure. After all, as Michael Porter put it, "strategy is about making choices." This is true of strategic transformation as well. When leaders determine the most crucial factors, they can use them as levers for change.[1]

One executive observed, "CEOs only have a few levers they can pull, but they *are big* levers."[2] Many assume that CEOs have limitless access and control over almost any resource or activity in the firm. While that may be true in theory, in practice most CEOs don't operate this way; they reserve discretion, avoid micromanagement, and rely on others to do their jobs.

In developing this book, I asked CEOs and other senior executives, "What are the big levers of critical action that—in your experience—made the biggest difference in transformation?" They told me stories of both successes and setbacks, and, drawing on their experience framing the issues for their organizations, they explained their implicit theories of transformation and shared the lessons they had learned along the way. Some had been through multiple transformations—some successful and some less so. Every company is a little different, and there were some idiosyncratic issues unique to individual leaders and their firms.

But across a wide swath of organizations, several common features consistently topped the list.

Four key levers are essential to successful strategic transformation. Let's refer to them as the "four factors." When organizations succeed in transformation, it is because they do these four things well. And when the transformation fails, these four are most often uncovered in the postmortem (see Figure 2.1).

These four factors are as follows:

- *Establish context: Define and communicate strategic intent and rationale.*
- *Engage stakeholders: Differentiate primary and secondary partners.*
- *Orchestrate mobilization: Convert vision into action.*
- *Cultivate change agility: Build dynamic capability.*

## THE FOUR FACTORS FRAMEWORK

Spoiler alert: CEOs are not the only ones addressing these four factors. In fact, part of the secret of successful transformation is that the responsibility is shared by others in the organization. CEOs own the transformation and are accountable for the outcomes, but they rely on many collaborators to implement these four factors.

As an aside, most executives appreciate the simplicity of this framework. In fact, they require it. They acknowledge the complexity of transformation and the myriad considerations involved, but as one CEO said, "I can't attend to fifty things." They need a concise framing of priorities to focus attention and monitor progress, while still capturing the intricacies of the process.

It is important to note that simple does not mean simplistic. These four factors make up an intentionally accessible model for transformation, but they involve many other requisite actions and obligations. It reminds me of what Supreme Court Justice Oliver Wendell Holmes said about effective jurisprudence: "The only simplicity for which I would give a straw is that which is on the other side of the complex—not that which never has divined it."[3]

Let's preview each of the four factors.

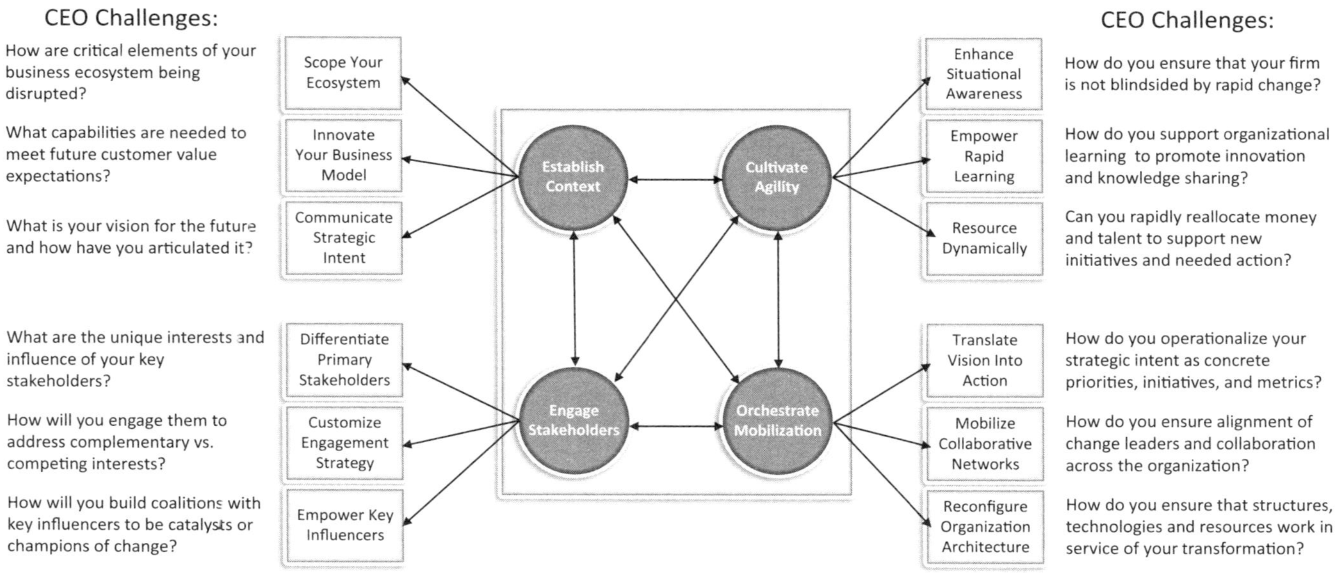

**CEO Challenges:**

How do you ensure that your firm is not blindsided by rapid change?

How do you support organizational learning to promote innovation and knowledge sharing?

Can you rapidly reallocate money and talent to support new initiatives and needed action?

How do you operationalize your strategic intent as concrete priorities, initiatives, and metrics?

How do you ensure alignment of change leaders and collaboration across the organization?

How do you ensure that structures, technologies and resources work in service of your transformation?

**CEO Challenges:**

How are critical elements of your business ecosystem being disrupted?

What capabilities are needed to meet future customer value expectations?

What is your vision for the future and how have you articulated it?

What are the unique interests and influence of your key stakeholders?

How will you engage them to address complementary vs. competing interests?

How will you build coalitions with key influencers to be catalysts or champions of change?

Enhance Situational Awareness

Empower Rapid Learning

Resource Dynamically

Translate Vision Into Action

Mobilize Collaborative Networks

Reconfigure Organization Architecture

Cultivate Agility

Orchestrate Mobilization

Establish Context

Engage Stakeholders

Scope Your Ecosystem

Innovate Your Business Model

Communicate Strategic Intent

Differentiate Primary Stakeholders

Customize Engagement Strategy

Empower Key Influencers

FIGURE 2.1. Four Factors of Transformation

## Establish Context

The first factor required for successful transformation is to establish the strategic context. Alvin Gouldner, one of the pioneers of organizational analysis, summed it up this way: "Context is everything." (Apparently, a man of few words.) What he meant was that organizational action makes sense only if people understand the circumstances surrounding it, the conditions precipitating change, and the outcomes they can anticipate as a result. Establishing the strategic context for transformation—if done well—answers the question "what's going on here?" A coherent diagnosis makes the job easier, clearer, and more likely to succeed.[4]

Let's unpack this a little more. Boiled down to its essence, the process of establishing the context for transformation involves two parts. The first is to distill the many influences driving change from inside and outside your organization into a "simpler story that calls attention to its crucial aspects."[5] You'll need to recognize them, make sense of them, and discern the opportunities available to the firm and the associated risks. This is the heart of strategic analysis. Doing this will help you gain understanding before taking action.

The second part of establishing context is to convey that understanding, and the perspective that it affords, to colleagues in your firm and other relevant stakeholders, communicating in a way that is compelling and actionable.[6]

There are a few critical reasons why establishing context is so foundational. First, it anchors your transformation in the broader reality of the business, including the current situation, the relevant past, and the expected future. Context gives you the background conditions and circumstances of time and place, providing what psychologists call "figure/ground" perspective and helping you distinguish focal objects from background, especially where this distinction is ambiguous. Context helps cut through the uncertainty to reveal and prioritize what is important—and why it is important—giving you clarity about what meaningful insights and inferences you might draw from events. In short, context shapes your understanding of the business within its environment.

But context is more than retrospective; it is also prospective. It gives you clues about how the future might be taking shape, suggests ways to synthesize and refine events, information, and data, and helps you interpret new information going forward. What should you attend to, and what patterns do you notice? What opportunities do you see coming, and what problems need to be solved? Context motivates change—or at the very least gives you incentive to find the avenues and tools to drive change.

These are straightforward questions, but the reality is that the answers are often not well understood. Trying to take action without understanding all the background elements can lead to errant decisions. Far too often, transformation efforts go off the rails before they get going, principally because leaders have not done a good job of establishing the strategic context for change.

In my experience, a few tasks are most critical for establishing the strategic context for transformation. They include the following:

- *Scope your business ecosystem.* Begin by conducting a business review, mapping changes in the broader value network, and spotlighting key environmental trends, opportunities, and threats. This helps you define the scope of the environment and establish criteria for making strategic decisions. Throughout this book, we'll discuss a variety of potential disruptors, particularly the impact of technological innovation and digital disruption.

- *Innovate your business model.* Determine future customer value requirements and audit your business capability gaps. Much of your strategic transformation hinges on this step. The first immutable rule of strategic transformation is that it needs to improve the connections between your capabilities and customer value.

- *Communicate your strategic intent.* Communicate with colleagues and other stakeholders, explain the rationale, and share your ambition to inspire others in the journey. They will not likely contribute to large-scale transformation without a compelling reason. Their motivation begins with shared purpose.

Establishing the context for change puts your organization on a more solid footing, with a clearer trajectory. As we go through this material, we'll address questions such as the following: What are the key elements of your business model, and how do these stack up against your evolving ecosystem of partners? What are the key disruptive trends that are redefining the parameters of competition and value creation in your industry? Importantly, how has this been communicated to others? Your answers to these questions set the stage for what Bob Johansen calls a new form of VUCA, one that stands for "vision, understanding, clarity, and agility."[7]

### Engage Stakeholders

The second factor required for successful transformation is to engage key stakeholders. We often define stakeholders broadly as "anyone who can affect, or is affected by, the actions of your company." In this sense, your strategic transformation involves a number of key stakeholders, and the success of your endeavour depends on their alignment and support.[8]

General George Casey described the challenge of stakeholder engagement when he was chief of staff for the U.S. Army. As he recalled, "Building external support was real senior leader business. No one taught me how to do this. I had to figure it out. It began when I realized that the higher I got, the more the keys to my success lay outside my organization, and that for the organization to be successful, I needed to spend more time influencing people outside of my control to support my efforts."[9]

Too many executives still underestimate the importance—and impact—of stakeholder engagement. Ironically, some believe stakeholder management is so inherent in their business that they don't give it explicit attention. Consequently, it doesn't play a strategic role.

Organization ecosystems are more complex than many executives initially guess. Value creation is a multiparty affair, and many of the interdependencies become so implicit that they are tacit and taken for granted. However, as you contemplate changes in your organization and business model, cracks may begin to form. Pay attention to those: They are likely pressure points for stakeholder engagement, or lack thereof. Think carefully about how your actions, investments, and strategies will affect your partners, and—just as importantly—how your partners will respond. What will be your strategy for engaging them?

Take transformation in the auto industry for example. As companies such as Ford, GM, Volkswagen, and others accelerate their journey toward electric vehicles (EV) and away from internal combustion (IC) engines, they confront a host of suppliers, partners, manufactures, employees, unions, regulators, distributors—and customers—who are also part of that transformation. Let's just look at suppliers. Research by PwC estimates that the contribution of power train and electronics to a car's value will increase from 44 percent in 2015 to 52 percent by 2025, with the battery pack accounting for up to half an EV's value. But this significant rise occurs at the expense of other components.[10]

In Europe alone, estimates are that perhaps 500,000 jobs will be displaced in the traditional supply network, and these losses will not be fully offset by growth in new EV suppliers. According to a report by the European Association of Automotive Suppliers, the traditional automotive supply and manufacturing sector, including related services like tire manufacturers and automotive support, employs approximately 7.3 million people in Europe alone.[11]

The challenge of stakeholder engagement in this case is that while customers and many shareholders might embrace the shift to EVs, supplier groups and labor unions might not. Whatever strategies these auto companies take toward transformation, they need to consider—and engage wisely with—their associated stakeholders.

That's our focus. There is a growing body of evidence that effective stakeholder management makes all the difference to your transformation success. And research by McKinsey suggests that senior executives understand this. Nearly 60 percent of respondents in the study said that "engaging stakeholders" ranks among their CEOs' top three priorities. However, despite this expressed need—and increasing commitment to stakeholder engagement—their success rate is much lower. Only 7 percent of executives said that their organizations frequently align the interests of stakeholders with those of their businesses.[12]

This is a troubling statistic, especially when you consider that this research data is across *all organizations*. The challenge of stakeholder engagement is even greater for organizations going through strategic transformation.

To help you gain traction in engaging stakeholders, we'll focus on a few key actions. Note how they are interrelated:

- *Differentiate your primary stakeholders.* Assess their influence on performance as well as their interests (the positive or negative impact of the transformation on them). This will elevate the importance of stakeholder engagement and make it an explicit part of your planning.
- *Customize your engagement strategy.* Modify your approach based on the importance of the relationship over time and the degree to which stakeholder interests are complementary or competing. One size doesn't fit all where stakeholder engagement is concerned, and your organization benefits by attending to the issues that are unique to each stakeholder or stakeholder group.
- *Empower your key influencers.* Find the key influencers who are in a position to make a difference. Because your organization is multifaceted, it is wise to consider which natural coalitions are advocates for transformation and have a vested interest in moving things forward and can be trusted to take the lead. Enrolling them early will generate broader involvement.

As you consider your own organization, think about questions including the following: Who are your key stakeholders, what are their interests, and how might they influence the success of your strategic transformation? Do you have proven approaches for engaging them productively, understanding their concerns, and managing their expectations? How do you align and empower key influencers and advocates to help define and lead strategic initiatives? Where are the potential pitfalls and how do you address them?

Often, given the urgency of performance, leaders focus their efforts too narrowly, and miss the broader scope of transformation. Stakeholder engagement is a discipline to ensure that all relevant parties are aligned in the transformation.

## Orchestrate Mobilization

The third factor required for successful transformation is to orchestrate its mobilization. This involves the purposeful design of coordinated action: equipping, deploying, and organizing the networks of people, technologies, and other resources needed to make large-scale change happen. There is an old aphorism attributed to various people, including Desmond Tutu, Saint Francis of Assisi, and Kung Fu Tze (Confucius) about how best to eat an elephant. The answer, of course, is "one bite at a time." Start with what's needed, then move on to what's possible, and soon you find you are doing the impossible.[13] Personally, I like this idea; it appeals to my sense of order and incrementalism. Regrettably, there's not much support for it when it comes to orchestrating strategic transformation.[14]

Some leaders understandably want to take the process "one step at a time." But the conventional wisdom of incremental and sequential change—improving first one part, then the next—is flawed. The approach might have worked in the past, during an era of relative stability and linear change. However, today most truly strategic transformation efforts "cut across business units and functions, target both the top and bottom lines, and engage a substantial share of the workforce."[15] Leaders need a different approach that fully embraces the complexity of organizations—and deals with it head-on—to bring about transformation.[16]

Piecemeal strategies that move one part at a time miss the mark in two ways. First, they are fragmented. And because your organization is multifaceted, the facets are interconnected and complementary. Move one without the other, and the first becomes a constraint for the second. You lose the synergies, or, worse, the pieces conflict. As Richard Rumelt, author of *Good Strategy, Bad Strategy*, put it, "To have punch, actions should coordinate and build upon one another, focusing organizational energy." Orchestration is difficult because it involves synchronizing and coordinating multiple elements of strategy, value creation, organizational design, technology, culture, and more. Either they all work together as a coherent system, or they don't. Small wonder that it is a challenge for many organizations.[17]

Second, piecemeal approaches aren't just fragmented—they're slow. Change takes time, but slow change often equals no change. The challenge of orchestration is to initialize movement, generate energy conversion, and sustain momentum toward a new and better place. In their book *Built to Change,* Ed Lawler and Chris Worley wrote, "A traditional organization must know how to disrupt the strong inertial forces in it that favor the status quo. Few organizations have a change capability—much less the inclination to change—so they fail to invest in orchestration."[18]

Momentum shifts depend on the collective intentions and ambitions of those involved. The tipping point for energy conversion occurs when there is buy-in and shared ownership of the vision of the future. It is strengthened through mutual expectations and values embedded in the organization culture. Movement toward its realization is supported by performance metrics, incentives, and rewards.

Orchestration is made more difficult in one other respect. Although the logic of transformation is inherently "from this to that," leaders need to run the current business successfully while they create or scale the new one. So, consider how your organization is building collaborative platforms for change. How are you resourcing these networks to focus on key initiatives? How are you upskilling the workforce and redesigning processes, data systems, and information flows to develop new capabilities? And finally, what are you doing to build a culture that champions change?

To orchestrate mobilization, it's important to keep a few key things in mind. Each emphasizes that transformation occurs by design. It is not just a human effort; it is rooted in a revised organizational infrastructure.

- *Translate vision into action.* Operationalize your vision for the future by establishing key initiatives that are pivotal in building capability to drive performance and value. These initiatives will help convert your vision into action and focus the organization on the most critical business imperatives and investments.
- *Mobilize your transformation networks.* To activate the transformation, alignment at the top needs to be clear to all, conveying one

unified voice to others; appoint a transformation team to lead key initiatives and harmonize cross-functional collaboration within the business; and leverage strategic partnerships to build capability and co-create value. Channeled toward mission critical outcomes, these efforts generate better enterprise-wide coordination, traction, and momentum within the organization as a whole.

- *Reconfigure the organization architecture.* The architecture of your organization can either propel transformation or hold it back. To mobilize the organization, streamline your structures around customer value; customize technology deployments to optimize operational, relational, and transformational impact; and refresh, reframe, or reform your culture to support the vision. Great orchestration focuses on those ideas and actions that have the greatest potential to deliver on key strategic imperatives, concentrating resources and energy to drive performance, and configuring the organization to ensure collaboration across the enterprise.[19]

## Cultivate Change Agility

The fourth factor required for successful transformation is to cultivate change agility. Jack Welch, former CEO of General Electric, once observed, "There are only two sources of competitive advantage—the ability to learn more about our customers faster than the competition and the ability to turn that learning into action faster than the competition."[20]

Learn faster; act faster. That's the essence of agility.

In chapter 1, I noted that strategic transformation is not a "once and done." In today's high-velocity environments where change is inexorable, strategic transformation depends on being continuously nimble and responsive, requiring a more anticipatory approach to change and discontinuity.

The facts bear this out. A recent *Forbes* survey of 1,000 global executives found that 81 percent considered agility to be the "most important characteristic of a successful organization." In a nutshell, these executives believe the rapidly evolving requirements of customers in a VUCA environment necessitate continuous flex and innovation.[21]

The incentives for achieving agility are also significant. Firms that do so attain faster time to market and innovation, as well as improved customer experience, product quality, and employee morale—all by over 50 percent.[22] In turn, these factors fuel revenue growth, profitability, and shareholder value.

In interviews for this book, executives consistently admitted that agility is a conundrum for them—they know it is increasingly vital in their business, but they admit they have yet to master it. Research by Gary Neilson, Karla Martin, and Elizabeth Powers supports that this is a challenge. In their study of 250 organizations, they found that most struggle to operate with agility. Approximately 60 percent of employees gave their companies a low rating, and when confronted with the statement "Important strategic and operational decisions are quickly translated into action," the majority answered no.[23]

Some executives see agility in reactive terms; that is, their goal is to be quick enough to cope with changes occurring in the environment. Rapid reaction is an important aspect of agility. But others see agility "more proactively, opportunistically, sensing possibilities, rapidly learning, and continuously innovating into new spaces." In their view, agility is not just a necessary organizational response, it is part of their strategic posture to shape the future.[24]

In other words, for some, agility is seen as an *instrumental* mechanism to help facilitate transformation. For others, agility is the *rationale* for strategic transformation; their aim is to drive the VUCA elements. At its zenith, agility generates innovation, which creates disruption for others, and the ability to gain a first-mover advantage.

The requirements necessary to cultivate change agility might be surprising. Part of the secret is creating the capacity for rapid adaptation and learning. But another part of the secret is maintaining continuity and stability in the face of change. That may seem counterintuitive at first. But the reality is that agile organizations aren't constantly reinventing themselves. Their approach to transformation is to stay focused and attentive while continuously adapting and updating the connections between their capabilities and value creation.

Here are a few general guidelines for managing agile transformation:

- *Enhance situational awareness.* Stay focused on purpose and strategic intent, develop deeper customer insights, improve your peripheral vision of boundary conditions, and probe the environment to detect and explore early trends. Lack of agility is often the result of being flat-footed when confronted with surprises. Improving your situational awareness gives you an early warning system.
- *Empower rapid learning and innovation.* Establish a climate that encourages initiative and rapid learning by empowering decision-making; enabling experimentation, testing, and learning; and incubating innovation.
- *Accelerate dynamic resourcing.* Share information widely, reallocate talent, and develop a more flexible budgeting process. These elements of *dynamic resourcing* will help your organization build a stronger core, which is important for increasing speed in the process of renewal.

One final point on agility: Notice that the title of this factor is *cultivate* change agility. The capacity to adapt quickly becomes an enduring characteristic of the organization culture, and it needs to be developed and shaped over time.

In doing background research for this book, I spent some time with Scott Price, CEO of DFI Retail Holdings Group. As we discussed his experience cultivating change agility, he emphasized, "Underline culture three times—it's that critical!" Part of the challenge is that culture is an intangible asset—it is very difficult to manage directly. Cultivating change agility involves some very tangible elements of the organization that shape the values, behaviors, and expectations that underlie change agility.

## THE SYSTEM OF STRATEGIC TRANSFORMATION

These four factors—establishing context, engaging stakeholders, orchestrating mobilization, and cultivating agility—are each important aspects of strategic transformation. And you likely see how they build on one another. They are complementary, and in combination, their impact multiplies.

For example, when your executive team establishes the context for transformation and clarifies the strategic intent, it becomes easier to engage stakeholders and customize your interactions with them. Reciprocally, by engaging stakeholders and knowing their interests and influence, you develop a better understanding of the context you're operating in and of the most important elements of your ecosystem. In contrast, failure to establish the strategic context for transformation will short-circuit stakeholder relationships, either because your initiatives are uninformed or because they are antithetical to stakeholder interests.

I'm sure you get this intuitively, but it is worth thinking through explicitly with your own firm. As you read this book, consider how each of the four factors influences or enables the others. For example, when you establish the context for change, you're priming the pump to orchestrate mobilization. When you communicate your vision and strategic intent, it becomes the impetus for prioritizing business imperatives and defining key initiatives. The combination of these sets up the means-ends connections, which in turn focus the deployment of your transformation teams. Stakeholder engagement envelops these initiatives and builds further momentum. And finally, when you cultivate change agility into this transformation, the organization takes on characteristics of a self-renewing system. That's the goal.

Now a small disclaimer: These four factors are presented sequentially in this book, but that's merely a literary convention. You can see how they are reciprocal and mutually reinforcing. The sequential presentation of chapters has an accessible logic, but it is a bit mechanical. Leading strategic transformation requires that you step back from the mechanics of the framework to manage the simultaneous connections of the entire system.

As shown in Figure 2.2, this four-factor framework builds on two key dimensions of contemporary strategic management: (1) organization-environment, and (2) divergence-convergence.

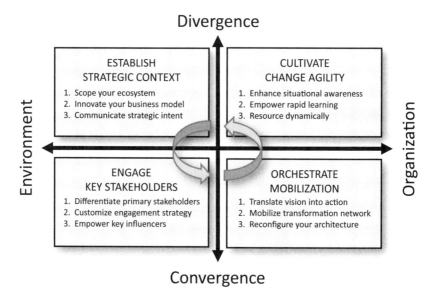

Divergence

| ESTABLISH STRATEGIC CONTEXT | CULTIVATE CHANGE AGILITY |
|---|---|
| 1. Scope your ecosystem | 1. Enhance situational awareness |
| 2. Innovate your business model | 2. Empower rapid learning |
| 3. Communicate strategic intent | 3. Resource dynamically |
| ENGAGE KEY STAKEHOLDERS | ORCHESTRATE MOBILIZATION |
| 1. Differentiate primary stakeholders | 1. Translate vision into action |
| 2. Customize engagement strategy | 2. Mobilize transformation network |
| 3. Empower key influencers | 3. Reconfigure your architecture |

Environment — Organization

Convergence

FIGURE 2.2. System of Strategic Transformation

### Environment and Organization

The first dimension of the framework reflects the connection between your organization and its environment. At its root, strategy is designed to improve how your organization positions itself within that emerging competitive landscape. Strategic transformation is predicated on the need to rebalance internal resources and capabilities relative to external opportunities and threats. Some aspects of transformation focus more on recognizing and attending to environmental change, while others emphasize changing the internal organizational configuration. Getting the right combination of these two is critical.

By way of application, consider how your leadership team would establish the strategic context for transformation. Analyzing your business ecosystem involves conducting a business review to determine whether your organization is properly situated in its environment, delivering customer value, and driving growth. This also involves conducting an internal analysis regarding key performance metrics and capability gaps. Ultimately, the challenge for your leadership team is to connect the external and the internal.

Engaging stakeholders also balances external and internal considerations. This occurs on two levels, the first obviously being that some of your key stakeholders are external (e.g., customers, suppliers, etc.) while others are internal (e.g., employees). But the organization-environment duality also defines the *relationship* with stakeholders. Take, for example, shareholders or the board of directors. On the one hand, they are part of your team: equity holders with a vested interest in the success of the firm. On the other hand, they are part of the environment: entities with independent interests to which they hold the firm accountable.

The challenge of strategic transformation is to maintain balance and alignment between the organization and the environment. Organizations get into trouble when this balance is lost. Too much emphasis internally during transformation risks the possibility that the firm will lose perspective on important environmental shifts or competitive dynamics (recall the IBM story in the last chapter). But too much emphasis on the external environment draws attention away from the important work of capability building and employee engagement, which can be just as destructive.

The essence of strategy—and the goal of transformation—is to realign the organization in its environment, reconfiguring internal resources and capabilities with external sources of value. You'll see examples of this throughout the book, particularly in our case studies of Mayo Clinic, Unilever, Microsoft, and others. Mayo Clinic's transformation was designed to realign its business model and delivery modes to reach more people in more places, dedicating its considerable expertise to improving health and well-being around the world. Microsoft's transformation was to pivot to a "mobile-first, cloud-first" environment and shift its structures, technologies, talent, and culture to this new environment.

## Divergence and Convergence

A second dimension underlying the overall system of transformation is the balance between the forces of divergence and convergence. *Divergence* implies that you're doing things differently, either from the past or from others. *Convergence*, on the other hand, implies bringing things together, unifying and integrating disparate elements to achieve coherence. There is a duality in organizational transformation that necessitates both.

During transformation, your organization necessarily departs from the past, creating new ways of working, new innovations, new structures, new paths to market, new business models, new sources of value—all forces of divergence—while at the same time bringing resources together, aligning interests, creating coherence and efficiencies that unify the overall system.

An important aspect of managing this divergence-convergence duality is that an increase in one requires a proportional increase in the other. In other words, the more divergence from the past, the higher need for convergence toward the future. This is perhaps most evident when considering employee resistance to change. If the change is small or incremental, with little divergence from the past, resistance is likely to be minimal—go with the flow. However, when the organization diverges substantially from prior practice, it creates more uncertainty and more risk for employees. Large change can make people freeze with fear. In these cases, your leadership team needs to make more substantial investments to communicate, educate, and motivate people to take the leap.

Similarly, transformation can increase the complexity in your business ecosystem and the diversity of your stakeholders, bringing richer resources and broader opportunities. But that also brings a divergence of interests and ways of working. Those divergent forces necessitate an equal investment to reconcile differences and reestablish convergence around an aligned business model. (More on this in chapters 3 and 4.)

Examples of this divergence-convergence balance can be found throughout the transformation process. Leaders see this firsthand when they orchestrate mobilization. The variety of strategic initiatives and the multitude of resources required can splinter an organization during transformation, leading to chaos and entropy. Leaders need to counterbalance the divergent forces inherent in these initiatives—all of which may be critical—with an equal degree of convergence, collaboration, and coordination. This is a point I'll elaborate on in chapter 5.[25]

## HOW TO USE THIS BOOK

With this overall system of strategic transformation as background, the next four chapters explore each of the four factors more deeply: establish the strategic context (chapter 3), engage key stakeholders (chapter 4), orchestrate mobilization (chapter 5), and cultivate change agility (chapter 6). In these chapters, we'll see some of the unique contributions each makes to the process of transformation.

The format of each chapter is as follows: Each begins with a short scenario from one or more of the example companies (Mayo Clinic, Microsoft, Unilever, etc.) as a prelude to the themes in the chapter. That will give you a quick glimpse of their transformation challenges and where they are in the process. The idea is to cue you into issues represented in the chapter.

Second, I'll share some symptoms of poor transformation: where things go wrong, why they go wrong, and how to spot the warning signs. You may recognize some of these symptoms based on your own experience, and that may help ground the topics in the reality of your firm. But rather than linger too long admiring the problem, we'll quickly move to the next section, "What You Can Do."

In each chapter, the "What You Can Do" section tees up three main subheadings in the chapter that cover key principles for moving transformation forward. I'll revisit the examples of Mayo Clinic, Microsoft, Unilever, NYPD, Chalhoub Group, and others to illustrate how the principles translate into their practice. As you read the chapter, you'll see how these companies progressed in their transformation, and sometimes where they stumbled.

At the end of each chapter, I'll conclude by summarizing the key points in a section called "Reality Check." The idea is for you to take time to reflect and do a quick self-assessment to calibrate where your organization currently stands regarding each of the four factors. After that, I provide some "Playbook Tools" to help you work with your team to apply the materials in your organization and take concrete action to build your own playbook.

In chapter 7, I'll provide some additional guidance about how you can use the framework and engage others on your team or within your organization to develop a game plan for transformation. This includes how to use the materials and diagnostics prior to undertaking transformation to better prepare, build capacity, and establish plans of action to improve your odds of success. It also includes what you can do during transformation to continually analyze where things stand and realign your efforts and interventions. Finally, the chapter includes guidance on conducting interim or after-action reviews.

Let's get started.

# 3 FACTOR ONE—ESTABLISH CONTEXT: DEFINE AND COMMUNICATE STRATEGIC INTENT AND RATIONALE

**KEY PRINCIPLE:** To be successful, transformation must begin with a clear strategic intent grounded in thorough knowledge of emerging trends.[1]

**BEFORE BECOMING CEO** of Mayo Clinic, Dr. John Noseworthy spearheaded the clinic's 2020 Initiative, a comprehensive study of the U.S. health care industry in order to guide Mayo's strategy for business transformation. The 2020 Initiative was designed to establish the context for change by identifying key parameters of disruption in the industry, determining the nature of interdependencies and innovation, and projecting how the nature of medical care—and competition within the field—was evolving. Within this strategic context, the 2020 Initiative drove Mayo's plan to transform with an eye toward 2030.[2]

Unilever's story was very different. When Paul Polman was hired as CEO in 2009, he inherited a business that was no longer working well and had developed a troubling legacy of underperformance. For nearly three decades, Unilever's management had been mired in a struggle between operating companies that prioritized growing local markets through diversification, and Category Coordinators, business-oriented teams focused on shoring up falling profitability. Unilever's matrix structure wasn't working, and as its market share and financial performance deteriorated, the company found itself faltering. By contrast,

Procter & Gamble, Unilever's main competitor, was charging ahead. During the financial crisis of 2008, Unilever's stock price plummeted 35 percent. Customers began defecting, shareholders were dejected, and employees felt demoralized. Obviously, this wasn't the best of circumstances under which Polman would begin a new job as CEO. But to turn things around, he needed to come to terms with the situation.[3]

And then there was Microsoft. When Satya Nadella was promoted to CEO in 2016, he knew better than almost anyone that his company needed a hard pivot toward cloud computing and mobile technology. To lead the transformation, Nadella needed to establish the context for change, not so much to uncover industry dynamics—Nadella knew very well how the industry was evolving because he had been leading Microsoft's cloud business—as to help others see what was happening and help them to stop relying on Microsoft's dominant position in PCs and desktop computing. Because the company was very profitable and had an enduring leadership position in the market over the prior decades, Nadella had to change the perspective and mindset of others in the organization.[4]

One more example involves the Chalhoub Group, a luxury retailer based in Dubai. In 2019, the firm encountered what CEO Patrick Chalhoub described as a perfect storm in luxury retailing. Weak oil prices, political developments in Europe, and a slowdown in the Asian economy all collided with the growth of the internet and e-commerce. Despite its considerable success over the years, Chalhoub experienced unprecedented upheaval, and significant change was necessary if the Group was to sustain its reputation for excellence.[5]

## THE CHALLENGE

Each of these stories illustrates the importance of the first factor of transformation: establishing the strategic context. Putting things in context helps us to better understand the circumstances driving change, the conditions that make it necessary, and the ways in which the organization will be more effective as a result. Some aspects reflect external elements of the broader environment, and some focus internally on the state of the business. *Both matter.* Some elements of establishing context emphasize information gathering, interpretation, learning, and diagnosis, while others emphasize sharing that knowledge, communicating, and shaping the expectations of people in the organization (and beyond).[6]

In this chapter, I'll elaborate on the stories of Mayo Clinic, Unilever, Microsoft, and Chalhoub to take a deeper dive into what some say is the "make-or-break" element of strategic transformation. Consistently and emphatically, senior executives say that any transformation must begin with a thorough understanding of the business ecosystem. And that understanding needs to shape the key decision parameters and narrative with others. Without first establishing context, change initiatives can easily be ill-informed or misguided.

## Symptoms of Missing Context

There are some pretty clear signs when a transformation process is launched without the crucial first factor. Perhaps trumpeting their "bias for action," leaders sometimes forge ahead boldly without establishing the strategic context for change. Unfortunately, this boldness can be hubris in disguise.

Some symptoms of missing context reflect that change was undertaken without the benefit of a comprehensive understanding or integrative point of view. Other symptoms are lagging indicators reflecting that leaders did not explain the rationale for change or clarify the "why" of transformation, where it was going, or how things would be better. See if you recognize any of the following:

**Solutions looking for problems.** Some years ago, I was hired to facilitate a strategic planning session for a large insurance company. The CEO was new and eager to make an impact. He assembled his direct reports, all of whom postured, pitched, and promoted their own agendas—competing with the others and trying to convince the CEO of what they believed were the best investments for the firm, devoid of broader considerations. A team of rivals such as this has some potential positives, not least of which is the diversity of opinions and perspectives that could obviate a tendency toward groupthink. However, I observed two negatives in this interaction that diminished its potential. First was how little these C-suite executives learned from one another—about the firm or about the broader context of their business. They advocated their own interests and didn't really listen to anyone else. The second observation was that their competitive win/lose tactics prevented them from aligning around a set of key priorities for the future. What was supposed to be a strategic planning session devolved into a tournament of self-interest and justification. The CEO had failed to establish the strategic context, and the result was a rather predictable quagmire of confusion.

In any transformation, particularly those involving business turn-around or new leadership, there is pressure to show progress and demon-strate results. While understandable, that urgency can lead to rash deci-sions that are uninformed by a thorough understanding of the situation. The result may be that in solving one problem we create several others.

**Disjointed, isolated, and incomplete change efforts.** Inad-equate understanding of context can also mean disregarding how change in one part of a company affects and is affected by so many other components and stakeholders; complexity can bog you down. In sessions with executives, I'll ask them what holds back change, and they often say, "The organization wants to pull us back to the status quo." Just as they start to make progress, entrenched routines, regulations, bureaucratic rules, and self-interested stakeholders an-chor the organization in the past. These countervailing forces need to be accounted for up front as key elements in the overall system of transformation.

The hallmark of systems thinking is a recognition of the intercon-nected nature of change: Each element in a system is linked to all the rest, in a mutually interdependent and reciprocally causal network. Change only one part in isolation from the rest, and the broader system pulls it back. As we saw in chapter 1, research by Willis Towers Watson showed that even when change is initially successful, the results recede. Part of the reason change is so often unsustainable is that the larger con-text of the system perpetuates the status quo.

This is especially true with digital transformation. Executive teams feverishly invest millions in technology upgrades, without situ-ating those investments within the overall strategic context of the organization, particularly with regard to customer value. As a result, they don't make corollary investments in processes, infrastructure, talent, culture, and the like (more on this in chapter 5). Many of these technology investments become internally focused and fragmented, failing to take into account the customer experience and broader industry evolution. As Gartner's Mark Raskino put it, "Sometimes an enterprise may misread a situation from the outset by, for example, failing to examine how digital forces will change an industry or having an insufficient corporate mission to see and seize product and business model innovation. Not having a strong understanding of what is happening in your industry can lead to a superficial or narrow scope of change for any digital transformation."[7]

**Nobody on the bus.** Not long ago, I was conducting a series of executive workshops in Australia. In one of the sessions, a participant told me a story of a turnaround initiative at the Metro city bus system. As the story goes, the bus system was underperforming because drivers were notorious for running late, routinely operating horribly behind schedule. To drive change (pun intended) and achieve better on-time performance, the management team incentivized bus drivers to follow strict timetables. Surprisingly, the drivers immediately hit the mark. And in a single day, the buses were all running perfectly on time. And they were completely empty! The compliant drivers were now rolling right by the bus stops, not picking up passengers. (But they were on time.)

We might reasonably doubt the veracity of some elements of this story, especially whether the drivers were truly oblivious to the implications of their actions. But the anecdote highlights the generalized lesson that compliance does not equal commitment. People can be unintentionally—or willfully—blind to the larger context of transformation and focus on what they're told to do without considering why.

Resistance to change is often a result of people not knowing the rationale behind or purpose for change—the *why*. Without that richer understanding, employees might dutifully comply (whether their compliance is in the spirit of the change or not)—or they might resist. When I ask managers why leaders don't convey the why of change, they admit it is because they often don't know it themselves. Yes, in an uncertain world where change is both necessary and ambiguous, detailing the rationale for transformation can be difficult. But that doesn't absolve executives from explaining it. It actually makes establishing the context for transformation more important.

## What You Can Do

These symptoms are familiar to many executives. Rushing forward with change initiatives without first establishing context is a common mistake. It is motivated by a sense of urgency and anxiety about the enormity of the process.

In chapter 2, I briefly outlined a few things you can do to set the stage more effectively for transformation, giving it a higher probability of success:

1. *Scope your business ecosystem:* Conduct a business review, map changes in the broader value network, and spotlight key environmental trends, opportunities, and threats.
2. *Innovate your business model:* Determine future customer value requirements and address capability gaps to create that value.
3. *Communicate your strategic intent:* Provide a compelling vision, rationale, and ambition to others in the organization.

Let's discuss each of these steps in more detail—one at a time—as we go through the rest of this chapter. A quick word of warning: In today's hyperdynamic environment, you need to move quickly because agility is a top priority. Establishing context proceeds more effectively if it is done on an ongoing basis. Don't wait until change is imminent and then try to learn all that you need. That job is nearly insurmountable given its complexity. Relatedly, don't fall into the trap of "analysis paralysis." The inability to make a decision due to overthinking a problem is often the result of gathering too much data without analyzing the underlying patterns to discern important trends. There are diminishing returns to each of the processes I'll discuss in the chapter. The job of the leader is to establish context while avoiding unproductive wrangling and move forward.

## STEP 1: SCOPE YOUR BUSINESS ECOSYSTEM

The essence of a business is outside itself.[8] When A. G. Lafley, former CEO of Procter & Gamble, looked back over his career, he concluded that there is one critical job that *only* the CEO can do. And that is linking the outside world—of customers, technology, the economy, society, and so on—with the inside world of the organization. To do that, Lafley said, the CEO must first "define the meaningful outside." In other words, it is important to scope the external environment and establish criteria for articulating what is most important among the myriad demands facing the organization. While you and I may not agree that *only* the CEO can do this work, Lafley's point that this is a crucial step is still valid.[9]

In today's business environment, your organization operates as part of a complex and evolving ecosystem of interdependent firms. Virtually no one is exempt, as no organization operates alone. Your transformation must take that into account. The process of creating, growing, and serving customers is a joint endeavor that involves a network of interconnected parties, each of whom brings some specialized set of capabilities and resources. Understanding the nature of those multilateral relationships—how that *ecosystem* creates value—is necessary for preserving its associated benefits and must also be an input into any plan for strategic transformation.

As a starting point, recognize that the complexity of your ecosystem can be an asset or a liability. Take just one example. A joint study by the Organisation for Economic Co-operation and Development (OECD) and World Trade Organization (WTO) illustrated how the increased growth of global value chains has resulted in more segmentation of production and services and, correspondingly, more interconnectedness of firms and entire economies. Today, more than half of manufacturing imports are intermediate goods (such as parts and semi-finished products), and more than 70 percent of services imports are intermediate services. These relationships confer advantages to buyers and suppliers, to large and small firms, and to manufacturing and service businesses.[10] However, there are associated challenges. We all experienced how, during the COVID-19 pandemic, the complexity of these networks exacerbated supply chain problems.[11]

The modularity of value chains—through outsourcing, offshoring, alliances, and the like—is not particularly new. Automobile manufacturers have been orchestrating complex networks of suppliers and distributors for nearly a century. But the OECD-WTO study makes clear that the scale and scope of these ecosystems is growing exponentially. Trade liberalization, cheaper and more reliable telecommunications, and information-management software have dramatically lowered the coordination costs among interdependent companies.

To many organizations, managing the complexity of these relationships is not easy, but they view it as a necessary cost of doing business that gives them access to cheaper labor or materials, specialized expertise and services, alternative sourcing, favored markets, and more. However, while some companies just tolerate the complexity, others see it as an asset.

Leading firms, such as Google, Amazon, and Airbnb, understand that the complexity of their ecosystems is a source of market power, based on network externalities. They have built their strategies around orchestrating increasingly complex ecosystems, where the value is derived from the relationships among parties rather than just the flow of resources. Oher firms are following suit, and building platform ecosystems is one of the primary drivers of digital transformation.

**Define the scope of your ecosystem.** A key aspect of establishing strategic context is defining the scope of your ecosystem. Let's take a lesson from Mayo Clinic. When John Noseworthy initiated Mayo's 2020 Initiative, he formed a steering committee to map the clinic's ecosystem of patients, providers, doctors, partners, and research centers within a matrix of target populations and potential growth initiatives. The process helped distill the complexity of a full spectrum of health care needs into an easily digestible framework that gave Mayo insights into how health care would evolve in the future. Externally, the industry was being redefined by two overarching factors: digitalization and the Affordable Care Act (ACA). Noseworthy and his team recognized that both the economic and delivery models of medicine were changing rapidly, and that would influence both the evolution of Mayo's customer/patient value proposition and the delivery systems, capabilities, and business models it needed for the future. As Dr. Gianrico Farrugia put it, "Really, you don't just fix health care by fixing health care, but you have to fix the whole system around it, from education, to government to regulation."[12]

In the midst of all this change, Mayo had been expanding its footprint beyond its three facilities in Minnesota, Arizona, and Florida. Mayo's ecosystem now included a network of seventy clinic-owned hospitals, specialized research centers, and education facilities, as well as multiple strategic alliances with partner providers in other parts of the United States and internationally.

Noseworthy and team needed to take all this into account to determine Mayo's best path forward and initiate a transformation that would require a significant change and augmentation to its business model. But Mayo Clinic also needed to consider all its key constituencies: doctors, nurses, staff, alliance partners, regulators, and so on. And perhaps most importantly, in establishing the context for change, Mayo needed to keep its patients and families front and center. The Mayo Model of Care highlighted the mission "to inspire hope and contribute to health and well-being by providing the best care to every patient through integrated clinical practice, education and research."

The 2020 Initiative gave Mayo Clinic a clearer understanding of the strategic context for transformation, how the industry was evolving, the circumstances behind it, and why change was necessary. And it gave Mayo options. Importantly, the process provided clarity to the steering committee, executive team, and board of directors—not just for making decisions about transformation, but also for communicating its rationale and allocating resources to the process.[13]

**Involve others in the process.** Noseworthy's decision to create a steering committee highlights the importance of involving others in the process of data collection and interpretation. A. G. Lafley's guidance notwithstanding, while it ultimately may be the CEO's job to link the outside with the inside, others in the organization can—and should!—participate in the process of defining the meaningful outside.

Sometimes, executives do what is known as a "Gemba Walk." (*Gemba* means "the actual place" in Japanese.) Executives go into the organization and seek input from the rank and file to gain a different perspective. Research clearly suggests that strategic transformation is more successful when employees are involved. There are a few key reasons for this. Up front, the experience and expertise of others can help improve the process of collecting information and interpreting sometimes-ambiguous signals from the environment. Research by Ed Lawler and Chris Worley found that companies built for change "make a large investment in conversations and reflection, particularly among the senior management." On the back end, when others have participated in the process, they tend to have a stake in its outcome. This sets the stage so that later, any strategic transformation will be led by, but not exclusively owned by, the CEO. (More on this in chapter 5.)[14]

Note also that involving others often includes connecting with external stakeholders in your network, a topic for chapter 4.

**Leverage Your Business Review**

Because business ecosystems are multifaceted, the process of analyzing them gets complicated very quickly. There is often a temptation—a logical bias really—to establish context by first scoping the external environment broadly to identify key trends in the industry. There's nothing inherently wrong with that approach; in fact, this work eventually needs to be done.

But in my experience, it's better to engage others by drawing a tighter analytical circle around your business.

Here's why. If the purpose is to establish the context for change, an immediate, proximate, and concrete way to do so is to evaluate the core state of your business. What's working? What's not? One of the most direct ways to do that is by conducting a business review, not just to identify performance gaps, but to scrutinize the key drivers of your competitive position and business performance. Roll up your sleeves and face the facts—both positive and negative. There are several ways to do this, but my advice is to get clarity on the following three key interrelated parts that form the foundation of your business model:

- *Customers.* Who are your target customers? What differentiated value are you providing? What are your channels to them? What are your relationships with them like over time? What are the key metrics, and how are you doing on each?
- *Capabilities.* What is your operating model? What are the end-to-end capabilities—combinations of processes, systems, and talent pools—that deliver value? What are key metrics for each, and how are you doing on them? How do you compare to your peers?
- *Financials.* What is your economic imperative? Specifically, what are your firm's financial position, long-term aspirational targets, key revenue streams, and cost structure? How are you doing relative to your plan, and where are the opportunities to improve? Do you need to rein in debt prior to transformation (lest it be underpowered)?

Your business model is, among other things, the story of your business. It conveys how things work as a system and how the pieces fit together. Conducting a business review is the groundwork for developing your strategy going forward (markets, channels, products, etc.), and it gives you context for communicating with employees. If you want to establish a rationale for transformation, there is no better way to do so than by telling a story of the business. As Joan Magretta, former editor of the *Harvard Business Review*, said,

> Because a business model tells a good story, it can be used to get everyone in the organization aligned around the kind of value the company wants to create. Stories are easy to grasp and easy to remember. They help individuals to see their own jobs within the larger context of what the company is trying to do and to tailor their behavior accordingly. Used in this way, a good business model can become a powerful tool for improving execution.[15]

An IBM study found that two-thirds of CEOs said that extensive changes were needed in their business models to compete in the future. Yet surprisingly few undertook the effort. Follow-on research by Mark Johnson, Clayton Christensen, and Henning Kagermann indicated that "few companies understand their existing business models well enough—the premise behind its development, its natural interdependencies, and its strengths and limitations." As a result, while strategic transformation and business model innovation are seen as valuable—even necessary—they usually do not happen.[16]

Wait, what? Executives really don't understand their own business models? Taken out of context, this phenomenon seems almost inconceivable. But think about it. What's your experience? Most managers, even senior executives, concentrate on a narrow part of the business, perhaps a function or a singular division. Their job is often internally focused, driving results in a particular area of responsibility, accountable to hit the key performance indicators (KPIs) and metrics by which their part of the business is calibrated. They miss the broader insights into the organization as a whole, and so they fall short when it comes to enterprise thinking.

When working with management teams, we often develop a thumbnail sketch of their business using a tool called a "business model canvas" developed by Alex Osterwalder. Maybe you've used it yourself. A quick mock-up for Mayo Clinic is shown in Figure 3.1.[17]

The beauty of the canvas is its simplicity. You can work through a series of related questions about customers, value creation, channels to market, capabilities, resources, and the economic fundamentals of the business: the very factors to consider when conducting a business review. It no longer surprises me to see how difficult it is for some management teams to chart their business model cleanly. It is more challenging than most imagine, until they do it themselves.

My advice is, don't wait. Make this a regular part of your business review.

Unilever CEO Paul Polman's transformation strategy was predicated on his first engaging the organization in a thorough business review. The process revealed myriad problems in Unilever's business model. In addition to the challenges of its matrix structure and competition among operating companies and category heads, Polman had to deal with the fact that the company's stock price continued to fall. Financial analysts were impatient for change and increasingly adversarial, so much so that Polman suspended giving quarterly earnings guidance. Revenues flattened and then declined. Developed markets in Europe and North

| Key Partners | Key Activities | Value Propositions | Customer Relationships | Target Customers |
|---|---|---|---|---|
| • Mayo Clinic Care Net<br>• Technology partners | • MMC=clinical practice<br>• Education<br>• Research<br>• Administration | • Preeminent provider of complex hospital care<br>• Keep patients healthy<br>• Meaningful experience<br>• Operational excellence<br>• [Risk: commoditize brand] | • MMC= inspire hope, contribute to health and well being by providing best care<br>• Patient centered care<br>• Long-lasting | • Patients Here<br>• Patients There<br>• Patients Everywhere<br>• Providers<br>• People/Consumers |

| | **Key Resources** | | **Channels** | |
|---|---|---|---|---|
| | • Medical knowledge<br>• Med school, etc.<br>• Proton Beam Therapy<br>• Center for the Science Health Care Delivery<br>• Ctr. Regenerative Med.<br>• Ctr. Individualized Med. | | • Clinic campuses (3)<br>• Mayo Health System<br>• Mayo Clinic Care Net<br>• Mayo Medical Labs<br>• Marketing events<br>• Social media<br>• Global Bus. Sol. (D2C) | |

| Cost Structure | Revenue Streams |
|---|---|
| • Physician salaries (Foundation doesn't share financial gains)<br>• Staff personnel expense<br>• Facilities, supplies and services<br>• Capital expense (new initiative requires significant investment)<br>• Acquisitions [potentially dilutive] | • Fee for service<br>• Medicare, Medicaid (CMS) reimbursement<br>• Pioneer ACO program – value add [Mayo opted out]<br>• Subscriptions-based alliance (Mayo and partner health systems)<br>• Support/gifts from benefactors (to new Centers) |

FIGURE 3.1. Business Model Canvas: Mayo Clinic. (Adapted from Alexander Osterwalder and Yves Pigneur, *Business Model Generation*, Wiley, 2010. This work is licensed under the Creative Commons Attribution-Share Alike 3.0 Unported License. Designed by Strategyzer.com.)

America had stalled, and emerging market growth slowed as well. Polman's early assessment was that 80 percent of the growth needed to turn the company around was in these emerging economies. But achieving more growth in these regions would prove difficult because over 50 percent of Unilever's current business was in developing countries, a higher proportion than any of its competitors.

Polman had challenges in the supply chain and in distribution as well. Although Unilever had a laudable reputation for supply chain management, Polman and team found too much waste and too many inefficiencies in the system. He knew Unilever needed to take costs out, improve quality, and work toward more sustainable sourcing.[18]

Among other analyses, the Corporate Social Responsibility (CSR) group conducted a "brand imprint" study to identify the environmental, social, and economic impact of Unilever brands. Karen Hamilton, who led the team, recalled, "We identified the major sources of our greenhouse gases, water and waste. This was soon after Paul become CEO and just before the UN's Copenhagen Climate Change Conference, so the data became vital input for the change that followed."

As part of his business review, Polman conducted a talent review and a culture audit. Based on this, within a year Polman had replaced a third of his top executives, including the chief financial officer, chief marketing officer, and heads of key business units. Polman observed that underlying Unilever's problems was a culture that was "internally focused and self-serving." In his view, the company needed to rekindle its enduring philosophy of "doing well by doing good." His challenge was to stimulate growth, reduce expenses, improve margins, reengage customers, and inspire employees. Polman's conclusion was that Unilever's business model was no longer appropriate and needed changing. Within this context, he set about reimagining the company.[19]

Unilever's situation is not unique. Many organizations go through cycles of decline, where business models need revitalization—if not complete overhaul and reinvention. But Polman is a particularly insightful leader who understood the implications of what he uncovered in Unilever's business review. And he used it as a foundation for establishing the context and rationale for business transformation.

## Map Your Broader Value Networks

One element that complicates your business review is the realization that delivering on your customer value proposition typically involves external partners. Some of these partnerships are arm's length and transactional, but others are closely aligned and interdependent. Establishing context for strategic transformation requires identifying your key partnerships, understanding the nature of interdependencies, and recognizing how they are evolving. Changing your business may strengthen some of these relationships and jeopardize others.

For example, Microsoft developed a hard-earned appreciation for the importance of partnerships as it began competing in the mobile phone market. Among many different partners in its ecosystem, Satya Nadella and team focused on a few critical ones: mobile phone vendors and app developers.

As Microsoft launched its Windows Mobile operating system, vendors were reluctant to work with the company. Rumor was that many feared Microsoft would dominate them the way it had done with PCs. Microsoft's legacy of near-complete market power—owing to its virtual monopoly in desktop computing—was scaring vendors off.

As a result of low market share, Microsoft couldn't induce app developers to join up. Software developers preferred to write apps for Apple's iOS and Google's Android than for Microsoft (which had a larger market share and bigger network). Like the phone vendors, app developers also had a history of negative experiences working with Microsoft. Absent a strong ecosystem of app developers, consumers were not drawn to the Windows Phone operating system.[20]

Expanding the circle, Microsoft had almost no experience working with telecom and mobile operators globally. These partnerships were crucial, of course, and could determine success or failure in the mobile phone market. Microsoft's acquisition of Nokia was intended to bring that capability in-house and bolster Microsoft's credibility, assuming it could pull off the post-merger integration.

However, the Nokia acquisition caused further concern among hardware vendors, who already felt threatened by Microsoft's previous decision to enter the "devices" business by producing its own Surface tablets. Instead of partnering with Microsoft, many hardware vendors concluded that they would now become competitors not only for market share but also for suppliers' resources.

What can we take away from this? Nadella understood that Microsoft had miscalculated and underestimated the criticality of its smartphone ecosystem. Reinventing the company would require getting that right.[21]

Most executive teams have a general appreciation of the complexities in their value network. But they often don't do the real work of examining the state of play in those interdependencies. Recall the IBM research suggesting a lack of analytical rigor around business models; this also applies to mapping changes in the broader value network.

At a minimum, there are three key facets of the network mapping process:

**Identify key partnerships.** Who are the critical parties (businesses, institutions, people) involved in the joint process of value creation? What roles do each play (supplier, complementor, distributor)? What activities do they perform? What services do they provide? Some of these partnerships are more important than others, but are any irreplaceable?

Research by BCG Henderson Institute suggests that collaborative networks fail most often because firms have not done a good job of designing the system, selecting partners, and clarifying the roles and responsibilities of key parties. Often this is because networks evolve incrementally over time, becoming an implicit part of the business. But organizations don't go the extra step of examining those networks *explicitly.* Where does your organization stand on this score?[22]

A second reason collaborative networks fail is that self-interested behavior destroys trust. Not surprising, right? Relationships fail when conflicts arise and trust is broken. It is no different in this context. Mistrust begins with opportunistic behavior, when one party is seen as taking more than its fair share. Or when information is hoarded or misappropriated. Or simply when one party does not deliver on its promise. When trust erodes, organizations tend to erect rules and stipulations as bureaucratic guardrails. This tends to inhibit flexibility, agility, and the capacity for change. And too often the partnerships devolve in a downward spiral of rigidity and exploitive behavior. Relationships become transactional; information is limited and flows only one way; and exchanges are relegated to negotiating price.

Don't make that mistake. Ask yourself: Who are your key partners? How (well) do you align with them, and how do you work toward common interests? What are the inflection points in your network where collaboration is most critical? What are the breaking points where collaboration falters? What are the associated risks to the organization (and to the relationships)? By being explicit about key relationships and evaluating where interdependencies might be fraying, you're in a better position to establish the context for change.

**Diagram resource flows and risk.** An important diagnostic in examining the health of your key partnerships is diagramming the actual resource flows, impact, and risk on the business(es). For example, one of the challenges of digitalization in today's environment is that it places a premium on managing data, information, and intellectual property exchanges among partner organizations. How does your firm manage data privacy and security? What systems and technology platforms support data sharing and exchange?

In addition to digital assets and information, you may want to get specific on the other resources—both tangible and intangible—that are critical to the partnerships. For example, how do financial resources (initial and recurring investments, revenue streams, expenses) flow among parties? How about your workforce, particularly with regard to critical talent: Are people shared or co-located? What opportunities derive from these resource flows, and what challenges may deteriorate the relationships?

**Evaluate the performance impact.** The net effect of these exchanges and resource flows has a direct impact on your organizational capabilities and value creation. Once you've zeroed in on the most crucial ones, you're in a better position to review performance standards and determine (among other things) how to monetize the collaboration. An important, if often ignored, part of this process is reviewing how value is shared and distributed once it is created. In order to support the resilience and sustainability of the network, partners should each be compensated in proportion to the value they create, at least in principle. The reality is that given both the direct and indirect effects of collaboration on performance, this calculus may become a little difficult. But that makes the job of evaluating it even more important.

Why do all this work? There are several reasons. First, it brings discipline to an essential and overlooked area of strategic context. By diagramming and evaluating elements of this broader ecosystem, you enable explicit analysis of and attention to them, allowing you to make more informed decisions. For his part, Unilever's Paul Polman emphasized the importance of mapping the firm's network with analytical rigor: "We spend a tremendous amount of time measuring the total impact of our activities across the whole supply chain—from the sourcing side to our factories to the consumer side. We are very data-driven."[23]

Like Microsoft, Unilever found that its network of partnerships was critical to its broader transformation. In evaluating its sustainability and environmental impact, Polman and team found that Unilever's own production processes accounted for less than 5 percent of the company's total greenhouse gas output. Suppliers generated 21 percent, and consumers generated an astonishing 70 percent. Consumers also accounted for 85 percent of its water usage. If Unilever was going to achieve its goal of reducing its environmental footprint, it would require change across the whole value chain, which involved an enormously complex set of partners. In addition to Unilever's 165,000 employees, operating companies, and diversified portfolio of brands, there were 5 million partners in the supply chain, and 2 billion consumers who used Unilever products daily.[24]

The second reason for doing this analysis is that, by making these interdependencies explicit, you're in a better position to calibrate how they affect the outcomes you are trying to achieve. To establish context for its strategic transformation, Unilever needed to account for those interdependencies. It was a big job, and Polman knew it. In his words, "For proper long-term planning, you've got to take your externalities into account. It's clear that if companies build this thinking into their business models and plan carefully, it will accelerate growth."[25]

This brings up a third reason for mapping your ecosystem: It's continuously evolving. These relationships are not static. Market dynamics create changes in the network. Even while you collaborate with your partners, they are competing and innovating to create more value. So are you. There's a coevolution among partners in the network that can lessen the influence of previously dominant suppliers, customers, or vendors, and it can bring entirely new players into the network.

It's important to determine which of your relationships are strongest and to predict how important they will be in the future. Establishing context for strategic transformation is in large part being able to understand and convey the ways these relationships are themselves transforming.[26]

In *The Sun Also Rises,* Ernest Hemingway described how someone goes bankrupt: "Two ways. Gradually, then suddenly." The same goes for changes in your ecosystem. Some are incremental, perhaps imperceptible, shifts. But they add up, reaching a tipping point. When that happens, change can come rapidly, and dramatically, causing disruption that is game-changing and irreversible. Let's turn to that next.[27]

### Spotlight Disruptors

Conducting a business review and mapping the larger ecosystem will help establish the backdrop against which you can spotlight key trends that determine the parameters of change shaping the future. These trends tend to fall into five broad categories: economic, technological, sociocultural, demographic, and political or regulatory. But there's an important distinction to make here. Some trends are well known but may not require much change in your business. Others are more disruptive, shaking the status quo.

Consider again the story of the Chalhoub Group and the disruptions it faced in retailing. CEO Patrick Chalhoub explained how the economic situation became more complicated: "The first big change was the drop in oil prices, which has shaken a lot of businesses and changed consumer habits. However, the second change was more important for me, and it was that our consumers changed a lot. So underneath this economic slowdown there was another, much deeper change, and it was the shift in our customers' mindsets."[28]

**Digital disruption and more.** Technology, of course, has been a big factor driving disruption. In retail, e-commerce has fundamentally changed the fashion and merchandising landscape. As websites such as Net-a-Porter, MatchesFashion, and Shopbop aggressively targeted Middle Eastern consumers by offering a wider range of products, localized collections, rapid delivery models, and competitive prices, the calculus for retail marketing began to change.[29]

Patrick Chalhoub knew time was of the essence. "Competition in the e-commerce market heated up in 2018, owing to Amazon's $580 million buyout of Souq, the largest e-commerce platform in the Arab world, and the $1 billion launch of e-retailer Noon, a joint venture between a group of investors led by UAE businessman Mohamed Alabbar and the Public Investment Fund, the sovereign wealth fund of Saudi Arabia."

E-commerce also weakened local distribution agreements and resulted in ever-wider choices and seamless service, which customers soon came to consider as the bare minimum. In addition, luxury brands that had championed their exclusivity (and higher price!) now needed to compete in a space in which consumers were empowered by and relied increasingly on social media and "influencer" marketing.[30]

Demographics accelerated change in the market. The high proportion of young people in the Gulf Cooperation Council, with a high internet penetration rate, mobile usage, and disposable income particularly in the Arabian Gulf region, meant that shoppers quickly migrated online for their luxury purchases.[31]

Pause for a moment to consider your own organization. What are the key disruptors in your industry? Are there external influences radically altering the way things work or the nature of competition? Disruption can come in many forms: technological advancement, a new regulatory framework, generational differences, and shifts in economic realities. Sometimes the changes are known, but the pace is uncertain—and often more rapid than most executives expect. This kind of change can present significant challenges and risk, eroding your competitive position and even leading to your firm's demise. But if managed strategically, disruption can bring opportunity for organizations that have the insight and agility to respond and adapt.

**The upside of disruption.** Disruption needn't be construed as negative; it has an upside as well. Economist Joseph Schumpeter described disruption as a "gale of creative destruction" that arises out of business competition and innovation that "continuously revolutionizes the economic structure from within, incessantly destroying the old one, incessantly creating a new one." As disruption shakes up industries, it creates opportunity. Strategic transformation is often designed to get out in front of change, driving disruption and innovation within the industry, establishing new competitive positions to which others must react.[32]

Mayo Clinic's 2020 Initiative was designed to do just that. Noseworthy and his team saw dramatic change on the horizon of health care. The Affordable Care Act (ACA) was expanding insurance coverage through broader state and federal Medicaid programs and insurance exchanges. Insurance companies, for their part, sought ways to reduce their expenses by creating narrower networks of lower-priced providers. The ACA had a provision for doctors and hospitals to become Accountable Care Organizations, which had a fixed-price reimbursement model for patients and were financially responsible for the care of those enrolled. Competition was also consolidating and scaling, with some very prominent regional and national competitors, like the Cleveland Clinic, Johns Hopkins, and others, driving innovation in medical care.

Noseworthy and team summarized their findings as a "perfect storm of reduced revenue and increased costs" due to an aging population, and "disruptive technologies" such as DNA sequencing.[33]

**Zero in on key trends fueling change.** How do you identify key disruptive trends? Begin with the realization that the most important ones are those that impact core elements of your business model. The key is to drill down to ascertain the influence of any disruption on (a) customer value or (b) capability. These have a direct impact on your economic model by affecting your revenue streams, cost structure, or both. And more broadly, they may redefine the nature of competition in your industry and your relative competitive position.

In our previous book, *Strategic Execution,* Ken Carrig and I discussed disruptive change occurring at Marriott International, SunTrust Banks, and Microsoft, among others. We saw digital transformation in the hotel industry—namely home-sharing platforms like Airbnb and online travel agencies (OTAs) like Expedia—redefining the customer value equation and recasting which capabilities would be needed to deliver on that in the future. At SunTrust, the future of banking was being shaped by financial technology (fintech, meaning digitization, mobile banking, cryptocurrency, and the like). SunTrust's merger with BB&T was motivated in part to scale investments in technology in order to compete with larger players in the industry.

And of course, Microsoft's transformation was driven by disruption in cloud and mobile computing. To ground its efforts, Nadella's executive team thoroughly analyzed macro trends in the industry and identified Microsoft's potential opportunities and threats associated with each of those trends. The company's top leaders agreed on the trends (e.g., cloud computing, mobile apps, etc.) but differed in their recommendations around financial investment. Scott Guthrie, Executive VP of Cloud and AI, summarized the debate as boiling down to research and development (R&D) investment: "What percentage of our overall R&D investment is focused on these trends that we all seem to agree 100 percent on?"[34]

Technological disruption is perplexing because it can lead to both fascination and fear. Research by KPMG emphasized the importance of putting it all in context. Over the 2010s, KPMG identified trends including cloud computing, data and analytics, artificial intelligence, enhanced user interface, and the like. But as the researchers put it, they "learned that viewing any of these signals in isolation risks missing the bigger picture, as new technologies and trends often converge to transform the very nature of an industry and how those in it need to respond."[35]

It may be impossible to overstate the impact of digital disruption in today's business environment. A recent study by McKinsey reported that only 11 percent of executives believed their current business models would be economically viable for more than five years. That's a vanishingly small number. Another 64 percent of executives said their companies needed to build new digital businesses to help them adapt.[36]

The question is *how*? In order to establish the context for transformation, it's important to understand technology's impact on your firm—both opportunity and threat—and then communicate its implications to your broader organization. Effective leaders take a discerning step back to gain perspective, determining the effect technology has (or will have) on their business models. Some factors fuel change and propel transformation, providing new market opportunities or a platform for new capabilities. Others inhibit change or represent technological headwinds that need to be addressed to achieve parity with others in the industry. Either way, it's the impact on strategy, rather than the technology per se, that matters.[37]

**Sometimes disruption is not obvious.** One pro tip for identifying disruptive trends: There is value in monitoring faint signals, as small changes often portend a vastly different future. A key tenet of Clayton Christensen's theory of disruptive innovation is that incumbents often ignore the disruption.[38] It's not that they don't see it but that they disregard or don't value it. Often if they see its future potential, they are encumbered by their own business model.

In her book *The Change Masters,* Rosabeth Moss Kanter advises that great change leaders "sense problems and weaknesses before they represent full-blown threats. They see the opportunities when external forces change—new technological capabilities, industry upheavals, and regulatory shifts. And then they identify gaps between what is and what could be. They find many ways to monitor external reality."[39]

**Construct future scenarios.** Sometimes key trends and their implications are clear and compelling. However, in increasingly uncertain VUCA environments, the future is less knowable. That makes any change more difficult. The value of identifying key trends isn't so much that it eliminates uncertainty and risk, but rather that it helps the organization isolate change drivers, analyze uncertainty and risk more thoroughly, build *future scenarios*, conduct stress tests, and establish some optionality around alternative courses of action. A 2022 McKinsey study suggests that in disruptive environments, developing "foresight capabilities" (using scenarios and stress testing) emerged as one of the core areas in which companies need improvement. Unfortunately, roughly half of executives surveyed rarely or never used scenarios and stress-testing exercises in strategic decision-making.[40]

Mayo Clinic's 2020 Initiative was all about scenario planning. Noseworthy and team developed three scenarios they wanted the committee to consider, each reflecting a different future for the industry and the company. Noseworthy led the committee through extensive debate and analysis of the pros and cons of each scenario and the options they reflected. The focus was on the external environment—the most important trends and uncertainties—but also on what each strategic option implied for Mayo's future standing in the industry. Ultimately, the committee settled on developing new business models as the best path forward.[41]

Scenario planning can be a powerful tool for establishing the strategic context of change. For some, the process is eye-opening. In conducting sessions with executive teams, I often begin by simply asking them to describe two scenarios: one where their firm achieves breakthrough performance and success, and the other where they experience decline and failure. While the success scenarios diverge wildly across businesses and industries, the "death" scenarios are often very similar. In debriefs with executives, their explanations run along the lines of: "The world changed, and we just kept doing the same thing." For many, it's a startling reminder that perpetuating the status quo incurs its own risks.

You have two basic choices to make regarding disruptive trends: defend against them as risk mitigation, or take advantage of them as opportunities. Let's take the next step: examining how disruption may affect your business model.

## STEP 2: INNOVATE YOUR BUSINESS MODEL

Once you have scoped your business ecosystem—by conducting a business review, mapping your broader network, and spotlighting disruptive trends—the next big step is to evaluate ways to innovate your business model around that future.

Unilever's Paul Polman determined that the company's financial troubles were inherent in its traditional business model. He described it this way: "We thought about some of the mega-trends in the world, like the shift east in terms of population growth and the growing demand for the world's resources. And we said, 'Why don't we develop a business model aimed at contributing to society and the environment instead of taking from them?'"[42]

Similarly, John Noseworthy described Mayo Clinic's shifting business model: "Mayo Clinic is a set of geographic destinations, but it is also a comprehensive platform of knowledge, expertise, and delivery proficiency for providing a variety of products and services to a spectrum of markets."[43]

The term "business model innovation" is one of those gee-whiz buzzwords that can be off-putting to many, intimidating to some, and impractical to others. I've seen enough executives' eyes glaze over to know we need to bring it down out of the clouds of theory to make it concrete and practical.

Simply stated, business model innovation is: (1) a change in your customer value proposition, and (2) a simultaneous change in your operating model of capabilities to drive that value. In other words, change what your customers expect, and change how you meet that expectation. That's it. Simple and straightforward. It is the heart of strategic transformation.[44]

You've perhaps seen some clear examples of business model innovation. Some years ago, Marriott sold off its hotel properties, freeing up capital for growth. As chief human resource officer Ty Breland said, "We're not in the real estate business." Marriott's value proposition is hotel management, service, and customer loyalty. Its investment in capabilities reflects that. Similarly, Coca-Cola sold off its bottling network, recognizing that its value was in the brand (and secret formula). Netflix initially rented out DVDs by mail but migrated to online and video on demand. The list of business model transformations goes on.[45]

Evaluating the potential of business model innovation is an important step in establishing context for transformation. Unfortunately, there's a lot of zealous pursuit of innovation and change that never receives enough scrutiny. (Recall the sobering research data showing just how many of these initiatives fail?) The purpose of the scrutiny is not so much to refute the premise of transformation—that need was established in step 1—but rather to put your approach under a light.

### Determine Future Customer Value

To begin this work, I find it useful to think three to five years into the future. Who will be your target customer, and what will they require of you? It's surprising how difficult it is for some executive teams to answer this question. Because of that, their discussions are often robust and can take some time. The research evidence is clear: Most executive teams have a tough time clearly articulating their *current* customer value proposition, let alone how it will change. They know their products and services, and even their channels to market. But they have a more difficult time explaining what problems they solve for customers, what "gains" they create, and what "pains" they alleviate. "Voice of customer" (VOC) analytics, which examine the gap between customer expectations and experiences, is a good starting point. These data are essential to understanding the customer relationship.[46]

Patrick Chalhoub saw this coming fast. Given industry changes, Chalhoub's leadership team recognized that customer expectations were shifting. In a company presentation, the Group summarized what its customers to wanted:

- Convenience—Guests are now time strapped—speed is a key for seamless guest experience.
- Consistency is base to build an omni channel experience.
- Relevance—The new guests expect real time interaction, personalized experience.
- Empowerment—Investing in guests to be the best brand ambassador.
- Agility—Guest retention is like a moving target, agility is key for success.[47]

Customers wanted convenience to shop where, when, and how they wanted; consistency, regardless of whether they purchased in store or online; and real-time, personalized service. Omnichannel retail significantly raised the stakes for the Group to provide customers anything, anywhere, anytime. And customers expected the same great experience whether it was online or in store. Patrick Chalhoub explained,

> Customers today want to have a fantastic experience, very good service, an absolute uniqueness ... They want storytelling. So it is not the end of retail—it is the end of retail that has no more meaning, or no more feeling than just the availability of products, because digital is just so much easier. Brick and mortar retail has to transform.
>
> We set up seven guiding principles and changed our vision from being a traditional distributor and retailer of luxury in the Middle East to becoming an agile organization that places convenience at its customers' fingertips. So, from being brand-focused, we have become customer-focused. Rather than having our customers coming to us, we are now going to them. The client today is totally empowered. So we have to make sure we have this client centricity.[48]

Mayo Clinic's 2020 Initiative also focused directly on its changing value proposition. Traditionally, the clinic's focus had been curing disease. Patient relationships were episodic; when people got (very) sick, they went to the hospital. And when they got well, they went home. While that proposition would continue, the 2020 Initiative invited Mayo to expand its value by keeping people healthy through long-lasting "meaningful experiences." Mayo's target customers expanded beyond patients to include clinicians, doctors, and partner hospitals that could benefit from Mayo's expertise. It even extended to consumers who wanted access to Mayo's advice and medical knowledge.

Noseworthy referred to these three customer segments as "patients here" (traditional patients who came to the clinic), "patients there" (those in the extended network of partner hospitals), and "patients everywhere" (anyone around the globe). Its channels to market diversified from the clinics in Minnesota, Florida, and Arizona to subscription-based alliances with hospitals, laboratories, and thousands of doctors worldwide. Mayo would even reach individuals through social media, marketing events, and digital health services.[49]

How viable was this new value proposition? That was the key question Mayo had to answer to establish context for change. Its scrutiny involved thorough analysis of expected results, including patient clinical outcomes, costs, revenue streams, and impact on reputation. It also involved analysis of potential risks. For example, some worried that this expansion of scope might dilute Mayo's reputation. Others were cynical, believing that it was about making more money. Noseworthy spent considerable time working through these issues and demonstrating how this approach was consistent with Mayo Clinic's mission. He referred to what William James Mayo, founder of Mayo Clinic, said back in 1910:

"The best interest of the patient is the only interest to be considered, and in order that the sick may have the benefit of advancing knowledge, union of forces is necessary."[50]

Dr. Mayo was a visionary, and this was his open invitation to continually evolve the clinic's value proposition and business model.

### Assess Capability Gaps

With (future) customer value as the focal point, the second part of business model innovation is adapting your operating model. That means scrutinizing your end-to-end capabilities to deliver on that new promise. Christine Wormuth, U.S. Secretary of the Army, reinforced this point very succinctly in her address to the Pentagon: "The Army is in a moment of transformation . . . There are new capabilities that we need to bring into the force."[51]

What's the best way to assess capability gaps? Typically, my advice is to start with the top three to five critical capabilities for creating value. Strategy requires prioritization, and transformation requires focus. My question to leadership teams is: Once you have identified the core capabilities, to what extent are they new? It's unlikely that you'll deliver on a new value proposition using *only* your old capability set. Some capabilities will likely remain unchanged; others will be adapted and improved; and still others could be completely new. The important question to answer is: What investments do you need to make right now to close the capability gap?

Capability gaps take two principal forms: corrective and prospective.

**Corrective capability gaps.** Corrective gaps refer to places where there is current underperformance. As my good friend Ken Carrig put it, "in any transformation, the first thing to do is stop the bleeding." Each capability is a combination of processes, systems, and people. Which processes aren't working, because they are too slow, they incur too many defects, or they cost too much? Which systems and technologies support those processes, and is the infrastructure providing the necessary information and decision support? Which key people—those in what I sometimes refer to as "A" positions—are most critical to the processes, and which have the most impact on value? What support do they need to perform at the highest level?

Corrective capability gaps may not be the most important for the future. But sometimes they are urgent and need to be addressed immediately, or they will hamstring transformation. As my clients in the Navy taught me, "You can't turn a ship that's not moving." Find the leaky parts of the boat, plug them, and get things floating.

**Prospective capability gaps.** Prospective gaps are somewhat different from corrective gaps. They represent *future* underachievement—places where the capability is not in place to deliver on the new value proposition. New talent and new ways of working are instrumental. New technologies are often the platform for prospective capability. These are important drivers of transformation because the investments must be made in advance, ahead of the curve.

When I ask leadership teams how long it will take to build new capability, they groan (and sometimes show a little trepidation). Putting new processes in place, investing in new systems and technologies, or simply acquiring, developing, and deploying new talent—these changes can take years. (Note: A culture audit should also be done at this stage to assess alignment for the future.)

The reality is that the cycle time for capability development is often longer than the time horizon for changing customer value. If you can't transform quickly enough, others will take away your business. The double whammy is that corrective and prospective gaps compound one another. As one anxious executive told me, "We don't have those capabilities, and our current organization is not capable of building those capabilities."

This is why establishing context is so important as a prerequisite first step in strategic transformation. It sometimes shines a light on the stark realities facing the firm. And maybe where to go to get help.

Chalhoub Group recognized that its traditional brick-and-mortar business model was becoming rapidly obsolete. It needed to adapt to the new customer expectations by transforming itself from a traditional distributor and retailer of luxury to a hybrid retailer bringing exceptional experiences directly to customers everywhere. As Patrick Chalhoub wrote in a company white paper, "To be successful, we will have to be aspirational, relevant, meaningful, and competitive, and adapt to the changes and to the new norm."[52]

In Mayo Clinic's 2020 Initiative, analysis showed that transformation to new business models would require significant capability development in areas that lay outside its legacy operations. Dr. Noseworthy's steering committee understood that the multi-billion-dollar investment in digital infrastructure was intended not just to bolster existing capabilities, but to invest in entirely new capability sets.

In terms of business-model innovation, Mayo Clinic's 2020 Initiative dramatically reconceived who the customer/patient was and what value Mayo could provide. It turbocharged Mayo's operating model with new capabilities, new paths to market, and new platforms of collaboration.

For our purposes here, it's important to realize that Dr. Noseworthy and his team didn't just hatch this plan and press forward. They established the context for strategic transformation by involving others in analyzing the ecosystem, the broader network of alliances, and the opportunities and risks associated with external disruption. Then they assiduously evaluated the potential value of new business models, their implications for patients, and the required investment in capability.

### Reconcile Your Financials

One last point about potential business model innovation. From a practical standpoint, you'll need to evaluate the impact of transformation on your financial model. You'll recall earlier in the chapter the importance of financials in conducting your business review. Project that forward now. This isn't just about determining the cost of transformation; it's about figuring out how it will influence your future cash flows and profit formula. Without the prospect of monetizing the change, your efforts may be for naught.

Research suggests that successful transformation addresses both the top and bottom lines. Keep things simple, and first focus on how transformation will influence key revenue streams. Will there be new revenue sources, perhaps through different channels? And how will existing sources improve or recede? Invariably this involves a recalibration of your revenue model of price and volume.[53]

Relatedly, what will be the impact on your cost structure? Strategic transformation almost always involves substantial capital expense. If your plan includes a turnaround, you will need to make some difficult decisions about capital allocation. Recall my earlier examples of Marriott and Coca-Cola selling off noncore businesses and freeing up assets for growth. How will your transformation change key expense categories, allocation, economies of scale, and margins? Although it is early in the process, it's not too soon to begin laying out the financial parameters of change.

## STEP 3: COMMUNICATE YOUR STRATEGIC INTENT AND RATIONALE

Let's pause for a second. We've worked through a lot in our discussion of analysis required to establish strategic context. The two main steps we've covered so far—scoping your ecosystem and innovating your business model—are the foundation for all the rest of strategic transformation. When leadership teams get clarity and alignment on these two, they are in a much better position to assess external dynamics and determine how the organization can reposition accordingly.

The third key step in establishing the context of transformation is to communicate the challenge—strategic intent, ambition, and rationale—to others in the organization. Remember, these are the people who actualize the transformation. And even though many of them have already been involved in the analysis stage, they are still likely to have questions about the *why, how,* and *what* of change.

In sessions with managers, we inevitably discuss the causes of employee resistance to change. When we peel back the layers of resistance, it boils down to *personal* uncertainty and risk related to *why* the change is necessary (i.e., its purpose), *what* the future looks like, and *how* they play a role. These are reasonable concerns, and that's why the job of the leader is to provide some perspective. Sadly, most leaders don't communicate well enough—or often enough—particularly during times of change. As a result, they find themselves trying to lead transformation on a foundation they've never built.

Some years ago, Bill Rogers, CEO of Truist Financial, told me, "The CEO has two jobs; to bring clarity from complexity and purpose to the work. If you do those two things, the doors open." Ultimately, that's the point of this third step in establishing context.

A well-framed statement of strategic intent can achieve this. In their book *Competing for the Future*, Gary Hamel and C. K. Prahalad describe three key features of strategic intent: direction, discovery, and destiny.

- *Sense of direction* conveys a unifying sense of where things are headed in the future, and the firm's long-term goals in terms of its market or competitive position.
- *Sense of discovery* implies a promise to explore new territory, creating a unique viewpoint about the future that differentiates the organization.
- *Sense of destiny* conveys the idea that the organization serves some higher purpose or societal good that connects with people emotionally.

When done well, your strategic intent captures the overarching purpose, aspirational vision, and competitive direction that frames transformation. And it communicates clearly to others what's in it for them—why they should care enough to join the journey.[54]

### Inspire the *Why* by Rooting It in Purpose

There are several aspects of the *why* of transformation, not least of which is, "Why do we need to change?" For example, Mayo Clinic's transformation was met with internal resistance, in part from deeply committed physicians who worried that new initiatives might divert resources from patient care. As Dr. Noseworthy put it, "Turning around a successful organization is not that easy." Hundreds of doctors "who assumed life was great weren't immediately eager to change how they work." Many of them were not fully aware of the many new initiatives and guessed that the change was about making money rather than world-class medicine. Noseworthy and team redoubled their efforts to rally the organization around the idea that the transformation indeed supported Mayo's mission.[55]

Similarly, in Satya Nadella's transformation of Microsoft, he was straight with his organization about why change was needed. In a letter to employees, he said, "Our industry does not respect tradition—it only respects innovation. This is a critical time for the industry and for Microsoft. Make no mistake, we are headed for greater places—as technology evolves and we evolve with and ahead of it. Our job is to ensure that Microsoft thrives in a mobile and cloud-first world."[56]

Notice that in articulating this strategic intent, Nadella established the context of transformation by explaining *why* change was necessary. As he put it, "Microsoft is one of these companies that have been super successful. One of the things that happens when you're super successful is you sometimes lose touch with what made you successful in the first place."[57]

But in laying out his vision for transformation, Nadella was also very focused on Microsoft's shared purpose and mission to make the world more productive. As he said, "When we talk about our mission of empowering every person and every organization on the planet to achieve more, it can't be just a set of words. It has to in some sense capture the very essence of who we are in all of the decisions we make, in the products we create and how we show up with our customers."[58]

Paul Polman framed Unilever's transformation as a response to a business environment that was "volatile and complex ... with more headwinds than tailwinds." He communicated to employees the need for a "Compass Vision," which was the cornerstone of the Unilever Sustainable Living Plan (USLP) to double revenues while simultaneously reducing its environmental impact and increasing its positive social impact around the world. The strategic intent was focused on (1) helping a billion people improve their health and well-being, (2) halving the environmental footprint of making and using Unilever products, and (3) "enhancing the livelihoods of millions of people as Unilever grows its business."[59]

This was an ambitious and aspirational vision for Unilever, and many were dubious. As shown in Figure 3.2, Polman believed the boldness of this vision would inspire and energize the organization, motivating employees to champion its cause. He believed it was a cornerstone of Unilever's philosophy of "doing well by doing good."

As Rosabeth Moss Kanter observed, "A vision remains just a dream unless it can inspire others to follow ... [Leaders need] to shape ideas into a theme that makes a compelling case for the value and direction of change—especially when you are pursuing a new idea that has not yet taken shape."[60]

FIGURE 3.2. Unilever Sustainable Living Plan (USLP) (Adapted from Paul Polman, "Captain Planet," interview by Adi Ignatius, Harvard Business Review, June 2012, https://hbr.org/2012/06/captain-planet.; Paul Polman, introduction to "Unilever Sustainable Living Plan: Small Actions, Big Difference," Unilever, 2011, accessed May 12, 2023, https://www.readkong.com/page/unilever-sustainable-living-plan-small-actions-big-8584553, 3.)

In my experience, a well-crafted strategic intent can serve as the "North Star" for strategic transformation. It provides light in the darkness, guiding the organization through change, providing direction for investment, and energizing its shared purpose. Given the inevitable chaos that ensues during transformation, it is good to have a clear North Star that will help you keep everyone's eyes focused on the horizon. When others ask, "Why are we doing this, and where is it all going?" you'll have established the context to provide a compelling answer.

### Shape the *How* by Rooting It in Culture

In addition to the *why* of change, the best leadership teams engage the organization around *how* transformation will transpire. When done well, this connects the strategic intent of the organization to its underlying culture.

Nadella described it this way:

> This starts with clarity of purpose and sense of mission that will lead us to imagine the impossible and deliver it. We need to prioritize innovation that is centered on our core value of empowering users and organizations to do more. We have picked a set of high-value activities as part of our One Microsoft strategy. And with every service and device launch going forward we need to bring more innovation to bear around these scenarios.
>
> Next, every one of us needs to do our best work, lead and help drive culture change. We sometimes underestimate what we each can do to make things happen and overestimate what others need to do to move us forward. We must change this.
>
> Finally, I truly believe that each of us must find meaning in our work. The best work happens when you know that it's not just work, but something that will improve other people's lives. This is the opportunity that drives each of us at this company.[61]

Nadella's plan to establish the context of transformation through cultural change was deliberate and thorough. As you'll see in the coming chapters, Nadella approached transformation both top-down and bottom-up, communicating a vision and reinvigorating Microsoft's culture of shared values. He framed the transformation of Microsoft as a cultural renaissance, and he invited employees and managers to "innovate together": collaborating to achieve a higher ambition, reinforcing its shared values and leadership principles.

He established three simple leadership principles as a starting point: (1) create clarity, (2) generate energy, and (3) deliver success. Next, he surveyed employees and conducted focus groups to assess which culture elements should be kept and which needed to change in order to drive transformation. As Chief HR Officer Kathleen Hogan noted, "There's a lot about Microsoft's culture and our heritage that we're proud of, that we never want to change ... But in our new world, how do we need to evolve?"

Nadella said, "I wanted to go back to the very genesis of this company. What is that sense of purpose and drive that made us successful? What was the culture that may have been there in the very beginning or in the times when we were able to achieve that success? How do we really capture it? So that's why I think about it as the renaissance as much as about fixing something that's broken."[62]

The approach worked. Employees found the challenge liberating and inspiring, and instead of the change bringing resistance, it reinvigorated the company's mojo and spirit of excellence.[63]

One proviso, or word of caution. The power of strategic intent is not in its deals, but in its compelling picture of the future. The plan for transformation is usually not fully baked at this point—that will come later. Resist the temptation to overprescribe or create overly detailed plans. Even if you had the details, which you often don't at this point, you might find yourself in the unenviable position of trying to sell your ideas to an incredulous, if not unreceptive, crowd. Employees may not be able or willing to accept the delta between where you are currently and where you're going. My grandmother used to say, "If you could see your whole life before you, you couldn't handle it." The same is true with strategic transformation. Big changes spelled out in exacting detail can be daunting, if not frightening, and might cause a rebellion before they are implemented.

It's better to focus on helping others understand why change is needed, where things are headed, in what ways the organization will be better as a result, and how you will work together to get there. Invite them along on the journey. This lays out the purpose, principles, and priorities of transformation. Granular processes and practices come later.

## REALITY CHECK

Aristotle said, "Well begun is half done." That adage may encapsulate the essence of this chapter. Successful transformation begins with a compelling strategic intent, grounded in a thorough understanding of emerging trends. Don't neglect the groundwork. A lot of effort goes into building the foundation for successful change.[64]

Paul Polman described the challenge of establishing context this way: "You have to be able to have an enormous appetite for the detail to drive [that] sense of urgency, to make that purpose come alive with storytelling. Then you need to have that broader picture ... by continuously being a few steps ahead, in terms of these systemic changes."[65]

Importantly, this work shouldn't wait until the need for change is imminent. It should be part of the ongoing business planning, review, and "strategy refresh" of the organization. Assess yourself on the key elements in the checklist in Figure 3.3. Reflect a bit on how they build on one another to provide a better understanding of needed change.

Take a few moments to do a realistic self-appraisal. Compare yourself and your organization to the examples in this chapter. In some cases, you may be ahead of the game. In places where you need to catch up, use the lessons learned to engage others in your organization around these issues. What could you do now to improve change readiness in the future? My suggestion is to view this self-reflection as a vital precursor to taking on any transformation project. I strongly advocate working through these challenges before experiencing the whirlwind of change (more on this in chapter 7). Carefully consider the following questions; you may find that writing down your answers, and comparing notes with colleagues, can help you get a more concrete picture of your context, business model, and reasons for change.

| | |
|---|---|
| **Scope your business ecosystem** | ☑ We clearly understand our business ecosystem, including the complex relationships among suppliers, partners, customers, competitors, etc.<br>☑ We continuously analyze the dynamic nature of our industry, sources of change, innovation, and potential disruption.<br>☑ We regularly evaluate our business model, our standing in the industry, and how we create value. |
| **Innovate your business model** | ☑ We work closely with our customers to understand and anticipate what they might need or expect in the future.<br>☑ We strive to lead the market, seeking new opportunities, new channels, and new products and/or services.<br>☑ We thoroughly assess capabilities needed for the future and make investments to build these ahead of the curve. |
| **Communicate strategic intent and rationale** | ☑ Our leaders create a compelling vision of the future that inspires new possibilities and a higher purpose.<br>☑ Our leaders clearly communicate the key factors needed to propel our success and breakthrough performance.<br>☑ We understand how by working together, we can all achieve great things. |

FIGURE 3.3. Checklist for Establishing Context

### Scope Your Business Ecosystem

How well does your leadership team understand the complexities of your business ecosystem and how its interdependent relationships are evolving? Is there rigorous analysis around this?

### Innovate Your Business Model

Strategic transformation involves significant changes to your business model. Does your leadership team make evaluating potential disruption in your current business model an explicit part of your business review? Doing so gives you more concrete insights into how the business might need to change. Equally importantly, the business model helps to tell the "story" of transformation to others in your organization.

### Communicate Strategic Intent and Rationale

Ultimately, a crucial reason to establish the strategic context of transformation is to communicate the strategic intent and rationale to others in the organization. These are the people who need to implement the changes and may be resistant because of uncertainty and perceived risk. How well has your leadership team communicated why change is necessary and how the business will be different and better as a result?

## PLAYBOOK TOOLS

As a starting point for building your playbook for strategic transformation, discuss the key points above with your team. Take time to isolate the key drivers of change, align on those, and build out from there. The following actions are helpful for clarifying the fundamentals needed to establish strategic context.

**Directions for Building a Playbook:** Work through the following activities together as a team. Aim to get consensus on your answers, and use Playbook Template 3.1 at the end of the chapter to capture the key points of your analysis.

- *Scope Your Business Ecosystem.* Use the business model canvas to scrutinize your organization as it exists today.
  - Customer value: Who are your key target customers? What is your customer value proposition (what "gains" you create and "pains" you alleviate)? What are your key channels to market, and what is the nature of your relationship with customers? How do these factors influence revenue streams?
  - Capabilities: Supporting this assessment of customer value, what is your operating model to deliver that value? What key activities, resources, and partnerships underlie your capabilities to deliver that value? Which matters most? How do these factors influence the main drivers of your cost structure?
- *Analyze Disruptive Trends.* Now look toward the future. Your organization operates in a dynamic ecosystem. What are the two or three key trends in your industry defining the parameters of change? How are they altering the requirements for future success? Use Playbook Template 3.2 at the end of the chapter to record your analysis.
- *Innovate Your Business Model.* Project three to five years into the future (determine for yourself the appropriate time horizon for your organization). How will your business context change?
  - Customer value: What will customers want or need from you in the future, and how is that different from today? Who will be your target customers, and how will you connect with them? What are the implications for your prospects of profitable growth?

- Capabilities: What key activities, resources, and partnerships will be required to deliver that value? To what extent are these new? Do you have significant capability gaps? Are these corrective or prospective gaps? Importantly, what investments do you need to make now to prepare for that future?

- **_Communicate Strategic Intent and Rationale._** Summarize the changes needed for future success. Craft a short (one or two sentences) statement of your organization's strategic intent and vision for the future. How will the leadership team communicate this to others in your organization in a way that they find compelling? How will leaders explain the competitive dynamics and the rationale for your transformation? In what ways can you connect the "why" of change to your organization's overarching purpose? Can you shape the narrative about change by rooting it in your organization's values and culture?

## WHAT'S NEXT? ENGAGE STAKEHOLDERS

Establishing the strategic context for transformation is an important prerequisite for change. And it sets the stage for the next chapter on engaging stakeholders. Your analysis of your business ecosystem will have revealed the complexities of your environment. With it, you will have a better grasp of how things are evolving, if not being disrupted. The success of your transformation will depend on understanding key stakeholders in the process and working with them to bring about change.

PLAYBOOK TEMPLATE 3.1. Business Model Canvas

| Key Partners | Key Activities | Value Propositions | Customer Relationships | Target Customers |
|---|---|---|---|---|
| | | | | |
| | Key Resources | | Channels | |
| Cost Structure | | | Revenue Streams | |
| | | | | |

Adapted from Alexander Osterwalder and Yves Pigneur, *Business Model Generation*, Wiley, 2010. This work is licensed under the Creative Commons Attribution-Share Alike 3.0 Unported License. Designed by Strategyzer.com.

PLAYBOOK TEMPLATE 3.2. Business Model Innovation

| Disruptive Trends | |
|---|---|
| Capabilities (Future) | Customer Value (Future) |
| Strategic Intent and Vision | |

# 4 FACTOR TWO—ENGAGE STAKEHOLDERS: DIFFERENTIATE PRIMARY AND SECONDARY PARTNERS

**KEY PRINCIPLE:** Successful transformation depends on effectively engaging a set of interconnected stakeholders in your ecosystem.

**UNILEVER'S TRANSFORMATION STRATEGY** was challenging because it involved an extraordinarily diverse set of stakeholders. When Paul Polman undertook the Unilever Sustainable Living Plan (USLP), he established very ambitious goals related to financial performance as well as environmental, social, and governance (ESG) issues. He declared that USLP would reduce greenhouse gases, use sustainably sourced agricultural products, reduce water usage, and help a billion people improve their health and well-being, among fifty other measurable targets. That was a heavy lift, and because Unilever had accepted responsibility for transforming the entire value chain, it had to confront the fact that many suppliers were initially not on board with the plan; in fact, they were only 14 percent ESG compliant. Consumers were not aligned either—recall they accounted for 70 percent of the greenhouse gas impact and 85 percent of the water footprint. Unilever's success required more than winning over dubious employees; it also needed the commitment of five million partners in the supply chain who likely would incur higher costs, two billion consumers who did not want to pay more for products, and anxious shareholders who had been seeing years of declining profits. Ultimately, Unilever's fate was not in its own hands. To succeed, Polman knew these key stakeholders needed to do more than just accept the proposed change; they needed to advocate for it and act on it.[1]

Airbnb has also faced some daunting challenges with its stakeholders. Since its founding in 2008, Airbnb had reinvented the hospitality industry and become the epitome of home sharing. Founder and CEO Brian Chesky led the firm through a dizzying period of growth, and by 2019, Airbnb had more than 6 million rental listings on its platform in over 100,000 cities across 200 countries. The number of hosts and guests continued to rise, and the company planned an IPO in 2020. Then the COVID-19 pandemic hit. As the epidemic spread rapidly around the world, reservations plummeted 72 percent, from about 31 million a year before and after a decade of rapid growth. Chesky put it this way: "A company dropping by 80% in eight weeks is like a car driving 100 miles an hour, and then hitting the brakes. There's no safe way to do that. Things are going to break." How would Chesky help Airbnb accommodate the interests and concerns of its vast array of stakeholders, including customers, hosts, employees, and shareholders?[2]

Another example of stakeholder engagement—in a very different type of organization—involves Bill Bratton and the New York City Police Department. Bratton was hired as police commissioner of New York City in 1994 to transform the force, reengage its 35,000 police officers, tackle out-of-control crime rates, reestablish closer relationships with local communities, placate an intransigent court system, and collaborate with local politicians and legislators. The task was daunting: It included myriad stakeholders with their own interests and concerns. However, rather than seeing these stakeholders merely as a constraint to his change agenda, Bratton viewed them as instrumental to the NYPD's success. As he noted, "You cannot police a community without effectively working with the community." In less than two years—and with no increase in budget—Bratton brought about a stunning transformation: Felony crime dropped 39 percent, murders decreased by 50 percent, and theft decreased 35 percent. Public confidence jumped from 37 percent to 73 percent, and job satisfaction among officers reached an all-time high.[3]

## THE CHALLENGE

This chapter picks up on the premise that strategic transformation involves ecosystem changes. It focuses on the second factor required for successful transformation: engaging your stakeholders. The challenge is how to build support among internal and external parties, each with a vested interest in the change. The keys to success lie in understanding their interests and influence in order to involve them in—or minimize their resistance to—the proposed change.

Recall the McKinsey study discussed in chapter 2 indicating that 60 percent of CEOs rank "engaging stakeholders" among their top three priorities. You may also recall that only 7 percent said they were able to achieve alignment between the interests of stakeholders and the business.[4]

### Symptoms of Stakeholder Misalignment

So where do things go wrong? The clearest symptom of stakeholder mismanagement is lack of alignment. Maybe you've seen this in your organization. Given the diversity of interests and approaches within your ecosystem, achieving consensus about the path forward is difficult. The task is made more difficult because, honestly, not everyone is on your side. Some of your relevant stakeholders are adversaries with competing interests.

Let's look at an example from one notable company: Uber.

**Roadblocks and dead ends.** When Travis Kalanick founded Uber, his vision was to disrupt—and dramatically transform—the taxi and limo industry through digital technology. Capitalizing on trends toward the "sharing economy" (as Airbnb was doing with homestays), Kalanick created a digital platform that connected prospective riders with gig workers willing to provide private transportation. The easy-to-use smartphone app allowed customers to summon a ride, routed the driver, gave estimated time and fare, and seamlessly automated the financial transaction, even giving riders and drivers a chance to rate their experiences. It was a huge hit. Riders loved the convenience over taxis, and drivers worked as entrepreneurial freelancers to earn extra money.

However, despite its initial success and rapid growth, Uber found itself ensnared in an array of controversies and disputes with a broad range of unreceptive stakeholders. Resistance took many forms. Regulators, competitors, Uber drivers, and even some customers and employees pushed back on what Uber was doing—and particularly *the way it was doing it*.[5]

As *Fortune*'s Adam Lashinsky put it, "Uber embraced rule-breaking as a business model, what with its catch-us-if-you-can flouting of local regulators." Instead of working within the existing framework of established regulations for limos and taxis, or trying to change the rules, Kalanick and team bulldozed their way into the market, ignoring the rules. For example, when the San Francisco Municipal Transportation Agency and the California Public Utilities Commission placed a cease-and-desist order on ridesharing, Uber ignored it, operating in open defiance, despite threats of fines and even possible jail time. Kalanick joked, "I think I've got 20,000 years of jail time in front of me." Similar incidents occurred in Boston, New York, and Washington, DC, as well as in France, Spain, Germany, and the United Kingdom. At the same time as the company was growing internationally, its relationships with some of its key stakeholders were unraveling.[6]

**Value destruction and loss of commitment to the vision.** In addition to Uber's legal wranglings with regulators, an increasing number of drivers began to complain that they should be recategorized as employees, not independent contractors. They began to value pay and benefits more than flexibility. Customers also railed against Uber's use of surge pricing during busy hours, and they expressed concerns about the security and privacy of personal data. There were even some rising concerns about safety after reports of drivers assaulting riders came to light. Some of Uber's employees—particularly women—were becoming disenfranchised in Uber's "frat boy" culture, which many viewed as misogynistic.[7]

As the company continued to grow, it was accumulating baggage with key stakeholders. Investors, for their part, were generally positive about Uber's financial valuation. But even here cracks were beginning to show. The intense rivalry and "street fighting" with competitors like

Lyft led Uber to require potential investors to sign a pledge not to take an equity stake in rival firms. That crossed the line for some investors. Billionaire venture capitalist Peter Thiel chose not to invest in Uber, describing it as "the most ethically challenged company in Silicon Valley."[8]

Talk about a bumpy ride! Some would suggest that many of these stakeholder battles were inevitable in an entrenched and inherently political industry such as public transportation. And there were definitely some outside forces agitating for a fight. But that context makes Uber's tactics even more questionable. Did it have to go this way?

Perhaps Kalanick embraced Facebook founder Mark Zuckerberg's adage about disruptive innovation: "Move fast and break things. The idea is that if you never break anything, you're probably not moving fast enough."[9] Maybe so, but things eventually got to a breaking point, and Kalanick resigned as Uber's CEO in June 2017. Dara Khosrowshahi was brought in from Expedia (another platform firm) to make changes and repair Uber's image, culture, and reputation in the eyes of a broad array of stakeholders.[10]

## What You Can Do

While remarkable, stories like Uber's are not uncommon. As a first principle, executives who view stakeholder engagement with a long-term perspective and as an opportunity to create enduring value tend to be more successful than those who approach it tactically or transactionally.

Paul Polman described how critical stakeholder engagement was to Unilever's success: "Delivering these commitments won't be easy. To achieve them we will have to work in partnership with governments, NGOs, suppliers and others to address the big challenges that confront us all. Ultimately, we will only succeed if we inspire billions of people around the world to take the small, everyday actions that add up to a big difference—actions that will enable us all to live more sustainably."[11]

As part of Unilever's plan, Polman engaged retailers like Tesco and Walmart, national governments, scores of non-governmental organizations (NGOs) like the Rainforest Alliance, and the United Nations. He understood that Unilever, as complex as it is, exists within the context of an even more complex ecosystem of stakeholders. As he put it, "By combining our own actions with external advocacy on public policy and jointly working with partners, we are seeking to create what we call transformational change—that is, fundamental change to whole systems, not simply incremental improvements."

In this chapter, I'll focus on key considerations outlined in chapter 2 to help you approach the process of stakeholder engagement more effectively, framing it around the requirements of strategy to improve your odds of achieving alignment. The main sections in this chapter are each organized around the three most important actions:

1. *Differentiate your primary stakeholders:* Assess their influence over performance as well as their interests (the extent to which your transformation positively or negatively impacts their organization). Those with high interest and high influence are among your primary stakeholders.

2. *Customize your engagement strategy:* Adapt your approach based on the importance of the relationship over time and the degree to which stakeholder interests are complementary or competing.

3. *Empower your key influencers:* Build coalitions with those natural constituencies in a position to make a difference.

## STEP 1: DIFFERENTIATE YOUR PRIMARY STAKEHOLDERS

All stakeholders are important. And some are more important than others. During transformation, it is important to distinguish your primary stakeholders from secondary ones. That's always the heart of strategic thinking—prioritize the few from the many. Conceptually, we might suggest that primary stakeholders include those with a clear vested interest in the transformation, either because they are impacted significantly or because they can substantially influence the outcome. Secondary stakeholders would then be those who, while relevant, may have less impact on the outcome.[12]

More practically, your primary stakeholders tend to be part of your business and directly involved in the process of value creation. This includes employees, customers, investors, suppliers, and partners. In some cases, they are so integral to the business that you may think of them as the *raison d'être*—the reason for being—that is aligned with your *purpose*. For example, A. G. Lafley, Procter & Gamble's CEO, used to channel Peter Drucker when he declared, "The purpose of a business is to create a customer." Shareholders also figure prominently in most public organizations. But remember, our focus here is not just how involved they are in the business, but how instrumental they are to the company's strategic transformation.[13]

To further refine the analysis, consider stakeholders outside of your business who are nevertheless critical to its ongoing operations, your license to operate, or some other key aspect. This can include, among others, government entities, regulatory agencies, communities, and NGOs. For example, McKinsey researchers found that a third of corporate profits are vulnerable to government intervention.[14]

Let's go one step deeper. Stakeholder groups are rarely homogeneous. Even within a group there is likely to be substantial variation. Take suppliers for example. Some provide undifferentiated commodities with abundant alternatives. Those stakeholder relationships may be more transactional. Suppliers who offer specialized, differentiated, or hard-to-replace inputs are much more critical. The longstanding Windows/Intel monopoly in PCs owed to this kind of stakeholder influence.

So how do you identify primary stakeholders in practice? A nuanced approach is to calibrate stakeholder influence and interests relative to the key dimensions of your transformation, customer value, and business model. Let's discuss stakeholder influence first, then move on to stakeholder interests. And then we'll put them together.

## Assess Stakeholder Influence

Let's first look at stakeholder influence. At a basic level, influence is simply the ability to affect or impact your organization. This can be through formal authority, leadership skill, political maneuvering, and other human interventions. But influence can also be rooted in the structures, systems, and processes of your organization. How your stakeholders are configured may play a role in shaping resource allocation, your capability requirements, and the channels you take to market. Finally, your stakeholders' resources—the materials, information, technologies, financial resources, and human capital—likely affect the way you operate. Our purpose here is to consider how these influences can impact your approach to strategic transformation.

Stakeholder influence can be both positive and negative. Some stakeholders can propel your transformation, and others can stop it in its tracks. Kurt Lewin's framework for change, which he called "force field analysis," was designed to help managers assess both the positive drivers of change and its negative restraints.[15]

As we assess stakeholder influence, the first task is to identify where they bring potentially value-enhancing opportunities—meaning those that facilitate transformation, make it easier, or improve the chances of breakthrough performance. The second way to assess stakeholder influence is to focus on mitigating risk during transformation. Where can stakeholders create challenges or diminish your performance and chances of success? Both are relevant: opportunity *and* risk.

In chapter 3, we discussed a process of mapping your network: (a) identifying key partnerships, (b) examining the resource flows, and (c) determining performance impact. That analysis is an important input to the process of assessing stakeholder influence.

Stakeholders can impact your business transformation in several ways. Here are a few of the most likely:

**Impact on your financials.** Strategic transformation requires you to consider both short- and long-term economic aims. Ask yourself: Which stakeholders impact your future revenue streams and cost structure the most? How do they influence your cash flow and profit and loss (P&L)? In the case of investors or creditors, are there some who have taken a larger equity stake in your business or a concentrated position relative to your financial leverage? How does their effect on your balance sheet propel change or restrain it?

As a first step, it is good to identify which stakeholders have the greatest sway on your financials—either the investment needed for transformation or the returns you are likely to achieve. Obviously, the more they affect future revenue streams and expenses, the more influence that stakeholder is likely to have. In such cases, a second step is to protect your financials, either by finding ways to preserve positive relations with that stakeholder, or by boosting your company's resilience to that influence, either by obviating it, mitigating it, or powering through it (or by both preserving positive relations *and* enhancing your resilience).

Successful transformation is more likely if you have existing growth, healthy margins, and greater optionality (multiple paths forward). The trouble is, many organizations that need transformation the most have none of these (meaning they have no growth, thin margins, and few options). That makes them especially susceptible to, or dependent on, stakeholder influence. That's why assessing the influence of key stakeholders, both positive and negative, is so important.

**Impact on your customers.** Stakeholders can also affect your customers. To assess this, consider which stakeholders can move customer demand and experience either positively or negatively. A large portion of your added value to customers is through your partners. Upstream, in what ways might those partners directly or indirectly influence product or service design, development, or brand image? Downstream, how might they influence the sales cycle, distribution, customer relationship management, and service? Which of your stakeholders help with attracting new customers or retaining existing ones?

Influence over current customer value is important, but in the context of transformation, the critical assessment is influence over *future* value. Recall my earlier example of automobile companies converting to EVs. Executives noted that the future is likely to involve less inventory on dealer lots—perhaps none—and sales that might take place 100 percent online. That requires big changes for dealerships, and as key stakeholders—with a good deal of customer clout—they may be hesitant if not intransigent. As Ford CEO Jim Farley acknowledged, "I think our dealers can do it. But the standards are going to be brutal. They're going to be very different than today."[16]

Don't forget that customers themselves are stakeholders! During transformation, you are likely to offer them something different—new features and benefits—but you may also ask them to give something up. As a result, some of your old customers may defect while you bring on new ones. This shift may be inevitable due to choices you make about channels to market, geographies, demographics, and the like. Successful transformation aims to blunt the negative impact of these stakeholder risks—and increase positive opportunity—by establishing strong customer loyalty, open communication, and multiple paths to market. Ultimately, these stakeholder relationships may be the arbiters of your success.

**Impact on your operations.** A third place to assess stakeholder influence is in operations. Consider the key factors required for maintaining continuity of operations during transformation and who has influence over those factors. Who can enhance production capacity and flexibility by affecting the volume, speed, quality, or cost of your processes? Which suppliers have critical inputs and resources? How responsive are they to shifts in demand? Which partners provide essential complements and value-added technologies, components, and services? Which distributors can open or choke your channels to market? How flexible are they to changes in demand?

To the extent that you have limited options for resourcing these inputs or would incur substantial switching costs, those stakeholders exert considerable influence over your transformation. For example, supply chain bottlenecks during (and after) the pandemic affected a wide swath of industries, ranging from computers to furniture and even baby formula. General Motors acknowledged that because of semiconductor shortages, it built around 100,000 vehicles that had to be set aside. These shortages were unforeseen, but they show the impact of suppliers on operations and illustrate sources of business risk during transformation.[17]

By the way, one obvious set of stakeholders that influence operations daily are your employees (and sometimes their union representatives). For example, Hollywood executives experienced substantial pushback from writers and actors as they made the move from traditional linear television to streaming and AI. The work stoppage associated with their strike brought the industry to a virtual standstill.

The broader lesson? Your odds of successful transformation increase when your firm finds ways to preserve the degrees of freedom to flex operations, achieve optionality through different sourcing strategies, and build robust capacity to assure continuity of operations if demand fluctuates.[18]

**Impact on your talent and culture.** All employees are valuable, and some are more critical to your transformation than others. I touched on this in the last chapter (Establish Context) and will elaborate further in chapter 5 (Orchestrate Mobilization). For our purposes here, consider which stakeholders influence the supply of your mission-critical talent—those skill pools with unique and valuable knowledge that we often refer to as "A" positions. This includes key leadership positions as well as specialized functional areas. Universities, headhunters, and recruiting firms are key stakeholders in this process. And research suggests that some of the best hires come from inside the organization through employee referrals.[19]

Recently I had an opportunity to do some work with one of the branches of the U.S. Department of Defense (DoD) in their effort to strategically transform the military. Among their biggest concerns was the recruitment, development, and retention of key technical talent in their civilian workforces. This labor shortage was hamstringing the DoD's timeframe and capacity for transformation. The analysis highlighted the importance of working with stakeholders in the defense-industrial base, federal and state agencies, universities, and local communities to develop and deploy at scale a workforce with the requisite skills, values, standards, and expectations (i.e., culture) needed to achieve service readiness for the future.

Remember, as you engage stakeholders for transformation, keep in mind that some of the most important jobs are ones that don't yet exist, because they represent *new skills* needed for the future—skills associated with new sources of value creation and that will anchor new organizational capability. Your ability to attract, develop, and retain talent is either a catalyst for change or a limiting factor if your pipeline is closed.

**Impact on your reputation.** Remember the adage, "You are known by the company you keep"? Organizations—and individuals—with whom you are associated may influence how others see you. Recall, for example, the reputational damage that Apple endured because of its relationship with Foxconn, a Taiwanese contract manufacturer with a problematic history of bad working conditions, labor abuses, and safety violations. Because Apple aspired to build a reputation for transparency and ethical behavior, Foxconn's actions proved especially problematic and damaging, even affecting Apple's stock price.

In many ways, this is not just about reputation. It directly relates to the larger issues inherent in being a good corporate citizen, especially regarding ESG concerns. Which stakeholders are particularly influential on these issues? Are they aligned with your values?

As you go through these assessments, look for patterns in your data. You will likely see that some stakeholders are very influential on one dimension but not others. Shareholders, for example, may have a strong influence over financials but a more moderate influence on other aspects of your business. Other stakeholders may not be as influential on any single dimension, but their impact accumulates and is aggregated across the range of dimensions. For example, labor unions can be very influential during transformation because they can affect financials, customers, operations, employees, and reputation.

Let's refer to the first type of influence as *intensity of influence* and the second as *magnitude of influence*. Intensity refers to how much impact there is in a particular part of your business. Magnitude is the overall scale of the impact. At the end of the day, you're looking to assess both intensity and magnitude. How you engage each stakeholder will depend on their influence profile. (More on that in the next section.)

Managers sometimes ask me whether the positive or negative influences cancel each other out. The answer is no, unfortunately they don't. Both positive and negative influences are important, and frequently you'll find that stakeholders can both positively and negatively affect an outcome (sometimes at the same time). For example, you need not search any further than your employees. They contribute energy and innovation in your organization, and they can also be a source of aggravation and dissent. It's their decision, their choice. And that's why engaging stakeholders and building trusting relationships is so important.

It gets more complicated when you consider that your stakeholders influence one another as well. The value of an ecosystem approach to transformation is that you consider multiple interrelationships and the degree of mutual interdependence.

Let's pause for a second. Before moving on, take a moment to do a rough assessment of your primary stakeholders, identifying perhaps six to eight that have the most influence on your transformation, customer value, and business model. (Note that as you consider this question, you may come up with more and more stakeholders, and that's fine as a first pass. But the process of honing your list gives you strategic insights.) Where in your value chain—financials, customers, operations, and so forth—do these stakeholders have the biggest effects? Which stakeholders are critical for propelling transformation, and which can bog down or derail your progress?

For some managers, this assessment results in a startling recognition of just how dependent their business is on others. This can be a vulnerability, and it underscores the importance of stakeholder engagement.

## Assess Stakeholder Interests

In addition to assessing stakeholder influence, it is equally important to understand stakeholder interests. Recently, I was invited to work with a senior executive team that was spearheading a big transformation with a group of powerful suppliers. One of the members admitted, "I wish I knew what motivates them. What do they care about, want, and need? What are their concerns and ambitions?" It was a moment of candor and honesty.

In a nutshell, the question of stakeholder interests boils down to: "How much—and in what ways—do your business plans impact them?" A growing body of research suggests that addressing those interests— and helping stakeholders to achieve their desired aims—can be instrumental to achieving *your* long-term value. Especially if you define value more broadly.

In 2019, the Business Roundtable codified its "Statement on the Purpose of a Corporation," signed by 181 influential CEOs. The statement delineated the need to create value for customers, employees, suppliers, communities, and shareholders. It generated substantial debate about the notion of "purpose," but virtually no disagreement that all stakeholders are potentially important. In fact, the notion of stakeholder capitalism is defined as companies seeking long-term value creation by considering the needs of all their stakeholders, including society at large.[20]

And it's important to remember that value is typically not a zero-sum game, with the spoils to be apportioned among stakeholders; rather, it is a system of mutual investment and return. There are direct and indirect effects in this dynamic system. How you engage stakeholders may impact more than your relationships with them; it may influence your broader image and reputation, even your internal identity as an organization.

We can approach this in an enlightened, philosophical way, and we can be very pragmatic. At a minimum, we can agree that if our strategic transformation depends on the actions of key stakeholders, we should learn more and consider "what's in it for them." This includes their level of interest, including both how much they care and what they care about specifically.

**Seek first to understand, then to be understood.** This sage advice about listening is originally attributed to Saint Francis of Assisi and is foundational to effective stakeholder engagement. How your stakeholders see things and interpret events is influenced by their needs and interests. Listening with empathy helps you learn and better understand where they are coming from.

When Bill Bratton became New York City's police commissioner, he understood the rugged political terrain of the job. He had held similar positions in Boston, and he recognized the importance of engaging stakeholders. He also knew that his plan for transformation would be supported by some and resisted (even sabotaged) by others. With the help of John Timoney (his trusted second, a twenty-year veteran and a "cop's cop"), Bratton identified advocates and naysayers among his primary stakeholders.

What's interesting about Bratton's approach is that he wasted no time before going to talk with the naysayers. Rather than arguing the merits of his plan to convince them, he listened to their concerns and ideas to learn about their interests.

Bratton also required his officers to convene regular community meetings so that citizens within each of the precincts could come together and share their concerns as well. Importantly, Bratton kept this up over time. He emphasized that he never wanted to go too long without touching base with the NYPD's key constituencies.[21]

There's good reason for that. Stakeholder interests change over time as events transpire and new information comes to light. Engaging with them over the long term to learn their interests creates the potential of discovery and understanding. It can also open the decision-making process to different perspectives, which might uncover more potential options going forward.

Unilever did something similar as part of its Compass Vision and USLP. Polman had his team lead a series of "Brand Deep Dives" to engage with consumers in their homes. Unlike typical marketing focus groups, these deep dives involved a succession of two-hour discussions with customers to learn about their interests, how they used the products, as well as "human themes" that connected them to the company and how it fit into their lives. As Marc Mathieu, senior vice president of marketing, put it, "We put people first, recognizing them as humans, not just consumers ... People today expect transparency and real-time engagement ... To develop a personal relationship with end users, the role of marketing has to change from creating a myth and telling it, to *finding a truth and sharing it*" (emphasis added).[22]

With better appreciation of your stakeholder interests, you might find common ground with them, winning them over by framing the discussion around how your plans align with their most important goals. Recall from our discussion of Mayo Clinic's transformation that doctors were concerned that the 2020 Initiative was only about making money. Dr. Noseworthy took time to meet with these doctors to convey how the plan for new business models would help achieve Mayo's mission of reaching more patients and saving more lives. He would not have succeeded in winning them over if he hadn't first taken the time to listen to them and focus on the long-term mutual interests.

Beyond the wholesale prospect of winning them over, listening to stakeholders gives you a chance to reframe the problem in order to jointly problem-solve and achieve mutual gains. Experts in negotiations often distinguish between position-based bargaining and interest-based bargaining. The former involves unyielding, opposing viewpoints (positions) and tends to end in either compromise or complete lack of agreement. Interest-based bargaining, on the other hand, involves collaboration and joint problem-solving to find win-win solutions. It is not at all uncommon in labor negotiations, for example, for employees and managers to have similar *interests*, such as safety or employment security, but very different *positions* on how to achieve those interests. Listening helps you parse out underlying interests.[23]

Listening is critical for building trust. Research by Edelman Intelligence suggests that stakeholders generally value more input. According to a survey by the 2021 Edelman Trust Barometer, 68 percent of consumers and 62 percent of employees thought they should have input in corporate decision-making.[24]

Being heard and having input are important for improving what my colleague Jim Detert calls "voice"—that is, the opportunity to express concerns and offer suggestions. That improves trust and strengthens relationships over time, helping them endure through rough patches. Even if stakeholders don't always get what they want, they are more likely to see the process as fair if they feel heard.[25]

Returning to Bill Bratton, there is a third reason why he listened to stakeholders (particularly naysayers). Bratton was no pushover, and he understood that if there was not going to be a meeting of the minds, he needed to learn what they cared about and discover what obstacles he would need to overcome to achieve success.

**Calibrate stakeholder interests.** Assessing stakeholder interest is not always easy, in part because their ultimate ends are not always indicated by what they say and do. What we see are their actions—tactics, strategies, and observable behaviors—and we try to reconcile these with what they purport to be their goals and interests. But the reality is that things don't always add up, and the frustrating "say-do gap" puts the relationship at risk.

I'm sure you've seen examples of this. So, while it's invaluable to listen to stakeholders and build relationships that can endure, it is also essential to gather more data that reflect the realities of the relationship over time. In my experience, stakeholder interests tend to fall into five general categories, as shown in Figure 4.1: Purpose, Position, Performance, Process, and People.

Return now to your list of most influential stakeholders. As you contemplate transformation, what are likely to be their chief interests? What data support that assessment? Recognize that these interests—and their relative importance—may change over time. And the longer you have had a relationship with them, the more likely their interests are to be accompanied by *expectations.* The bottom line is that your transformation plans may alter the calculus on some of these interests and expectations. It bears repeating that if your strategic transformation supports their interests or elevates what's possible for your stakeholders, they will likely be on board with you. If your plans jeopardize those interests or work in opposition to them, that puts them at risk, and they will likely not support you. In fact, they may well oppose you. (Keep in mind that their "level of interest" in your plan is directly proportional to the impact it has on them.)

For example, consider Airbnb and its hosts (the property owners). When the COVID-19 pandemic hit, Airbnb was besieged with thousands of guest requests for cancellations and refunds. Because of Airbnb's clear commitment to preserving long-term customer value—and doing the right thing—the company revised its "extenuating circumstances" policy, allowing guests to cancel reservations and receive full refunds. By May 2020, the refunds had totaled $1 billion. Hosts had to forgo that revenue—leaving them exposed financially—and many understandably wondered why Airbnb was taking care of the customer but not them. Nearly 50 percent of those hosts depended on rental income to pay their mortgages and rental fees.[26]

Airbnb's policy change had apparently disregarded the interests of hosts and violated their expectations. CEO Brian Chesky was faced with a situation where some hosts left the platform, while others brought litigation against Airbnb. Chesky responded in a letter to hosts that read in part, "Please know this decision was not a business decision, but based

| Interest | Description | Example |
|---|---|---|
| **Purpose** | Stakeholders may be purpose-driven, focused on achieving their mission, vision of the future, and foundational values. Some see it as their *raison d'etre*; the reason for being perhaps at a philosophical level. | Non-governmental organizations (NGOs), non-profits, community organizations, educational institutions, religious organizations |
| **Position** | Stakeholders may be interested in positioning, competitive advantage, status, or improving their relative standing in the industry or professional community. Some may find real benefit in your affiliation, a relational asset with spillover effects to their own brand. | Professional service firms with enviable client lists, law firms with high profile cases, investment firms with high-net-worth clients. |
| **Performance** | Stakeholders may be interested in the practicality of performance outcomes. Often defined in financial terms (profits, margins), and may also include other aspects of goal achievement relative to customers (sales, market share) or product functionality and performance. | Consumer products firms focused on share price, market share, new product portfolio. Retailers concerned about recurring revenue, customer retention, inventory turns, and stock outs. |
| **Process** | Stakeholders may be particular about the manner in which they work with you; that is, the process. This may include tangible elements, such as the design of workstreams and systems integration, data sharing, etc. It may include intangible elements such as decision making, trust, integrity, and ethics. | Contractors concerned about safety protocols. Six sigma organizations establishing aligned ways of working that do not compromise standards. Tech firms that prioritize data exchange, storage, privacy and security. |
| **People** | Stakeholders may be concerned about the well-being of people, job satisfaction, employment security, opportunities for advancement, retention, etc. This may include access to talent or the ability to acquire and transfer knowledge. | M&A firms concerned about headcount or culture compatibility. Professional services firms that leverage rainmakers. |

FIGURE 4.1. The Five Ps of Stakeholder Interest

on protecting public health ... We have heard from you and know we could have been better partners ... When your business suffers, our business suffers. We know that right now many of you are struggling, and what you need are actions from us to help, not just words."[27]

Chesky's letter was a clear signal that he was listening to his stakeholders, but he would need to go further to address their interests and expectations if he hoped to get the organization back into alignment.

## STEP 2: CUSTOMIZE YOUR ENGAGEMENT STRATEGY

It is very common for organizations to formalize stakeholder management. For example, corporate boards of directors are explicitly created to align the interests of shareholders with the governance of the firm. Other departments and centers of excellence are often created around key stakeholder groups. Consider, for example, the number of organizations that have investor relations departments, public relations offices, customer relations management, employee relations functions, and the like. The value of these formalized approaches to stakeholder management is that they enable firms to build structures, processes, systems, and capabilities around ongoing day-to-day stakeholder interests, and to allocate top talent to the effort.

Successful leaders understand that in addition to those formalized structures, strategic transformation requires a more personalized, hands-on approach. In the context of transformation, the most important reason to assess stakeholder interests is to determine how best to customize an engagement strategy with stakeholders. The broad spectrum of engagement approaches, from least to most engaging, includes the following: informing, consulting, involving, collaborating, and empowering.

How do you choose? As a starting point, you may find it useful to map stakeholders along the two dimensions underlying our discussions so far in this chapter: (1) degree of *influence*: power to impact the transformation, and (2) degree of *interest*: extent to which it impacts them. It's a useful heuristic because your engagement strategy depends upon where a stakeholder lies within this matrix (shown in Figure 4.2). But keep in mind—like everything else in strategic transformation, this mapping is dynamic and changes over time.[28]

### Involve Primary Stakeholders

"Keep your friends close, and your enemies closer" is an ancient proverb attributed to Sun Tzu (though you may recall this line from *The Godfather*). Some powerful stakeholders—those with great influence and great interest in your business—may be your advocates. Rely on them and nurture their goodwill.

Boards of directors, for example, are especially vital stakeholders during a transformation. Because profit margins may diminish during the first phases, your top team must have board support before venturing in. More generally, a board's governance responsibility for key decisions affecting the direction of the organization makes it a critical ally in strategic transformation.

Microsoft's board was generally supportive of Satya Nadella's transformation and stayed mostly out of the whirlwind of change, giving him

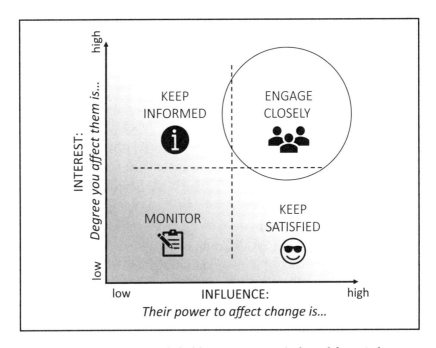

FIGURE 4.2. Customize Stakeholder Engagement (Adapted from Aubrey Mendelow, "Stakeholder Mapping," *Proceedings of the 2nd International Conference on Information Systems, Cambridge, MA* 5, no. 2 (1991): 91.)

the autonomy he needed. In selecting Nadella as CEO, the board showed confidence in his ability to change Microsoft's direction and steer it into spaces where others might not. Despite the inevitable pressures of activist investors, Microsoft's board gave Nadella room to run and did not try to intervene or micromanage. As board chair Bill Gates put it, "Satya is a proven leader with hard-core engineering skills, business vision, and the ability to bring people together." (And the fact that the stock price jumped quickly didn't hurt his case.) To keep their support and reinforce their advocacy, Nadella communicated frequently with the board and kept them apprised of his progress.[29]

Nadella also recruited Gates to work on new products and technology, and the two cooperated closely. Although Gates had formally retired, Nadella realized that no one had as much influence or star power as he did. He knew Bill Gates as the face of transformation would generate excitement about (and confer legitimacy on) a new future.

Of course, not every powerful stakeholder is benevolent. Some have great influence and great interest—but are NOT your advocates. Their interests are not aligned with yours. Regardless, friend or foe, during strategic transformation, it is vital to stay connected with these powerful constituencies, use a high-touch approach, and manage the relationships directly. They are likely the core of your primary stakeholders and may well be central to the viability of your business model and plan for transformation.

To tailor your engagement strategy, you'll need to determine the extent to which these stakeholders' interests are *complementary or competing*. In reality, with any stakeholder, it is very likely that some of your interests will be complementary, while others will be competing. You want to make sure to manage the mix.

**Complementary interests: Collaborate.** In instances where your stakeholders' interests are *complementary* to yours—consistent, supporting, or value-adding—you can more easily achieve alignment and move forward more quickly. Collaborating closely with these allies can help you achieve mutual gains and shared outcomes. Don't leave this to chance. At a minimum, you need to make your interests clear to these partners. And as far as possible, explain the logic of your business model evolution, customer value, and capabilities. They will likely gain insight from this. The more integral they are to those plans, the more detail they'll need. In the best of cases, they share your vision for the transformation. Ideally, the win-win solution is that your collaboration generates opportunities for more value, both for you and for them.

Unilever was fortunate that some of its suppliers saw Compass Vision and USLP as a chance to enhance sustainability and ESG priorities, while others saw it as "greenwashing" and a source of additional constraints on their businesses. But importantly, almost none of those suppliers was indifferent to USLP, because the transformation affected all of them.

Polman's strategy was to involve suppliers directly and collaborate with them in the process. He was able to learn about their positions and enroll them in the plan. The results were very encouraging: The supply chain responded with passion and creativity, embracing the strategic challenge and driving positive change. For example, early success included implementing sustainable sourcing policies with small farmers. With this kind of engagement, in just three years, Polman was able to increase the proportion of sustainably sourced products in the supply chain from 14 percent to 48 percent.[30]

Polman also met with all his brand leaders, inviting them to assess the environmental, social, and economic impact of the products. His category heads assigned a team to evaluate the environmental footprint of the company's entire portfolio. The result of this engagement strategy was better alignment among key stakeholders around a set of recommendations and innovations that formed a strong platform for implementing USLP.

Polman's experience reinforces the point that engagement with critical stakeholders needs to be personalized and continuing. It is time-intensive, of course, but the payoffs are most worthwhile.

As an aside, these meetings and exchanges should be direct, timely, and personal (face-to-face when possible), to demonstrate the importance of transparency and the value of the relationship, not just the task.[31]

As Polman described it, "As we opened up our model and more transparency, we also ended up building more trust with our stakeholders, with our partners in the value chain that we worked with. But what is very clear, it is first and foremost, very motivational for our employees."[32]

**Competing interests: Compromise or confront.** While ideally your stakeholders have complementary interests, some of your primary stakeholders will have *competing interests*—that is, their objectives may be inconsistent with, or even antithetical to, your own as you move forward with transformation.

These can be delicate if not difficult situations, because your business plan probably requires their involvement, not just acquiescence. For example, during transformation some employee groups may resist change because they favor job security and consistency. Change is risky to them. Senior leaders can force the issue, commanding employees to comply, but this may deteriorate alignment and jeopardize employee relations in the future.

So, dealing with competing interests can be tricky. Often it comes down to a trade-off between accomplishing your task objectives and preserving the relationship for the future. When preserving the relationship is important if not essential, achieving compromise tends to be a worthwhile goal.[33]

Recall Brian Chesky's *mea culpa* with Airbnb hosts. He had decided to allow guests to cancel reservations and get full refunds without adequately involving hosts in that decision. And hosts were the ones directly affected by the decision. The backlash could have been worse than it was. Chesky emphasized the importance of long-term relationships with hosts and tried to find a solution. As a compromise, Airbnb committed $250 million to reimburse hosts for up to 25 percent of their lost funds. Chesky and the other Airbnb founders personally contributed $17 million to a relief fund from which super hosts—those with top ratings—could draw funds for mortgage payments.[34]

Notice that in seeking compromise, Chesky was transparent and emphasized the importance of the long-term relationship with hosts to restore goodwill and trust. He also made them whole financially. With those two priorities as a foundation, it was easier for Chesky to pursue a compromise path of "give a little, get a little" going forward. The lesson? Reciprocity doesn't need to be simultaneous, but the ledgers eventually need to balance. Ultimately, Chesky and the hosts aligned around joint objectives and shared mission for the company. In my experience, this is one of the best ways to balance competing priorities, and perhaps to move toward complementary interests.

But let's not be too idealistic. The Airbnb story had a happy resolution. However, in instances where competing interests cannot be managed through compromise, it may be necessary to confront opposition. The reality is that stakeholder engagements sometimes involve tough conversations. It's all about managing expectations.

For example, early in his tenure as CEO of Unilever, Polman told shareholders that the company would no longer publish quarterly annual reports or offer earnings guidance for the stock market. Polman declared that Unilever would now take the long view. He even went a step further, urging shareholders to invest elsewhere if they didn't "buy into this long-term value-creation model, which is equitable, which is shared, which is sustainable."[35]

There's obvious risk involved in confronting powerful stakeholders the way Polman did. But he understood the importance of taking decisive action on an unpopular decision, establishing realistic expectations, and establishing his position in leading the transformation.[36]

Bill Bratton also faced numerous powerful stakeholders with competing interests. Recall that when he began his transformation of the NYPD, he identified naysayers among his primary stakeholders and took pains to learn their concerns and interests. As with any change, there were some in the community who were happy with the status quo and took issue with Bratton's plans, particularly his emphasis on "zero-tolerance" policing (based in part on the idea that addressing minor infractions prevents bigger crimes). Because Bratton understood the (competing) interests of naysayers, his engagement strategy with them was to isolate them, build the broadest coalition possible among other stakeholders, and bring irrefutable evidence to discredit the opponents' claims.

For example, one of Bratton's most serious obstacles came from the objection that prosecuting small "quality of life" crimes would overwhelm the city's courts with a burdensome caseload. Bratton sought support from the mayor's office, which had considerable sway with district attorneys, the courts, and the jail system. Bratton's team provided data to the mayor's office showing that the court system could handle minor quality-of-life crimes, such as loitering and disorderly conduct, even though it preferred not to. While acknowledging the potential for a short-term rise in cases, he indicated that the evidence was clear that in the longer term, this approach would lead to a reduced workload. Recognizing that the mayor's office was giving Bratton "top cover," the courts appealed to the local legislators. Bratton and the mayor conferred with each other weekly and broadened their coalition to include the news media, in particular *The New York Times*. Through a deluge of articles, press conferences, and interviews, Bratton took every opportunity to put "zero tolerance" front and center of the debate. Eventually, he won in the court of public opinion.[37]

Not every transformation involves this kind of political wrangling. But many do. Some very powerful stakeholders—stakeholders with whom you are interdependent—may have interests and agendas that will not align with yours. Remember, one of our premises about business ecosystems is that participants both cooperate and compete. Engaging with them over time helps you shape your relationships. Understanding when to collaborate, when to compromise, and when to confront powerful stakeholders is key to your success in bringing about strategic transformation.

And this highlights why establishing context (in the prior chapter) is an important prerequisite for strategic transformation. It gives you clarity on the reasons for change, the critical aspects of your transformation, and the strategic intent going forward. That gives you stability in the back-and-forth volleys of stakeholder engagement. It's not that you can't adapt or won't make concessions or compromises over time, but a good understanding of your context and the network of interdependencies among your stakeholders results in a strong foundation for finding mutual interests for collaboration.

### Placate Secondary Stakeholders

My advice generally is to focus mostly on those primary stakeholders who are directly consequential to your transformation—that is, those with the most influence and the most interest. Achieving success with them goes a long way toward building momentum for change.

However, there are other stakeholders who, while not as obviously important, can make a big difference as well.

**High influence, low interest: Keep them satisfied.** Some of your stakeholders have significant influence but limited interest. For example, some suppliers or vendors who aren't affected much by your transformation plans may simply go along with them. As long as their business isn't affected, they're good. Similarly, powerful government or regulatory agencies may take a wait-and-see approach.

As the saying goes, "let sleeping dogs lie." Your highly influential but benignly disinterested stakeholders need to be kept satisfied. If your transformation does not require a particular stakeholder to make substantial changes themselves—meaning it has little impact on them—they are more likely to accept your objectives. However, because they have high influence, it's wise to consult them about your plans, seeking input and gaining advice. This is more than simply a tactic to keep them placated. Their influence is likely derived from their close involvement in and understanding of your business. Interactions with them may give you useful perspective.

Polman expanded Unilever's engagement with government agencies and NGOs. At the request of the UN secretary general, Polman joined the UN Global Compact, in which global businesses committed to the environment, human rights, and anti-corruption measures. In addition to these stakeholders, Unilever partnered with industry organizations such as the World Business Council for Sustainable Development. It also developed relationships with UNICEF, Save the Children, Oxfam, and the Rainforest Alliance.

A word of caution and perspective: These kinds of engagements are time-consuming and could realistically have led Polman to lose focus. However, in his view, just the opposite happened. It helped Unilever to reframe its commitments to include social impact as well as sustainability. And rather than taking his eye off the ball, the broader stakeholder engagement gave Polman insight and perspective for the USLP transformation.[38]

As he put it, "We have set a bold ambition to achieve change within our own company—through our brands, innovation, sourcing and operations. But we are only one company among many, and the change needed to tackle the world's major social, environmental and economic issues is big—and urgent."[39]

**Low influence, high interest: Keep them informed.** Some of your stakeholders have high interest but low influence. Routinely, this includes those outside your business who are affected by what you do. NGOs, for example, frequently represent the interests of communities that are impacted by an organization but lack the clout, resources, or experience to advocate on their own behalf. This category can also include those within your business who are not in powerful positions.

Although these constituencies may not have a material impact on the outcome, it is wise to keep them informed and updated because of their interest and the degree to which transformation affects them. Depending on the context, this might be either through a "push" strategy, where information is disseminated to interested parties to inform them of plans and events, eliminating surprises, or a "pull" strategy, where the information is provided upon request.

Following the pandemic, some neighborhood communities expressed concern that Airbnb was too "hands-off" regarding safety issues and crime in some of its properties. Even though Airbnb doesn't own the properties, and can't actively monitor them, Chesky established safety measures, set up a 24/7 neighborhood hotline, banned parties on all properties, set up a "risky reservation" cue to look at any suspicious activity, and built a team that uses AI to detect and suspect behavior. As Chesky put it, "If we are part of the problem, we are going to work with cities, that's why we've done numerous agreements with cities, to create restrictions. We actually do want Airbnb to get more and more into long-term housing. We want people to feel invested in the community."[40]

Takeaways from this? Don't underestimate the latent power of a secondary stakeholder group. Influence can be compounded across interested and motivated stakeholders who lead coalitions that have more aggregate influence. A famous example is the Department of Education and teachers' unions. Prior to 1980, teachers' unions within the United States had limited influence over public policy within the federal, state, local, or individual school systems. But the National Education Association (NEA) successfully lobbied the Carter administration to create the Department of Education (DoE), giving it federal control over public education. Since that time, the DoE staff has grown to over 4,000, and the influence of teachers' unions has grown significantly as a result.[41]

Other less famous examples of stakeholder alliances abound. Industry associations, shareholder advocacy groups, international labor unions, and many NGOs represent these kinds of aggregate influences. Coalitions among relevant parties make stakeholder engagement potentially more complicated. However, by tracking these relationships on an ongoing basis and watching their evolution, it's easier to see the state of play, track how the game is changing, and anticipate their responses over time. Experienced executives know that stakeholder engagement is not a one-time or a delegated job, and they manage the transformation with this in mind.

At the end of the day, it may not be possible to achieve total alignment with all your stakeholders or to ensure that those stakeholders are in alignment with one another. Your ecosystem is not that orderly. But the success of your transformation depends on addressing their interests and influences in a way that facilitates change and addresses its complications.

## STEP 3: EMPOWER YOUR KEY INFLUENCERS

So far in this chapter, we've covered ways to differentiate your primary stakeholders, as well as ways to customize your engagement strategy with them. The third critical step in stakeholder management is to empower key influencers who are advocates for transformation. One CEO told me, "It is very difficult to lead strategic change entirely from the C-suite—the organization is too complex, and you are too far away from the action." It's better to identify and empower a core group of influencers—a critical internal stakeholder group—who operate as a de facto coalition to embrace change, accept responsibility, initiate momentum, and draw others to join in the transformation. Harvard's John Kotter, perhaps the most recognized thought leader on change management, refers to this as "the guiding coalition."[42]

In virtually any strategic transformation, there will likely be a natural cohort of individuals, typically within the middle management ranks, who fit this bill. Sometimes they are intrinsically motivated to lead the charge, and sometimes they need to be coaxed. As Chan Kim and Renee Mauborgne observed, "Because most organizations have relatively small numbers of key influencers, and those people tend to share common problems and concerns, it is relatively easy for CEOs to identify and motivate them."[43]

And this key influencer group is a valuable stakeholder in the change. Consider the following questions:

- Is there a natural cohort in our organization that has both the interest and the influence to initiate and catalyze change?
- Do they see the need for transformation? What additional engagement is needed to secure their collaboration?
- What authority and resources would they need to take action and lead as a change coalition?

In Bill Bratton's case, his key influencer group was composed of precinct commanders—midlevel officers with operational credibility—who were core drivers of the transformation. Bratton identified these commanders as key influencers not because of their personalities or personal persuasions but because of where they sat within the organization (i.e., their "A" positions). Each commander had a large span of control, managing 200 to 400 officers, creating powerful inflection points in the organization's structure. Above the commanders, the department had a narrow structure; below them it broadened considerably.

To engage the commanders, Bratton brought them face-to-face with the need to change, helping them see the reality of the situation and then empowering them to tackle it head-on. Rather than merely painting an inspiring vision for them to follow, Bratton made them catalysts of the transformation by holding semi-weekly meetings to review performance and crime statistics within each precinct. Transparency and accountability were strong motivators, and soon the commanders began sharing information and data, challenging and learning from one another, modifying their approaches, and sharing best practices.

The commanders embraced the transformation. Rather than perpetuating the old culture of blame, they embodied a new culture of high-performance learning. They didn't just "buy in" to the transformation; they *owned it*. It wasn't Bratton's plan, it was theirs. And the effect cascaded down through the organization as commanders implemented their versions of Bratton's briefings. And then it had a domino effect, improving performance and reducing crime, in Bratton's words, "block by block, precinct by precinct, and borough by borough."[44]

The power of Bratton's approach derives from our original premise about stakeholder engagement: strategic transformation occurs through the interconnected efforts of others in your ecosystem. This is especially effective when these stakeholders have credibility grounded in experience and influence based on trust. In reflecting on his philosophy about empowering change, Bratton quoted Theodore Roosevelt, the first commissioner of the NYPD: "The best executive is the one who has sense enough to pick good men and women to do what he wants done and self-restraint enough to keep from meddling with them while they do it."

He also emphasized the importance of shared vision and collaboration: "You cannot be successful if you're leading a group of people who don't share your passion, who don't share your vision, who don't share your goals. And you cannot be successful if you don't share theirs. If you're not willing to allow them to share with you their ideas, their passions so you can effectively force-multiply your own with theirs."[45]

## REALITY CHECK

Let's summarize key points in this chapter. As in the previous chapter on establishing context, I invite you to do two things before moving on. First, spend some time reviewing the checklist in Figure 4.3 to do a quick assessment of your organization. How well do you manage stakeholder relationships currently? If you're like many managers, you're generally

| Differentiate primary stakeholders | ☑ We analyze our various stakeholders to determine their influence and identify the role they play in our business. |
| | ☑ We spend time with our stakeholders to better understand their interests, motivations, and expectations of us. |
| | ☑ We prioritize our relationship with a core subset of primary stakeholders who are most important to our success. |
| Customize your engagement strategy | ☑ We are quite strategic in how we engage advocates as well as critics to bring about the best possible outcomes. This is not left to chance. |
| | ☑ We actively partner with stakeholders who have complementary resources, skills, and interests. |
| | ☑ We work to align the interests of shareholders, customers, employees, and others to achieve long-term mutual gains for all. |
| Empower key influencers | ☑ We build coalitions with key influencers in the organization to be catalysts and champions of change. |
| | ☑ Our leaders routinely empower teams to bring about positive change. |
| | ☑ In our organization, empowerment and accountability go hand in hand. |

FIGURE 4.3. Checklist for Engaging Stakeholders

aware that stakeholders play a role in strategic change, but perhaps you haven't assessed their roles thoroughly or specifically. There's obviously value in that.

Second, think about how you could close the gap between where you are and where you need to be with these stakeholders. Recall that at the beginning of the chapter, I shared research showing that while executives understand the importance of stakeholder engagement—and are spending more time on it—their success rate achieving alignment is quite poor.

As you went through the chapter, were there questions or concerns that kept cropping up? What have you done well, and where do you need the most improvement? How can you engage others in your organization around these issues? What lessons can you draw from the company examples in this chapter?

## Differentiate Your Primary Stakeholders

How much effort do you put into distinguishing your most important stakeholders? There's a lot of buzz around the importance of stakeholder management, but much of it is philosophical and even political. Very little of it is strategic.

Your transformation takes place within the context of a complex and dynamic network of interdependencies. The value you create and the advantage you derive are based on those interdependencies. Unfortunately, you are unlikely to succeed if you haven't mapped the terrain of those relationships and planned for how you will engage with them. As your transformation gets underway, the terrain may change as interests and influence evolve.

### Customize Your Engagement Strategy

You need to tailor how you engage stakeholders to their unique interests and expectations, as well as their influence over your transformation. One size doesn't fit all. If their interests are complementary to yours, you're in a much better position to collaborate successfully to co-create more value for both you and your partners. If they have competing interests or resist your vision for the future, you'll need to find ways to reach a compromise with them or develop effective approaches to confront and defuse their opposition.

Every stakeholder is important, and every stakeholder is different. But there are patterns or similarities that help you customize your strategy for engaging different stakeholders. Your most important ones need personal attention and ongoing interaction. To the extent possible, being transparent and treating them ethically helps build trust and a sense of fairness. Others may only require periodic updates and information to keep them in the loop. But given the limits of time and resources, your approach to engagement may be different.

Either way, as much as possible, take a long-term view. For example, during the COVID-19 pandemic, many organizations laid off workers to cut costs and save cash. Others burned through cash to do whatever they could to keep staff employed. When consumer demand bounced back, companies that limited layoffs were in a better position to restore performance and customer value.[46]

### Empower Your Key Influencers

Finally, think about those within your organization who would be the natural candidates to take the lead in guiding a coalition of change.

Sometimes this is based on where they are within the hierarchy (typically not the C-suite), and sometimes it is based on their expertise. But like all critical stakeholders, their power tends to be based on their influence in the organization, particularly those lower in the hierarchy, and their inclination or interest in seeing the transformation succeed.

## PLAYBOOK TOOLS

As you did at the end of chapter 3, take time—with your team—to get stakeholder analysis down on paper. The idea of stakeholder engagement is intuitive, and yet there is a stark contrast between acknowledging the concepts and doing the actual work. As a starting point for building your playbook for stakeholder engagement, take time to parse through key aspects of your most important partnerships.

**Directions for Building a Playbook:** Work through the following analysis as a team. Get consensus on your answers and chart your key points using Playbook Template 4.1, at the end of the chapter.

- *Stakeholder Interests and Influence.* Delineate which internal and external stakeholder groups have a vested interest in your business transformation? Who is affected and whose support do you need?
  - List the key stakeholders who are (a) affected by the changes you propose, and/or (b) affect the success of the initiative.
  - Influence: What type of power or influence might these stakeholders have over the outcome? How might they respond—positively or negatively—to the proposed strategic change? What leverage do they have?
  - Interests: For each stakeholder group, what are their key interests? What do they care about most, and how might the proposed strategic change involve them? Why might they oppose the change, or support it? Are their interests complementary or competing?
- *Stakeholder Engagement Strategies*
  - Map your stakeholders along these two dimensions: (a) *influence*: power to impact the initiative, and (b) *interest*: the degree to which it impacts them. Note that these may be categories of

stakeholders (e.g., distributors) and/or individual stakeholders (e.g., a key component supplier). Hint: Sometimes maps of stakeholders crowd too many parties in the top right corner. As a team, discipline yourselves to distribute your ratings pragmatically. Use Playbook Template 4.2 at the end of the chapter to record your analysis.

– Engagement strategy: Given how you have mapped each stakeholder, how would you engage them? What approach would work best? How would you minimize the negative implications and maximize the positive in order to gain support and create shared value? Be specific and think through how your approach would affect both the relationship and the outcomes of the transformation.

- *Empower Key Influencers.* Identify individuals who are uniquely positioned in your organization and who have the influence and interest to form the core of your transformation team. These individuals are perhaps readily identifiable because of their vested interest in the transformation. How would you involve them now to gauge their interest and capacity to serve? (More on this in the next chapter.)

## WHAT'S NEXT? ORCHESTRATE MOBILIZATION

Before we move on to the next chapter, remember that the transformation framework in chapter 2 reflects a system of change priorities, balancing external and internal pressures (the essence of strategy) and reconciling the forces of divergence and convergence (dynamic organization). To this point in the book, we have focused primarily on the external factors. Establishing context for transformation requires an assessment of how the environment is shifting, the powers of disruption, and the opportunities for business model innovation. Stakeholder engagement also has an external focus, oriented toward achieving alignment and convergence in order to co-create value.

In the next chapter, we'll shift gears a bit, focusing more on the internal dynamics of the organization and ways to orchestrate the allocation of resources for transformation.

| STAKEHOLDER | INFLUENCE | INTERESTS |
|---|---|---|
| 1. | | |
| 2. | | |
| 3. | | |
| 4. | | |
| 5. | | |
| 6. | | |
| 7. | | |

PLAYBOOK TEMPLATE 4.2. Engagement Strategy

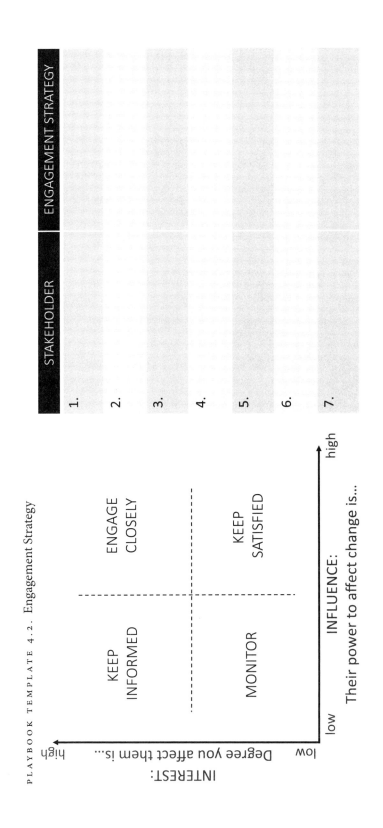

| STAKEHOLDER | ENGAGEMENT STRATEGY |
| --- | --- |
| 1. | |
| 2. | |
| 3. | |
| 4. | |
| 5. | |
| 6. | |
| 7. | |

INTEREST:
Degree you affect them is...
high ← low

KEEP INFORMED | ENGAGE CLOSELY

MONITOR | KEEP SATISFIED

low     INFLUENCE:     high
Their power to affect change is...

# 5 FACTOR THREE—ORCHESTRATE MOBILIZATION: CONVERT VISION INTO ACTION

**KEY PRINCIPLE:** Successful transformation hinges on orchestrating a multitude of organizational resources to achieve a bold ambition.

MAYO CLINIC PROVIDES a great example of orchestration. To accomplish Mayo's plan to pursue growth and innovation through new business models, CEO John Noseworthy needed to convert that grand idea into actionable goals and a concrete set of strategic initiatives across the enterprise. It was one thing to inspire transformation with a compelling vision for the future. It was another to translate that vision into action. Noseworthy would engage his steering committee to clarify priorities and lay out a multifaceted action plan to drive performance.[1]

Unilever's challenge was similar. CEO Paul Polman had purposely devised the Unilever Sustainable Living Plan (USLP) to be very bold, and very broad, involving a panoply of stakeholders with varying interests. In the previous chapter, you learned a bit about how he engaged those stakeholders. Beyond that, to get traction and show real progress, Polman needed to coordinate the efforts of many parties inside and outside the organization. To focus their efforts, he established clear priorities and performance metrics for USLP, and he mobilized a transformation team to encourage collaboration across the enterprise. As you can imagine, the logistic challenge was daunting.

Microsoft's transformation was equally complicated. Satya Nadella's pivot to "cloud-first, mobile-first" was more than a new strategy. The orchestration challenges were like those of Mayo and Unilever in some respects, but Microsoft's transformation was rooted in what Nadella believed was a cultural renaissance—an effort to reinvigorate the spirit of collaboration and innovation that had eroded over the years. The culture refresh would be accompanied by a new structure, new processes, and a new set of key priorities. Nadella's job as leader was to achieve alignment in this new organization, and then underpin it with a new organizational architecture where all key parts—and parties—were integrated to the whole.

Chalhoub Group's digital transformation began with a series of unfortunate missteps, illustrating the challenges and risks of pivoting to a new business model before mastering the capabilities to do so. Chalhoub's leadership team recognized the need to adapt to industry changes. From a traditional Middle Eastern luxury distributor and retailer, it would transform into a hybrid retailer bringing exclusive experiences to customers everywhere. As Patrick Chalhoub wrote in a company white paper, "To be successful, we will have to be aspirational, relevant, meaningful, and competitive, and adapt to the changes and to the new norm." But change was not easy, and the company learned some hard lessons along the way.[2]

## THE CHALLENGE

Each of these examples highlights the third factor of strategic transformation: orchestrating mobilization. This involves identifying a set of initiatives with the best prospects to drive transformation, and then marshaling the resources and configuring the organization to achieve your strategic intent. In this chapter, I'll discuss the key aspects of effective orchestration and share more about how the leadership at Mayo Clinic, Microsoft, Unilever, and Chalhoub Group undertook this journey.[3]

### Symptoms of Poor Orchestration

As with the other requirements for successful transformation, there are symptoms—or side effects—of poor orchestration that you'll want to avoid. Some of these reflect a lack of clarity and focus during the ear-lier steps of transformation, resulting in confusion and misalignment. Some symptoms relate to the absence of coordination and collaboration across the organization—people may be energized but run off in dif-ferent directions, resulting in chaos and even conflict. Still other symp-toms of poor orchestration relate to the misallocation of resources. The structures, processes, and systems that must be configured to support change sometimes work at cross-purposes, binding up the organization. As a result, things bog down and the organization has a difficult time mobilizing change.

Let's look at a few of these symptoms in the context of Chalhoub Group's digital transformation.

**Cacophony and discord.** Lack of alignment results in so much noise. The whole point of orchestration is to coordinate and align dis-parate elements to achieve a unified outcome. When people work in silos, it often results in miscoordination, arguably the biggest threat to orchestrating transformation.[4]

Patrick Chalhoub has openly discussed the Group's difficulties in transforming from its brick-and-mortar retail model to the fast-paced environment of e-commerce. This was new territory for the firm, and its leadership team didn't have experience—or technical expertise—in digital retailing. Initially, Chalhoub's digital strategy involved a decen-tralized approach, setting up stand-alone websites for its business units, such as Level Shoes, Level Kids, Wojooh (a cosmetics store), Tryano, Ghawali, Lacoste, and Swarovski, among others.

But the approach was too fragmented, and progress too slow, as the company tried to develop a compelling digital story that cohered across its many brands. The result was a lot of noise in the system and not enough coordination. The organization was moving in too many dis-jointed directions, and its strategy began to lose coherence. And while the decentralized approach was perhaps initially easier to deploy, it made things more complicated for the customer.

To adjust, Chalhoub did a one-eighty and set up a centralized "digi-tal competence" center in Sharjah (the third-biggest city in the United

Arab Emirates) to develop online initiatives. The centralized team charged with this goal was technically strong but was "too far removed from the business. There were a lot of bottlenecks because they were not able to move at the speed of the business," Chalhoub said.[5]

**Perils of incrementalism: Too little too late.** This experience highlights the risk inherent in a lack of coordination. Patrick Chalhoub described the company's early mistakes this way:

> As soon as we felt the importance of being more digital, more connected, we took the first step, but it was, I would say, late. We should have taken it before.
>
> Our first step was to create a digital center in order to enter the digital world. However, although we felt that we were moving in the right direction, we weren't necessarily doing it in the way that was sustainable for the future. The reason is that, at first, we felt that going digital was just a marginal part, whereas it wasn't, it influenced everyone and everything. We couldn't have only one part of the organization looking into this, as we had initially thought, but we had to make sure that everyone was included.
>
> It took us six months to formulate our digital strategy, but when we did it in July 2016, we felt that it shouldn't be only digital transformation, but the overall transformation of the organization, including the change in our culture, our behaviors, our processes, and so on. It was about making sure that people made quick decisions using digital technology in order to be relevant to the consumers, who, at their end, were also moving very quickly.[6]

Too slow and too fragmented. Patrick Chalhoub deserves a lot of credit for recognizing the problem and making an immediate course correction. Orchestrating transformation requires a comprehensive approach, synchronizing and integrating across the whole organization. There are a lot of moving pieces, and evidence suggests that when organizations fail, it's often because they neglect one (or more) of those pieces.[7]

### What You Can Do

Chalhoub' s experience is a cautionary tale and highlights the difficulty of orchestrating change, particularly in new competency areas, when multiple elements of your business model are changing and your customer expectations are evolving.

Because orchestrating transformation involves the coordination of so many different resources, it can get overwhelming quickly. In this chapter, I'll share three key steps in the process that make it more effective:

1. *Translate vision into action:* Clarify key priorities and devise a focused set of strategic initiatives to drive performance and achieve your vision.
2. *Mobilize your transformation network:* Demonstrate leadership alignment at the top, activate a transformation team to lead cross-functional collaboration, and leverage partnerships.
3. *Reconfigure the organization architecture:* Streamline structures and processes and customize tech deployments.

Each of the main sections of this chapter address these three steps. As you can see, there's a lot to cover. Let's get at it.

## STEP 1: TRANSLATE VISION INTO ACTION

As you recall from chapter 3, large-scale transformation *must* clarify for all concerned how the business will be different and better as a result—that is, how it will create more value. Most transformation efforts fail because they lose focus and momentum, succumbing to the inevitable forces of inertia that perpetuate the status quo. Evidence suggests that even with all the urgency that surrounds digital transformation in today's environment, organizations have a poor track record when comes to delivering tangible results.

So, a translation process of sorts needs to take place, to convert your strategic intent into more operational terms and take you from somewhat abstract—if inspiring—ideas (purpose, vision, mission) to more concrete, focused priorities and initiatives. This not only gives transformation a solid footing, but it also links tangible actions to measurable outcomes. That's where the rubber meets the road. Let's discuss how to convert your vision into action.

Ask yourself these questions:

- Have we established clear priorities that reflect the core business imperatives behind our vision for the future? How well are these known throughout the organization?

- Have we devised a set of concrete strategic initiatives that deploy resources and talent to mobilize the organization and focus our energies to build the future?
- Do these initiatives hang together with a coherent logic that reflects our overall strategy? Are they instrumental for building critical capability for transformation?

### Clarify Key Business Imperatives

To channel resources and energy, you need to prioritize your critical business imperatives to guide and channel your focus. Steve Jobs argued that focus is about the discipline of saying no: "People think focus means saying yes to the thing you've got to focus on. But that's not what it means at all. It means saying no to the hundred other good ideas that there are. You have to pick carefully. I'm actually as proud of the things we haven't done as the things I have done."[8]

Given the complexity of orchestrating change, the limits of attention, and inevitable resource constraints, it is necessary to make choices and identify the precious few—perhaps three to four key business imperatives—that define, prioritize, and operationalize your strategic intent.

Think about this for a second. What are the critical priorities or imperatives in your firm? How well are these understood? In Microsoft's case, Nadella's first message to employees made clear what he thought it would take to succeed: "As we look forward, we must zero in on what Microsoft can uniquely contribute to the world. The opportunity ahead will require us to reimagine a lot of what we have done in the past for a mobile and cloud-first world, and do new things."

Nadella focused on three "must-do" priorities for transformation: (1) getting products and technology right, (2) developing platforms and ecosystems, and (3) integrating Nokia into the fold:

> We are the only ones who can harness the power of software and deliver it through devices and services that truly empower every individual and every organization. We are the only company with history and continued focus in building platforms and ecosystems that create broad opportunity. ... While the deal is

not yet complete, we will welcome to our family Nokia devices and services and the new mobile capabilities they bring us.[9]

As much as Nadella had inspired Microsoft employees to innovate and "do more," he also concentrated their energy on the handful of high-value priorities that would take the company forward and define the parameters of its success. It helped clarify Microsoft's strategic intent and operationalize where it would focus in a cloud-first, mobile-first environment.

Paul Polman did something similar at Unilever. He laid out three key priorities for Compass Vision and USLP: (1) improve the health and well-being of more than a billion people, (2) halve the environmental footprint of Unilever product manufacturing and use, and (3) work across the entire value chain to enhance the livelihoods of millions of people. "We have set out to make a difference to those big issues that matter most ... We are focusing on three areas where we have the scale, influence and resources to make this big difference."

These three strategic priorities were operationalized as nine "pillars" (e.g., nutrition, greenhouse gases, waste, sustainable sourcing, etc.), and further translated into fifty specific, measurable targets.[10]

Metrics matter, and Polman grounded his lofty ambitions for a more sustainable world in concrete measures and performance targets to show progress. Too many executives miss this step, failing to connect the strategic intent with the operational imperatives. Establishing key priorities helps crystallize strategic intent by focusing on critical outcomes, particularly around customer value. The associated metrics, in turn, help dimensionalize those priorities in terms of measurable performance data.

Remember, none of this is static. Conventional wisdom holds that your strategic intent, key objectives, and metrics are more powerful when they are clear and concise. And I agree with that, in principle. In practice, however, these things evolve over time. In my experience, the strategic intent and ambition of the transformation needs to be inspiring and directional to motivate and guide change. As noted in chapter 3, a statement of strategic intent does not incorporate all the details. Initially, you likely don't *have* all the details, and even if you did, you might not want to convey them all at once. Strategic priorities, in turn, are often delineated based on input from others in the leadership team—and this is as it should be. As the transformation unfolds and new information becomes available, it is important to recalibrate and adjust as appropriate.

In Microsoft's case, the system evolved. Nadella stayed focused on Microsoft's mission to "empower every person and every organization on the planet to achieve more." Over time, its key priorities morphed to: (1) reinvent productivity and business processes (e.g., Windows 365, AI-backed tools, LinkedIn); (2) build the intelligent cloud platform (e.g., server and enterprise services GitHub, Azure, MS Cloud, data center); and (3) create more personal computing (with tools like Teams, Edge, Bing, Surface, Xbox, etc.). These revisions reflected the new realities of Microsoft's transformation journey, and they were used to focus R&D spending, business operations, and financial reporting.[11]

## Devise a Coherent Set of Strategic Initiatives

Key business imperatives operationalize your strategic intent. Strategic initiatives are the pivotal actions by which you deliver on it. Take Mayo Clinic, for example, and the challenge of operationalizing its strategic intent. Given its breadth and ambition, there was a good chance it would lose focus. Noseworthy and team believed that effective implementation of its "new business models" strategy required a concrete and clear goal. To that end, the steering committee set a stretch target of 200 million consumer "touches" per year. A consumer touch was defined as a "meaningful experience" whose value is attributable to Mayo Clinic and that gives "the consumer what they want, when and where they want it, and on their terms."[12]

With 200 million touches, Mayo had translated its strategic intent into one boldly ambitious goal. Now the trick would be devising a set of strategic initiatives to achieve that goal. Where were the targets of opportunity with the most potential? If you think of your key priorities as the outcomes or ends you're trying to achieve, strategic initiatives are the means (actions and investments) needed to get there. And the means-ends (actions-outcomes) connections must be synchronized.

**Develop a portfolio with an underlying strategic logic.** Unfortunately, the process of orchestration often becomes disjointed at this point because executives build their initiatives around isolated "pain points," or perhaps corrective capability gaps as described in chapter 3. These often seem reasonable and sometimes are justified as low-hanging fruit. The problem is, on their own, these initiatives lose coherence, don't sync up, and don't collectively deliver on the key priorities and strategic intent. Pursuing a wide array of independent and unconnected initiatives— letting a "thousand flowers" bloom—may not be a good idea here.[13]

A more successful approach is to build a portfolio of coordinated initiatives around a strategic logic that propels transformation. That's what Mayo Clinic did.

Mayo's digital transformation was based on a very systematic approach to resourcing a portfolio of strategic initiatives. As shown in Figure 5.1, Noseworthy's steering committee created a matrix that juxtaposed needed capabilities with three distinct customer categories. Mayo categorized

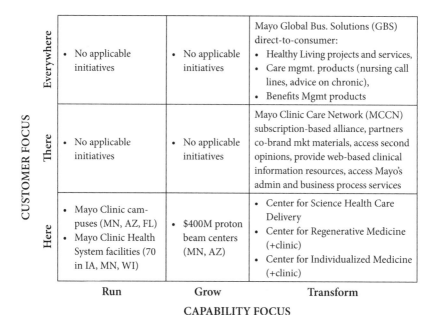

| CUSTOMER FOCUS | | Run | Grow | Transform |
|---|---|---|---|---|
| | Everywhere | • No applicable initiatives | • No applicable initiatives | Mayo Global Bus. Solutions (GBS) direct-to-consumer: <br> • Healthy Living projects and services, <br> • Care mgmt. products (nursing call lines, advice on chronic), <br> • Benefits Mgmt products |
| | There | • No applicable initiatives | • No applicable initiatives | Mayo Clinic Care Network (MCCN) subscription-based alliance, partners co-brand mkt materials, access second opinions, provide web-based clinical information resources, access Mayo's admin and business process services |
| | Here | • Mayo Clinic campuses (MN, AZ, FL) <br> • Mayo Clinic Health System facilities (70 in IA, MN, WI) | • $400M proton beam centers (MN, AZ) | • Center for Science Health Care Delivery <br> • Center for Regenerative Medicine (+clinic) <br> • Center for Individualized Medicine (+clinic) |

CAPABILITY FOCUS

FIGURE 5.1. Mayo Clinic: Rubric for Strategic Initiatives (Adapted from Regina A. Herzlinger, Robert S. Huckman, and Jenny Lesser, "Mayo Clinic: The 2020 Initiative, Harvard Business School Case 615–027.)

capabilities in three buckets: (1) *run*: continue to operate current business areas efficiently and effectively; (2) *grow*: expand capability and improve performance; and (3) *transform*: develop new capabilities in new arenas. These three capability categories were paired with customer categories, as discussed in chapter 3: *here*: patients in Mayo facilities; *there*: patients and providers in the broader network; and *everywhere*: people globally.

The result was a coherent set of strategic initiatives that included a range of new approaches to the physical delivery of care, such as concierge medical services to increase convenience and access for patients, and an array of web-based services.[14]

There are several points to highlight about Mayo's strategic logic. First, the approach included initiatives that would continue to deliver results for Mayo's current business (e.g., "run-here") while also transforming to the new one. This is often referred to as organizational ambidexterity and is another reason orchestration is so challenging. Second, the strategic logic gave Noseworthy's team a rubric for simultaneously generating and evaluating initiatives based on their potential to deliver value. At every turn, the team could assess the degree to which the initiatives supported the goal of 200 million touches. It's an intuitive notion, but don't miss the key point: *identify the strategic initiatives that are pivotal with the most potential to take the transformation forward—to achieve your strategic intent—and place your bets there.*[15]

**It's all about capability building.** The key to these initiatives was their capacity to build capability for Mayo Clinic. Think about the premise of business model innovation in chapter 3. Organizations undertake strategic transformation when they are not adequately organized or resourced to deliver on their new value proposition. To get where they need to go, the initiatives must close the capability gap(s) by upskilling or reskilling; acquiring new talent in key positions; developing new ways of working; and reconfiguring the structures, processes, systems, and culture needed for the future. (Recall the "prospective" capability gaps mentioned in chapter 3.)

Typically, these initiatives are phased over time with an eye toward short-term wins and longer-term outcomes. Resources are allocated accordingly, especially capital investment, which will likely reflect the degree of risk and uncertainty of the initiatives, as well as the extent to which the organization has current capabilities to execute at scale. Pilot programs and proof-of-concept initiatives help the organization to learn and demonstrate value before increasing investment.

The purpose of orchestration is to ensure that these key initiatives work in concert with one another. Noseworthy established a set of co-ordinated initiatives, each with its separate workstream, that *collectively enabled* Mayo Clinic to transform and deliver new value. The approach helped Mayo develop new lines of business more quickly and coher-ently. As a result, it could implement them at scale.[16]

Once you develop a strategic logic and a coordinated approach to your key initiatives, it is easier to mobilize resources and allocate capital, technology, data, and infrastructure, as well as deploy talent, to each one. A rubric like Figure 5.1 gives you the criteria for prioritizing these investments. And once the key initiatives are prioritized and resourced, it is possible to add in other smaller complementary projects and pilots with more modest budgets. As a set, they roll up to a larger contribu-tion, and importantly, they can generate a good deal of learning (more on this in the next chapter).

Let's pause for a moment. All this discussion about strategic initia-tives is, in some ways, putting the cart before the horse. Before they are completely fleshed out, it is important to identify who will be leading the charge.

Typically, the process of operationalizing strategic intent and clari-fying strategic priorities and initiatives is the purview of the CEO and senior executives. But very early on, the top team will be in discussion about who will take the initiatives forward. And very likely those people will have been involved in the initial planning phase, providing input, expertise, and experience. Let's turn to this topic now.

## STEP 2: MOBILIZE YOUR TRANSFORMATION NETWORK

"First who, then what." Jim Collins was right that the most successful leaders surround themselves with strong teams. And that has a special twist in the context of transformation. Two points in chapter 4 were a prelude to this discussion of orchestration. First, transformation is difficult to lead solely from the C-suite, and while the CEO and senior executive team have important roles, transformation needs a lower center of gravity. Most of the critical momentum shifts take place lower down in the organization.[17]

The second point is the importance of empowering key influencers to "own" and precipitate change. Bill Bratton did this in the NYPD by engaging precinct commanders. Multiple teams are likely to be working simultaneously, and they must operate as a collaborative network. Getting the right mix of talent is critical, both within teams and across teams. Let's discuss this in more detail.

As a starting point, ask yourself these questions:

- Have we established leadership alignment at the top of the organization, demonstrating mutual commitment and accountability for the transformation?
- Do we have key personnel leading the transformation, establishing collaborative networks across key functions and business units?
- Do we collaborate well with our partners to garner key skills and resources needed to develop and deploy capability quickly? What is our experience with strategic merger and acquisition (M&A)?

## Demonstrate Leadership Alignment

In prior chapters, I've emphasized the importance of leadership alignment, and it bears repeating here with special emphasis. When Ken Carrig and I were doing background research for our book *Strategic Execution,* CEOs told us repeatedly that alignment was the most important factor driving breakthrough performance in their firms. Without that, they cautioned, nothing much else mattered.

Why? Because organizational complexity is a powerful force working against alignment. To achieve coherence and commitment to the vision for transformation, CEOs and senior leadership teams need to demonstrate three things: (1) a clear strategic intent, (2) a shared expectation for high performance, and (3) accountability for results.[18]

Satya Nadella prioritized alignment in Microsoft's transformation. "Coming together as teams fuels this on a day-to-day basis. And having the Senior Leadership Team (SLT) set both pace and example means a lot to me. I have discussed this point in various forms with the SLT and have asked for their 'all in' commitment as we embark on the next chapter for the company. We need to drive clarity, alignment, and intensity across all our work."[19]

A pivotal moment that demonstrated alignment to others was when the members of the SLT gathered onstage at their global summit to inaugurate a new era of leadership. Chief HR Officer Kathleen Hogan recalled, "I can't tell you how much positive feedback we've gotten on that. It was five minutes, but it was symbolic, and I think it goes to this alignment point. People want to see that the leadership team is aligned. They're in it together. And if you can create that, it can be a huge accelerator."[20]

To reinforce alignment over time, Nadella established a weekly standing meeting with his direct reports to discuss progress on Microsoft's strategic priorities. After those meetings, each of the leaders met with their respective groups as well—and the meetings continued to cascade to more levels within the Microsoft organization. Hogan observed that "everyone's voice matters, and anyone can ask a question ... Satya did a great job creating clarity around our focus on personal computing, on the cloud and productivity, and again that clarity then allows people to drive alignment around it."[21]

## Activate Your Transformation Team

In truth, Nadella replaced some members of his team. Not all were aligned or properly positioned. But those personnel changes were important and sent a message throughout the organization.

The importance of talent and leadership cannot be overstated. In any transformation, the right team makes all the difference. In the previous chapter on engaging stakeholders, I emphasized the merits of empowering key influencers: those who see the importance of transformation, are in a position to make a difference, and will help evangelize it and catalyze momentum. These individuals are likely to be the core of your transformation team.

However, I am continually reminded by leaders that trust is more important than experience in building this team. CEOs routinely appoint individuals to change leadership positions because they trust their commitment to the organization, their dedication to the transformation, and their personal loyalty to the leader themselves.

Increasingly, CEOs appoint a *chief transformation officer* (CTO) with responsibility and authority to challenge, press, and stretch the organization, while also mobilizing resources and enabling connections. The CTO often works with a *program/project management office* (PMO) to coordinate strategic initiatives, facilitate progress, resolve problems, and share best practices.

The CTO is a key orchestrator of change—assembling, developing, and resourcing cross-functional collaboration to take the transformation forward. Ironically, the CTO typically doesn't have formal authority over members in the network; line managers retain responsibility and accountability for day-to-day operations. The CTO directs the change process to make certain that the job is resourced and coordinated well. The CTO takes the lead in building synergies among people, data, and infrastructure, creating a high-functioning network of allies. This network operates across the existing organization, and in fact it needs to move more quickly than the rest of the organization.

In Unilever's case, Paul Polman appointed Keith Weed as the *de facto* CTO by promoting him to the senior executive team and giving him responsibility as both the chief marketing officer (CMO) and the lead for both sustainability and communications. In those combined roles, Weed coordinated the USLP sustainability strategy. As Weed put it, "We wanted to signal that sustainability was not about 'corporate social responsibility' as an isolated activity. It was everyone's responsibility. So we abolished the CSR office to underline our belief that marketing and sustainability were two sides of the same coin. It was a belief that became reflected in our strategy."[22]

Weed's job was a big one, and his seat on Polman's senior executive team gave him credibility with other top leaders. It also gave him a window into broader corporate issues. However, while he soon aligned with the senior leaders, he acknowledged that "gaining acceptance was tough

... We realized that it was going to take a long time to embed something on this scale deeper in the organization."

For support, Polman gave Weed leadership of a talented twelve-person sustainability team who had been measuring Unilever's environmental footprint. All the members of this group had deep-rooted business experience, and they garnered more commitment from senior leaders. As top executives learned more about how USLP would impact their businesses, they not only didn't resist it, but they also invested in the capabilities and resources needed to support it.

Gail Klintworth joined the team and was promoted to chief sustainability officer. In her role, she couldn't mandate change to the businesses, but she served as a catalyst and facilitator of it. To help business leaders realize the promise of USLP, she designed a strategic initiative called USLP Refresh that supported them in implementing the program. She assigned members of her team to each of USLP's strategic priorities, and she asked them to collaborate with category and brand teams to review their business models. This helped connect them with additional resources and build the capability to execute USLP.

At the same time as Klintworth was working on USLP Refresh, Marc Mathieu, SVP of Marketing, launched his initiative, Crafting Brands for Life (CB4L). The purpose of CB4L was to more closely associate Unilever's brand strategies with USLP principles and reinforce that it wasn't just products but lifestyle. The CB4L program involved a series of 1.5-day workshops to engage Unilever's 6,000 marketers around linking their brands to USLP, helping them move beyond brand positioning to develop a brand purpose aligned with the strategy.[23]

What's notable about Unilever's approach is that a relatively small transformation team built out commitments and support with others in the organization, both vertically and horizontally, expanding the network driving transformation.

The Chalhoub Group set up its transformation team in a very similar way. Recall that Patrick Chalhoub acknowledged the company's early challenges in digital transformation were the result of being too slow and too fragmented. He needed a core team to accelerate change in a coordinated way across the entire organization. Chalhoub set up the

SHIFT team, under the leadership of CTO Rania Masri, to help business units develop initiatives focused on new ways of working—a new culture, new processes, and new technologies—to ensure continued growth and longevity of the business. Masri described the team's goal to future-proof the company: "We have planned a 900-day transformation movement with the overarching vision to transform from a traditional distributor and retailer of luxury in the Middle East to a hybrid retailer bringing luxury experiences to the fingertips of customers everywhere. Our 'SHIFT' team works alongside our existing corporate segments and business units to help include and guide all our units in this shared transformation journey: connecting our customers seamlessly and offering an exciting experience for all."[24]

Masri and the SHIFT team did three key things to mobilize the transformation. Working with Chalhoub's array of businesses, they (1) defined the key priorities for transformation, (2) communicated those priorities to others within the firm, and (3) aligned the organization around them. "Forming a small team of disruptive thinkers, our mission was to find the points stifling agility and growth and to light small fires across many teams to challenge [and] find solutions ... In our unconventional methodology that focuses on the 3 P's—People, Processes and Platforms—we were able to define, communicate, and align the organization around what was important to achieve. Over the span of the 900-day project, we created the movement and the foundation to the change that would come."[25]

**Building a team of teams.** The Chalhoub and Unilever transformation teams each operated as a *de facto* team of teams. There are a few key things to note here.

First, the teams were simultaneously small and large. Each was composed of a modest group of about a dozen professionals, but the way they engaged others throughout the organization served as a talent multiplier. They were able to accomplish so much more because of the networks they built.

Second, the work of the transformation teams was inherently cross-functional. Over the years, I've learned that most strategic challenges are, in fact, cross-functional. This is likely your experience too. Although any one strategic initiative may have a concentrated functional or specialized focus, the work of the transformation team transcends those functions and business areas. Consequently, the team needs not only deep functional expertise, but also linking and bridging skills to enable relationship development, collaboration, and knowledge sharing across the enterprise.[26]

Third, the transformation teams didn't exert formal authority over most of their members; rather, they recruited people in the existing business units to collaborate with the transformation team to devise and implement the initiatives. This isn't unusual and is especially important because it keeps the horsepower for transformation in the business units.

Fourth, the transformation team guided strategic initiatives top-down (originating with the senior team), but it enabled real progress to manifest bottom-up. This is consistent with findings from research conducted at Bain: "The best ideas for game-changing initiatives most often come from deep within the organization, but their success depends on the ability of top executives to spot them, elevate them, and support them with the right kind of investment. The transformation teams not only helped identify and implement strategic initiatives, they enabled the business units to try things, adapt, and learn. The applications and innovations were then showcased throughout the organization."[27]

Finally, the development of ideas, performance improvements, and new ways of working—in other words, capability building—occurred within the existing businesses. This isn't always the case. Many times, strategic initiatives require tiger teams, greenfield operations, new acquisitions, external partnerships, and the like. But both Unilever and Chalhoub found that when the seeds of change germinate within the existing business units, it generates more buy-in from those involved. That gives the transformation better and quicker lift. And consequently, because performance improvements reinforce the change, they don't need to be sold or mandated from above. Instead, in the best cases, the business areas "own" the transformation, generating more momentum. The new organization (capability) emerges from within the old one, rather than supplanting it.

**Many hands make light work.** Evidence from these examples and others shows that a small transformation team can pack a powerful punch. And the impact is multiplied when the team brings others into the mix. Some excellent research by McKinsey's Kevin Laczkowski, Tao Tan, and Matthias Winter found that scope of involvement is a very significant factor. Their research showed that successful transformation was more likely when companies "mobilized a substantial chunk of their workforce—at least 8 percent—to drive transformation initiatives." Top-quartile companies deployed more than 20 percent.[28]

The idea makes sense: More involvement gives firms a chance to pursue more initiatives, and each initiative adds to the total. As I noted earlier, when you have a strategic rubric that establishes integrated workstreams, mobilization is more coherent, allowing for a larger number of smaller initiatives that collectively produce big results, each in service of the whole. In the McKinsey study, 68 percent of the initiatives had budgets of less than $250,000, and only 16 percent were budgeted at $1 million or more. Over half of the transformation value came from the smaller initiatives ("smaller" was defined as less than 0.5 percent of the transformation value). In other words, little gains rolled up to big wins.

In dynamic environments where disruption and volatility upset the status quo, leaders need practical ways to scale transformation and innovation quickly and effectively. Hierarchical and bureaucratic approaches tend to slow that down. By giving small transformation teams the latitude to build broad collaborative networks, engaging many in the organization around a clear set of strategic initiatives, drawing on their collective experience, and giving them freedom to shape the initiatives, transformation can come more quickly. (More about this in the next chapter on cultivating change agility.)

### Leverage Partnerships, Mergers and Acquisitions

By now, it should be clear from these examples that great orchestration involves cross-functional collaboration to build new capabilities and deliver value. Let's extend that logic further. As you know, the complexity of your business ecosystem requires collaboration with external partners. This is especially true when your organization is missing some foundational elements of needed capability.

Take Chalhoub Group's two aborted attempts at building e-commerce platforms. Each was ineffective for different reasons, but they revealed Chalhoub's lack of experience in the digital domain and its lack of capability to get the solution right.

In response, Chalhoub Group formed a joint venture with Farfetch, an internationally known e-commerce marketplace. Farfetch founder José Neves noted that the deal had to be done on an accelerated timetable, with the goal of growing the Middle East business "very, very fast."

The deal made a lot of sense because Chalhoub and Farfetch had complementary assets and capabilities. Chalhoub had a powerful portfolio of luxury brands, and most of Farfetch's revenue was from luxury brands, including Valentino, Givenchy, and Burberry. The agreement involved Chalhoub sharing its distribution and marketing services with Farfetch's e-commerce platform and curated content in Arabic. In return, Chalhoub's luxury brands connected to a successful platform. Farfetch also provides service, fraud control, data security, and the like. Chalhoub Group is responsible for fulfillment and delivery.

The joint venture allowed Chalhoub to scale capability rapidly and dramatically alter customer value. "This partnership will be a huge acceleration for our transformation," Patrick Chalhoub said.[29] The benefits were reciprocal. Farfetch CEO José Neves observed, "With Chalhoub we have the ability to leverage their brick-and-mortar presence. They have some amazing own concepts. The combination of our omnichannel technology and Chalhoub's brick-and-mortar retail footprint brings the best service level that anyone in the industry can offer ... Together we have a unique competitive advantage."[30]

Mayo Clinic also used partnerships to drive transformation and established a set of alliances with other health care providers, formalized as the Mayo Clinic Care Network (MCCN). The partnerships gave other medical centers access to Mayo's expertise through a web-based clinical information system, including a platform called eConsult that provided second opinions on complex cases. The partners also co-branded marketing materials with Mayo and had access to its administrative and business-process services. (Note that Mayo's customers were no longer just patients, but also included clinicians and administrators.)

In return, the MCCN enabled Mayo to scale and extend its reach very rapidly. Within only three years, the network had expanded to thirty partners in sixteen states, Puerto Rico, and Mexico City. This was instrumental in achieving the goal of extending patient care. In addition, the network became a feeder system to Mayo's flagship facilities, where partners referred patients with complex cases for further care.[31]

**Value of complementary assets.** Note a few things about these partnerships regarding orchestration. First, they mobilized assets quickly—much more rapidly and effectively than if the firms had tried to grow and scale capability on their own. Second, the partnerships were valuable because they blended complementary assets. Strategic partnerships can be useful even if they only duplicate your skills and capabilities, adding scale and avenues for growth. But the real value-add during transformation is when they bring skills and resources that complement or augment your capability set, enabling you to achieve more. Third, these partnerships were focused on the longer term and provided opportunities to learn. In fact, research suggests that the ability to glean knowledge and build capability internally may be the ultimate reason to enter a strategic partnership. In the context of strategic transformation, some of these alliances may be transitory, enabling you to gain ground quickly, while some may be more enduring.[32]

**The value and risk of strategic M&A.** In some cases, particularly when strategic initiatives involve more dramatic capability pivots, a valuable option is merger and acquisition (M&A). Acquisition and divestiture can rebalance a firm's business portfolio. By divesting chronically underperforming units or those with low strategic value, you'll free up capital for growth and new capability development. M&A activity may provide access to new markets, technology transfer, new products, new channels, and new skills all along the value chain.

In some cases, it is possible to acquire an entirely new business model. For example, since becoming CEO of Microsoft, Satya Nadella targeted over eighty-five acquisitions, many of them directly associated with Microsoft's transformation to a cloud-first, mobile-first environment. The Nokia acquisition was obviously part of that, as were the acquisitions of LinkedIn, GitHub, Skype, Yammer, aQuantive, Activision, and Nuance.

However, the M&A path to transformation is not without considerable risk. As Harvard economist Clayton Christensen observed, "Companies rightly turn to acquisitions to meet goals they can't achieve internally. But there is no magic in buying another company."[33] Microsoft's big investment in Nokia was a dud, and it eventually wrote off over $7.8 billion and cut 7,800 jobs. Other acquisitions were more successful, but the failure rate of M&A is 80 to 90 percent (when the criterion is increasing the combined firm value). Value is often created for the acquired firm, but not the acquiring.

Research by PwC revealed the reasons why. The chief causes for poor post-merger performance include mismatched company cultures, technology incompatibility, and the loss of key talent. Talent is particularly troubling in that 65 percent of executives in the PwC study said that accessing new talent was among the most important goals of the acquisition, but only 10 percent reported significant success in post-M&A employee retention.[34]

The challenges of post-merger integration are made more difficult during strategic transformation, with the inevitable leadership changes, layoffs, technology and system integration, process revamp, and culture change.[35]

Mayo Clinic also had some experience with M&A before it undertook its 2020 Initiative. And during the transformation to a new business model strategy, Noseworthy and his team considered some acquisitions. But their analysis and previous experience led them in to conclude that M&A is not always a shortcut to transformation, in part because it involves substantial risk. As Mayo CFO Jeff Bolton recalled,

> What became apparent early on was that potential [acquisition] targets were dilutive from an operating income perspective and came to the party requiring substantial capital for traditional delivery of services. But the real thing we found was that the integration into the Mayo culture was a "heavy lift." We had to devote a ton of resources to bring these organizations into the Mayo Clinic model of care.[36]

In the end, Noseworthy and team concluded that acquisitions might help financially, but they couldn't reconcile how it would aid patient care. And that was the strategic priority.

Other CEOs are more bullish on M&A as a strategic transformation tool. When done appropriately, and when the integration achieves operational and cultural alignment, then the incremental value and capability synergies can be realized. Like other aspects of strategic transformation, M&A needs to be closely aligned—and in service of—business model innovation.

## STEP 3: RECONFIGURE YOUR ARCHITECTURE

Let's take the next step. So far, we've talked about two key actions for orchestrating mobilization: (1) converting your vision into action by clarifying key priorities, and devising an integrated set of concrete initiatives, and (2) mobilizing your transformation network by ensuring alignment, and assembling a team to build collaborative partnerships across those initiatives. This is the nature of orchestration—it involves mobilizing and synchronizing a multitude of resources.

Now let's tackle the third piece: reconfiguring your organization architecture. Back in chapter 2, we saw that strategic transformation needs to balance and integrate forces of divergence and convergence. Orchestration is an apt metaphor in this case: As in an orchestra, divergent parts, each making a unique contribution to the whole, come together in harmony and create something beautiful (forgive my cheesy eloquence—I think successful organizations are a thing of beauty).

But let's not get lost in metaphor. Orchestrating transformation requires a focus on separate strategic initiatives, each with its own investments, actions, and outcomes. At the same time, these initiatives need to be brought together to move forward and achieve the overall vision and strategic intent of the organization.

Nowhere is that divergent-convergent tension more evident than in the design of the organization's architecture. Recall that organization architecture is composed of the structures, processes, systems, and even culture of the firm that collectively make up the infrastructure for your business model (see Figure 5.2).[37]

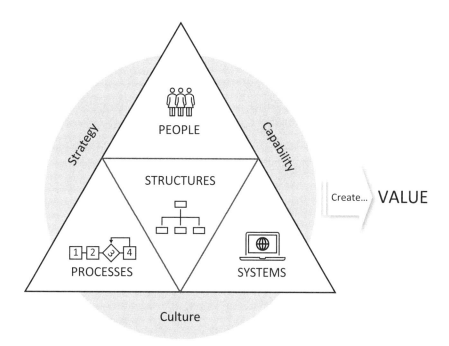

FIGURE 5.2. Organizational Architecture.

**Differentiation and integration.** Structures, processes, and systems are important because they set the design parameters for *how* work gets done. Your structures delineate divisions of labor and lines of authority. Your processes stipulate repeatable, scalable action sequences that define workflow standards. In turn, your systems and technologies are conduits for data and information that support better decision-making. Your reward systems focus behavior and energize motivation toward desired outcomes. These elements of architecture together manifest aspects of culture, representing the sometimes explicit, often implicit, norms and expectations for how we engage one another and mobilize performance.

In the context of transformation, your architecture must balance two dimensions: differentiation and integration. *Differentiation* refers to the separations among tasks, areas of responsibility, and specialization required for efficient execution. Think of it as designing the parts of the system—and as you're aware, transformation involves a lot of parts.

*Integration*, on the other hand, knits all those parts back together via a mechanism that enables coordination, collaboration, and exchange of information/resources.

**Inertia versus momentum.** The other tension inherent in the organizational architecture is that between inertia and momentum. In my experience, your organization architecture will either propel transformation or hold it back. Rarely is the effect neutral. The reason is that an organization's architecture has inherently bureaucratic features. That's not all bad. Without some standardization and formalization, the organization would have very little stability, predictability, or efficiency. Too much bureaucracy, on the other hand, and the organization gets too rigid. Rigidity can keep the organization operating in the past, while you're trying to forge the future. Many managers express frustration that change inevitably requires "bureaucracy busting" because outdated policies, procedures, and processes hold back progress. Reward systems can be especially pernicious, incentivizing behaviors that are antithetical to change.

So, what's the solution? The short version is this: Streamline your architecture to ensure that information and resources get to the people who need it, clarify authority, and reward productive collaboration along the value chain. Make certain this is aligned in service of capabilities that drive (new) customer value.[38]

The point is to simplify and refine your organization architecture to reduce drag and inertia. Realign it to build the energy that drives transformation. To be candid, this is where my discussions with executives sometimes go a little sideways. It's hard work, and occasionally I get the question, "Does everything need to change?" Well, yes and no. Like much else we've discussed, some parts are more critical than others to create a tipping point for change. Think of it as operating at two speeds. Those most critical to value (and transformation) need to be realigned immediately. Those less critical can maybe wait a little while.

But the acid test for your organization architecture hinges on these three questions:

- Have we streamlined our structures and processes to enable better decision-making, more efficient workstreams, and better line of sight to customers?

- Do our structures and processes enable key nodes of collaboration? Are decision rights clear and roles adequately defined?
- Have we scrutinized our technology investments to determine how our digital transformation is in clear service of overall business model innovation?

## Streamline Your Structures and Processes

Let's start with structures and processes. One of the tenets of architectural design is "form follows function." (You've likely heard the expression.) The design of your organization (its form) should be configured to achieve its desired outcome (its function). If you're trying to achieve a new outcome—new capability, new value, new business model—you'll likely need to change the form of your organization. The obverse of this—doing things the same old way but expecting different results—is, as Albert Einstein noted, a little nutty.

Satya Nadella inherited a difficult legacy of structural changes at Microsoft. His predecessor as CEO, Steve Ballmer, had reorganized eleven times during his tenure. Microsoft was (and is) a complicated portfolio of divisions and business units, and Ballmer's penchant for restructuring had become almost an annual ritual, leaving some employees dreading, as one executive labeled it, "YAR" (yet another reorg).

However, his last reorganization—dubbed "One Microsoft"—was extraordinary. It fundamentally altered the structure of the company to support better collaboration and agility to "enable innovation at a greater speed."[39]

Prior to Nadella, Microsoft had been structured as a set of autonomous product divisions, each working with relative independence. This design had advantages and disadvantages. On the plus side, unencumbered business units could respond more rapidly to separate customer concerns and market shifts. But in Microsoft's case, the structure resulted in fragmentation, competition, and an inconsistent face toward customers.

To achieve better integration and alignment—and a unified face toward the customer—the One Microsoft initiative was designed to drive "better execution from product conceptualization and innovation right through to marketing and sales." The new design needed to reinvigorate collaboration, break down barriers and silos, and reinforce enterprise alignment. As Ballmer described it, "We are rallying behind a single strategy as one company—not a collection of divisional strategies. ... We will see our product line holistically, not as a set of islands. We will allocate resources and build devices and services that provide compelling, integrated experiences across the many screens in our lives."[40]

Microsoft reorganized from a product structure (with eight separate product teams) to a functional structure designed around four engineering teams that represented a de facto value chain for the new "devices and services" company: (1) operating systems, (2) applications, (3) cloud, and (4) devices. Importantly, each function needed to collaborate with the other adjoining functions, in order to see its efforts pay off in getting products to market. With this restructuring and clarification of purpose, competition abated and cooperation increased.

On top of the functional structure at Microsoft was a latticework of connections. Each of the major initiatives had a champion who drove cross-company teamwork, integrating the different business areas so that the entire staff committed to the initiative's success. As Ballmer described it,

> There is a process element and a culture element ... Process wise, each major initiative of the company (product or high-value scenario) will have a team that spans groups to ensure we succeed against our goals. Our strategy will drive what initiatives we agree and commit to at my staff meetings. Most disciplines and product groups will have a core that delivers key technology or services and then a piece that lines up with the initiative. Each major initiative will have a champion who will be a direct report to me or one of my direct reports. The champion will organize to drive a cross-company team for success, but my whole staff will have commitment to the initiative's success.[41]

The logic behind Microsoft's approach is straightforward: Streamline the organizations, simplify authority structures, reward collaboration, and establish enterprise goals around each strategic initiative to deliver customer value. Some of the inevitable white noise in the system wouldn't go away immediately—Microsoft is a very complex organism. But clarity and collaboration where it counts are hallmarks of good transformation.

When Nadella became CEO, he kept this fundamental architecture, only making a few tweaks and some personnel changes. "One Microsoft" was dedicated to the goal of working across business units to achieve the company's mission.

Still, although it had already begun, the process wasn't easy. As one executive observed, "One Microsoft is working to overcome years of a legacy where we had strong decentralization and strong organic divisions. Some would argue we took that too far, and there was a fear of certain groups even competing with each other. [In our new way of working], this is saying any solution or service that we have has to have One Microsoft and an end-to-end solution for the customer's benefit."[42]

There are a couple takeaways from Microsoft's restructuring. In my experience, there is no one type of structure that works best in all cases. Functional, divisional, matrix, and more—all have their pluses and minuses. During transformation, the goal is to simplify and clarify structural underpinnings of change.

Microsoft's approach did two things. First, it overcame inertia and got the firm moving toward a new future by streamlining structures, clarifying roles and responsibilities, and establishing common goals pointed toward a shared vision of innovation and the cloud-first, mobile-first ideal.

Second, Microsoft's approach balanced needed differentiation and integration. The new structure created vertical centers of excellence and specialization in key functional and engineering/technology areas, leveraging expertise within the entire company to reinforce critical capabilities. And the champions and integration teams for each strategic initiative helped span horizontally across those areas to improve collaboration and speed to market.

Remember, every structure has its downside. Division of labor is necessary for efficiency but creates gaps in the organization, cracks that can become crevices and separations that hurt collaboration. As a solution, my advice is to *organize one way and manage the other*. By that I mean that the best leaders find these structural gaps and help to create bridges over them. They do this by balancing formal structures with informal connections. One of the advantages of Nadella's approach is that he balanced differentiation and integration where it was needed most for Microsoft.[43]

### Integrate Your Digital Transformation

Like organization structures and processes, your technology platforms are part of your organizational architecture, and a central aspect of orchestration. The role of technology in strategic transformation is so ubiquitous (and critical!) that many simply refer to the entire process as "digital transformation." But don't make the mistake of conflating the two. It is true that virtually all strategic transformation today includes a digital aspect. Businesses and organizations spend over $4 trillion a year on information technology alone. Yet, despite that investment, it is unclear whether all this technology spend is delivering results.[44]

As I've noted previously, one of the challenges of digital transformation is that it becomes an entity unto itself, detached from the larger context of the business. And this is the single biggest reason transformation goes off the rails. Why? Because technology is the original "shiny object" that draws our attention and can detract from other requirements of transformation. Technological innovation continually produces new and tempting solutions to problems that aren't always well understood.

So, the first and most important admonition about orchestrating tech deployment is *don't lose sight of the business*. What does that imply? Like other elements of the organization architecture, technology is a tool in service of strategic transformation and needs to be integrated with overall business model innovation.

Recently, I was advising an executive team whose company was undergoing digital transformation. The CEO had hired a consulting firm to lead the effort, but the consultants would not—or could not—articulate how the multimillion-dollar investment would enhance the customer experience and value proposition. Their focus was instead on technological advancement. It was a source of considerable consternation for the CEO, and this hamstrung the initiative, killing momentum.

To avoid this scenario in your own organization, get clarity on the following: First, can you draw a line between technology investment and customer value? Most organizations cannot, except in vague terms. Second, which technologies are most critical in building capability to deliver that value? Where do you need further deployment to build capability? Third, is there a discipline around technology investment that shows an explicit ROI, and even better, a link to P&L, building specific metrics into business targets? The McKinsey study mentioned in chapter 3 reported that fewer than 25 percent of companies have a "clearly defined process that prioritizes the most strategically important efforts." That's a pretty small number. There is often tension between technology-push and customer-pull, but if the goal of your tech deployments is to improve customer value, then any initiative must be preceded by in-depth input from customers.[45]

Most senior executives are not digital natives, so my advice is to focus less on the technology per se and more on evaluating its business application. In a rather shorthand way of thinking about this, we can assess technology's impact at three levels: operational, relational, and transformational.

**Operational impact: Improve processes and productivity.** At a fundamental level, technology is often the driver of your operations. From a process standpoint, technologies can alter the design and functionality of workstreams, increasing efficiencies by augmenting processes, improving quality and speed, or perhaps even incorporating automation.[46]

From the standpoint of decision support, digital technologies provide access to more, better, and faster information, data analytics, and insights, which can dramatically increase productivity and value. And of course, increasingly, digital technologies such as AI and machine learning may do more than supplement and complement employee skills and knowledge—they may substitute for human input.[47]

Through the lens of your core capabilities, think about which technology upgrades provide opportunities to enhance your operating model. Technology investment is often focused on achieving lower cost and higher productivity. However, in the context of strategic transformation, technology's operational impact is arguably most powerful when it enhances your core capabilities and generates additional value that differentiates your organization. Take, for example, Chalhoub Group's initial technology investments, which were designed to do just that.

As part of its transformation journey to hybrid retailing, Patrick Chalhoub recognized the importance of leveraging customer data. But the reality was that the process of collecting the data, organizing it, extracting customer information, and offering personalized services was time-consuming, costly, and often unsuccessful. Chalhoub needed a better system to improve productivity of operations. In response, the company implemented a new point of service (POS) system, Oracle Retail Xstore's platform, which provided associates with quick and relevant customer information (purchase history and preferences), inventory data, and mobile payment capability.[48]

The Group had already been using some customer data to identify patterns in the group- and business-unit-level purchasing. However, its data strategy didn't support more granular analysis that could help make recommendations to individuals based on their previous purchases. "At a group level we can deliver in-depth analysis of our customers across brands looking at their purchasing behavior. But for now, we are not yet equipped with a technology that allows predictive analysis, but it is part of our strategy," Chalhoub added.[49]

Chalhoub's goal was to move beyond the operational impact of technology to the next level: its relational impact.

**Relational impact: Enhance connectivity and integration.** The relational impact of tech lies in its capacity to increase connectivity with others in your business ecosystem, improving collaboration and customer engagement. By helping to overcome the limits of time and location, technology increases the range of potential relationships and economic partners, expanding your relevant networks and creating opportunities for more diverse, dispersed, and virtual connections.[50]

This is more than human connectivity. It also includes shared databases and linked systems creating integrative capability. Blockchain, for example, can maintain a record of transactions across broad peer networks. Advances in the internet of things (IoT) use sensors, software, and other processing technologies to connect and exchange data among physical objects, devices, and systems via communications networks. More prosaically, the "technology backbone" of your business may be a customer relationship management (CRM) system or an enterprise resource planning (ERP) system. Given the increase of cloud computing and software as a service (SaaS), even smaller organizations are investing in integrative management systems that improve relational connectivity. For example, research by the Aberdeen Group found that 65 percent of small businesses use some ERP system, and 98 percent of top-quartile businesses are doing so.[51]

For its part, Chalhoub Group's transformation required it to go beyond the operational impact of technology to enhance its relational value across its network of retail brands and with customers. As Patrick Chalhoub put it, "We use customer data to connect to clients. We have to understand our clients and service them better." Technology should enable a smooth customer experience and leverage customer data to improve service and offer personalized recommendations. "If I can bring the best of these services to my stores, then fantastic," said Chalhoub.[52]

Sometimes the distinction between the operational and relational impacts of technology is nuanced. It might also be useful to think about the operational impact in terms of improving the efficiency, decision support, and productivity of internal processes and capabilities. The relational impact is more about linking those operations and coordinating processes and data into an integrated system to improve collaboration and customer/stakeholder connectivity.

**Transformational impact: Creating new business models.** The transformational impact of technology is gauged in terms of its effect on your entire business model. This includes using technology to create new platforms, channels to market, (tech-enabled) products, capabilities, and value propositions. This also moves beyond a focus on process improvement and services to an explicit focus on revenue generation.

Chalhoub Group's joint venture with Farfetch affected the business in both operational and relational ways. But even more so, its impact was transformative, changing the entire business model (to omnichannel), altering the customer value proposition, and enabling new capabilities. The platform serves as an e-commerce marketplace that gives customers access to a wide selection of curated luxury brands, through customized search (refined by a multitude of buyers) and the ability to view and purchase online. Patrick Chalhoub said, "With Farfetch's technology and support we hope to be online faster to service our customers in the Middle East and all over the world."[53]

Platforms like Farfetch are changing many businesses and industries, giving rise to technology-driven business models that disrupt industry value chains. Digitalization, for example, affects upstream partners, and can alter your supply chain ecosystem. And it can alter downstream distribution and customer engagement too, giving platforms an opportunity to create what Nicolaj Sigglelkow and Christian Terwiesch call "connected strategies" that turn "occasional, sporadic transactions with customers into long-term continuous relationships."[54]

Let's put all this in the context of your organization. The main point of this section is that technology deployment needs to clearly support the business transformation, and that means building capability to drive value creation. Unfortunately, tech investments often prove ineffectual because they are not grounded in the business strategy. That's the first disconnect. Remember, your strategic transformation depends on assessing where and how technology can improve operational efficiency, relational connectivity, and/or new business models. All three are potentially important, and they build on one another.[55]

The second disconnect is that too many firms overlook the fact that technology works in conjunction with other elements of organization architecture. It is not independent. In order to take advantage of technology, organizations likely need to modify their processes and, as a consequence, their structures. And with new technology comes the requirement for new skills. Many firms' record on talent sourcing is fairly dismal. But making tech investments without acquiring tech talent is like buying hardware with no software. Finally, as we'll discuss next, transformation typically cannot happen independently from cultural change. Simply adding technology to old processes, structures, skills, and cultures is like paving cow paths.[56]

At the end of the day, orchestrating transformation largely comes down to reconfiguring the organizational architecture to support enterprise-wide initiatives to achieve your strategic objectives. Strategy offers a formal logic for the organization's goals and provides clarity for collective action. In the end, orchestration is the process of mobilizing all these resources and coordinating action to achieve your desired outcome.

## REALITY CHECK

Let's take time for a reality check. How well does your organization convert strategy into a set of actionable initiatives? Do you use these to reconfigure the organization, mobilize resources, and energize collaboration to drive performance? There is a lot that goes into orchestration, and it is some of the hardest work of transformation. You can understand why so many firms struggle. As in chapters 3 and 4, I invite you to take some time to review the checklist in Figure 5.3 and assess where your organization is currently. If you're not going through transformation now, you can think of these as questions about orchestration potential. Is your organization orchestration-ready? If not, you may want to figure out why.

Second, think about how you make improvements to build capability for orchestration. It is of course better to work on this now than

| Translate Vision into Action | ☑ We have articulated clear priorities that operationalize our strategic intent and focus the organization on what matters most. |
| --- | --- |
| | ☑ We have established a coherent set of initiatives and performance metrics that guide our strategic investment and action. |
| | ☑ Our strategic initiatives all tie together in order to help us build new capabilities for the future. |
| Mobilize Your Transformation Network | ☑ We have strong alignment at the top of the organization, and this energizes the entire enterprise. |
| | ☑ We routinely work in cross-functional and cross-business teams to build collaboration across the enterprise. |
| | ☑ We coordinate with external partners to leverage complementary skills, knowledge, and resources. |
| Reconfigure Architecture | ☑ We have streamlined our organization structures and processes to improve workflow, decision-making, and collaboration. |
| | ☑ We have clearly defined process to prioritize technology deployment toward the most strategically important efforts. |
| | ☑ Our culture supports the values, expectations, and behaviors necessary to drive our business forward. |

FIGURE 5.3. Checklist for Orchestrating Mobilization

during the whirlwind of actual transformation. If you're in the process of transformation now, these points may give you a checklist to work on. How can you engage others around these issues? What insights can you draw from the examples of Microsoft, Mayo Clinic, Unilever, and the Chalhoub Group?

### Translate Vision into Action

How clear are people in your organization about what strategic intent means for them? In many instances, when I ask people about their company's strategy, they give me vague platitudes. When I press harder, they default to telling me about their job. There's a big void between strategic generalities and tactical action. During transformation, it is very important that leaders operationalize strategic intent.

The odds of successful transformation improve when you have an ambitious vision for the future. But that vision needs to be defined in operational terms that help focus attention and energy on key strategic priorities, to enable you to lay out a clear set of initiatives according to which you can allocate resources and take action.

Sounds easy. But it isn't. In this chapter, we saw examples of companies who worked through the process of translating vision into action. Perhaps more importantly, those cases illustrate some key principles that may give you guidance in your own organization. The principles and practices for operationalizing strategic intent are useful for all organizations, whether they are going through transformation or not. The process is a fundamental building block of strategic action.

### Mobilize Your Transformation Network

*What* is an important question in orchestrating transformation (i.e., What are we going to do?), and operationalizing strategic intent refines the "what" in more actionable terms. *Who* is also a very important question (i.e., Who is going to lead this? Who is on board and will collaborate?). There are a few takeaways and things to think about from this chapter. For example, you may use a chief transformation officer (CTO). Many firms do, and some don't, but regardless, it is important to have clear leadership and alignment at the top. Most employees take cues about the importance and accountability for change by observing the signals from the top team.

But as important as the top team is, the real work happens lower in the organization. This is why your transformation team, while perhaps small, needs to be the hub of an expanded network of collaborators. Those collaborators may be part of a set of temporary cross-functional teams working on key strategic initiatives. And they may be working in their ongoing business roles. Either way, the teams build capability for the organization, and they initiate movement toward the new business profile, gaining traction and showing progress.

### Reconfigure Your Architecture

Finally, consider all the structures, processes, and systems that are the tools for getting the work done. Structures clarify responsibilities and decision authority; processes lay out the sequence of action; and systems channel needed data and information to make better decisions. They're invaluable—and they're usually designed to do yesterday's work, not today's or tomorrow's. That's why your architecture needs to be reworked, or it will hold you back.

The same goes for culture. It can propel you forward, hold you back, or lead you to veer in a different direction. In this chapter, I shared some guidance about how other firms approach realigning their architecture. My advice is *not* to copy them, but to learn from them and apply the principles to your own organization's needs.

## PLAYBOOK TOOLS

To continue building your playbook for transformation, take time with your team to sketch out the key elements of orchestration to mobilize the organization. This is one of the most multifaceted aspects of transformation, and it's easy to get stuck in the weeds. Resist that tendency by keeping your eyes on the strategic elements. The following actions are helpful for clarifying the fundamentals needed for orchestrating mobilization.

**Directions for Building a Playbook:** Work through the following activities as a team. Use Playbook Template 5.1 at the end of the chapter to get consensus on the following:

- *Vision into Action.* Refer to your prior work at the end of chapters 3 and 4. Given your vision and strategic intent, identify two or three business imperatives that operationalize your ambition for the transformation. These are the "must-win battles" that will define your organization's success on the other side of transformation.[57] What metrics and performance data will calibrate progress toward these imperatives?

- *Strategic Initiatives.* Devise a focused set of three to five strategic initiatives to mobilize the organization and accomplish your business imperatives. Ultimately, there may be more than three to five initiatives, but start with these as the key ones. Initiatives may include developing new offerings (product/service), new channels to market, new capabilities, new technologies, etc. Some initiatives likely have multiple subcomponents, but they should work together in a cohesive manner. Importantly, be explicit about how these initiatives will help you build new capability to drive better value.

- *Mobilize Your Transformation Network.* Who will lead the transformation? The CEO and top leadership team own the process and are accountable for the results, but real progress occurs through broader collaboration among others in the organization.
  - Activate Your Transformation Team. At the end of chapter 4, you identified a set of key influencers who were well positioned to potentially form the core of your transformation team. Refine that thinking now. Who would constitute your transformation team? Typically, this is a small cadre of trusted leaders who are advocates. It may also include some close external partners. Does your team require the appointment of a CTO and/or PMO? It is not too early to mobilize that group and demonstrate alignment at the top.
  - Mobilize Cross-Functional Collaboration. Use your transformation team to identify candidates to lead each of your

strategic initiatives and build broader collaborative networks. Most strategic initiatives have cross-functional elements, so at this stage, determine which organizational units should be included, and what role each plays in the cross-functional team (CFT). Identifying individual team members may come later and may be delegated to the transformation team.

- Mobilize Resources. Each strategic initiative (and CFT) will need additional resources. These may include additional talent, data, technology, infrastructure, capital expense, etc. What budgeting requirements are immediate to mobilize action, and which can be deferred?

- *Reconfiguring Organizational Architecture.* Your transformation network operates as a "team of teams" where each CFT conducts its own work, while collaborating with other teams. To improve their chances of success, take time to consider which factors are likely to inhibit effective lateral connections across the network, and what changes made now would better enable it. Use Playbook Template 5.2 at the end of the chapter to create a short list based on the following questions:
  - Structures: Do authority structures, role definitions, decision rights, etc. promote lateral coordination, information sharing, and decision-making? What factors might be inhibiting that? What factors enable collaborative work? What structural changes are needed to achieve your objectives?
  - Processes and Policies: Are processes and workflow streamlined in order to create better collaboration and line of sight to customers? What factors might be inhibiting that? What factors enable effective and efficient workflow? What process or policy changes are needed to achieve your objectives?
  - Technology: What technology investment is needed to impact operational, relational, and transformation outcomes? Where are the technological deficiencies that inhibit your transformation? What is currently in place that facilitates your efforts? What are the recommended technology investments that are critical to achieving your objectives?

– Human Resources (HR): Do issues of talent management, performance management, rewards, training, leadership, and/ or culture promote collaboration? What factors might be inhibiting that? What factors enable collaborative work? What HR-related changes are needed to achieve your objectives?

## WHAT'S NEXT? CULTIVATE CHANGE AGILITY

As you've worked your way through the four factors of strategic transformation, it's perhaps easier to see how establishing context (chapter 3), engaging stakeholders (chapter 4), and now orchestrating mobilization (chapter 5) are interdependent. Each plays a significant role in transformation, and they are mutually reinforcing. The next chapter builds on this and addresses the requirements—and challenges—of cultivating change agility in the organization so that continuous adaptation, learning, and innovation allow you to thrive in a world of perpetual disruption.

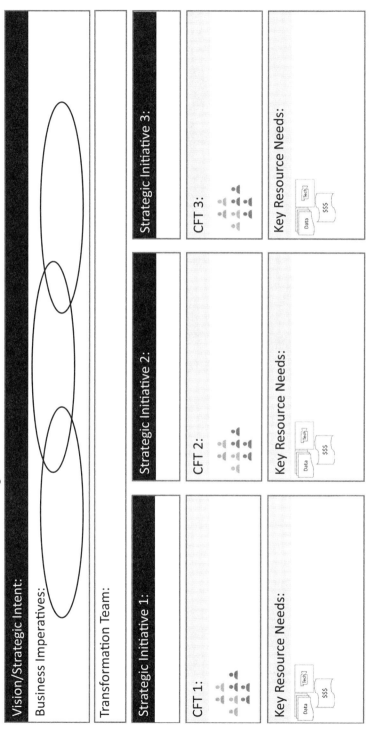

| Organization Architecture: | Inhibitors | Enablers | Required Action |
|---|---|---|---|
| Structures: Do authority structures, role definitions, etc. promote lateral coordination, information sharing, and decision-making? | | | |
| Processes and Policies: Are processes and workflow streamlined in order to create better collaboration and line of sight to customers? | | | |
| Technology: What tech investment is needed to impact operational, relational, and transformation outcomes? | | | |
| Human Resources: Does talent management, rewards, training, leadership, and culture promote collaboration? | | | |

# 6  FACTOR FOUR—CULTIVATE CHANGE AGILITY: BUILD DYNAMIC CAPABILITY

**KEY PRINCIPLE:** Strategic transformation builds dynamic capability and change agility.

**AS YOU'LL RECALL** from the last chapter, the Chalhoub Group got caught flatfooted when the retail industry shifted to e-commerce—highlighting the problem of agility. The company endured some painful lessons in its conversion to hybrid retailing. But even after making the transformation, Chalhoub Group needed to stay responsive to customers in new ways, because the customers themselves were also adjusting to game-changing technology, and the business environment was burgeoning with more disruption. Change was constant, and innovation and adaptation were part of Chalhoub's new business model. As Patrick Chalhoub described the situation, "So, it wasn't about going from point A to point B anymore, because point B was continuously changing."[1]

Like Chalhoub Group, Microsoft confronted challenges of agility in its pivot to a "mobile-first, cloud-first" strategy. Its ten-year delay in addressing industry disruption and embracing the potential of cloud computing caused Microsoft to trail behind Amazon's 71 percent market share. By some accounts, there were leaders within Microsoft who had consciously marginalized mobile and cloud investments so that Microsoft's legacy desktop products wouldn't be displaced. The shift to mobile and cloud computing required Satya Nadella to create an organization that was nimble enough to respond quickly in the new era of rapidly evolving technology. What would Microsoft do to achieve that kind of agility?[2]

Finally, Mayo Clinic, too, learned the value of agility as it evolved its 2020 strategy into its next iteration; the 2030 strategy, dubbed "Bold Forward." In 2019, Gianrico Farrugia succeeded John Noseworthy as CEO and set in motion aggressive goals to turbocharge Mayo Clinic's pursuit of digital transformation and new business models.

And then the COVID-19 pandemic hit. As Dr. Farrugia recalled, "We certainly never imagined that the year after approving our 2030 strategic plan to cure, connect and transform health care, it would be in the throes of a global health crisis. And really, those first six to nine months have arguably been the most challenging in Mayo Clinic's history." But despite the challenges, Mayo Clinic provided medical care to 65,000 patients with COVID-19 and achieved the lowest mortality rate in the world. And through it all—actually *because* of the experience— Mayo Clinic accelerated its transformation. Farrugia noted in 2021, "I think as an organization, we've made close to a decade of progress over the course of one year. So, all this work in the digital space, including using artificial intelligence to inform decision-making, has been ongoing for many years at Mayo Clinic. But it was the pandemic that pushed us faster and further than we could have imagined."[3]

## THE CHALLENGE

These stories illustrate the challenges involved in the fourth factor of strategic transformation: cultivating change agility. The transformation journey involves some discrete episodic shifts and—just as important— some continuously adaptive and responsive elements as well. As alluded to in chapter 2, a contemporary premise of strategic transformation is that change is not a "once and done." In the VUCA environments in which we find ourselves, organizations need to develop the capacity to adjust on the fly, sensing and responding to unforeseen opportunities or threats. They need to develop an ability to learn rapidly and convert that learning into action. The essence of dynamic capability is that change agility is embedded in the organization as an ongoing element of its strategy. Strategic transformation is designed to achieve that capability.

## Symptoms of Poor Agility

What stands in the way of achieving more agility? There are several barriers, and we can generally categorize them into three buckets: (1) cognitive, (2) affective, and (3) structural. Often, we inadvertently build these constraints ourselves.

**Fixed mindsets.** Literary theorist Kenneth Burke observed, "A way of seeing is also a way of not seeing."[4] As we focus intently on one object, we neglect another. Recall the story I shared in chapter 1 of my early career experience at IBM. Let's return to that now.

Despite its many advantages, world-class talent, cutting-edge technology, and market dominance, IBM seemed to be caught off guard, unprepared for the industry shift from mainframes to PCs. How could this possibly happen to the market leader? Critics often contend that IBM had become complacent and arrogant, resting on its laurels and not listening to its customers. But honestly, my experience was just the opposite. IBM was assiduously focused and engaged with its biggest and best customers, developing leading-edge technologies and industry-advancing innovation.

The trouble was, the PC itself was not actually a leading-edge technology. But it was a huge market disruptor. The customers who were buying it were not large or sophisticated. They were individuals and small businesses who had never bought a computer before. The market shifted, and IBM missed the shift. Ironically, its passion for computing made it more myopic. It had a fixed mindset—an unwavering way of processing information—resulting in tunnel vision, "chin-down" management, and a tendency to ignore other inputs.

**Threat rigidity.** Like the cognitive constraints that plagued IBM, agility is often hindered by disposition or emotion as well. Change fatigue, for example, is a common malady among employees and managers who have endured the heavy weight—and personal risks—associated with organizational transitions. It causes them to deny, delay, and defend the status quo against further change. Psychologists call this "threat rigidity," meaning people freeze under pressure or harden their response sets. Ironically, rather than dialing up an agile response under conditions of disruptive change or uncertainty, some do just the opposite: They double down on familiar patterns. And if performance suffers, they force their way forward insistently, often defaulting to micromanagement or strict supervision.[5]

One of my good friends, Tim Baldwin, told me the story of his high school football coach, who used to declare in a tough game, "We're going to run off tackle dammit, or we're not going to win!" Tim mused, "Yeah, coach, you might be missing the point here." Rather than adapt to the circumstances, the coach was using old solutions for new problems—a common response.[6]

**Structural shackles.** In the prior chapter, on orchestration, I noted the importance of balancing inertia and momentum. Let's take that one step further. Newton's first law of physics asserts: An object in motion tends to stay in motion, and an object at rest tends to stay at rest. In other words, all objects tend to oppose a change to their current state.

Agility—or a lack thereof—is not just a human response; it is an organizational one as well. It can in fact be a manifestation of an organization's architecture. The structures, processes, systems, and cultures that underly your firm's core capabilities can propel performance or hold it back during periods of change. If we're not careful, our core capabilities can become core rigidities, and old architectures reinforce that.[7]

As noted management guru Ram Charan explained: "The hard work that a CEO must do to drive that tempo happens in breaking through entrenched organizational constructs to nurture a culture that values the doer over the manager, and small teams over giant org charts. CEOs are successful in developing this working model when they simplify the most important processes, clarify governance to reduce ambiguity in decision making, pare down the number of managers, and celebrate team progress. As important, they build a culture that learns so the business can adapt quickly."[8]

**The mad scramble.** Finally, a debilitating symptom of poor agility is what you might call the "mad scramble." Given disruptive change, executives sometimes overreact, responding chaotically and without careful consideration of unintended consequences. A key theme in chapter 3 is that establishing context is foundational to transformation to guide a coherent strategy for action. This is especially true for moving with agility as well. Without a clear understanding of the circumstances, solutions can be shortsighted. Making crazy is not the same as being agile.

During the pandemic, for example, when money was cheap and the market was hot, tech firms made a mad scramble to hire talent, recruiting thousands of programmers, analysts, and developers in part because everyone else was doing it. Fear of missing out (FOMO) drove some very good firms to react hastily, copy others, over-hire, and become needlessly bloated. Later, when the market cooled and recession fears took over, these same firms rapidly jettisoned thousands of employees.

"I got this wrong," said Meta CEO Mark Zuckerberg, "and I take responsibility for that." "We hired too many people," said Salesforce CEO Marc Benioff, "and I take responsibility for that." "I grew the company size too quickly," said former Twitter CEO Jack Dorsey. "I apologize for that." The mad scramble for talent was not strategic, and it cost these organizations.[9]

## What You Can Do

These examples illustrate how difficult it can be to embed change agility in your organization. Moving quickly is difficult. Moving continuously is more difficult. In this chapter, I'll share some of the key things senior executives say they've learned about developing change agility in their organizations.[10] Johnny C. Taylor, CEO of SHRM, said, "This is all about the culture of the organization." And that culture derives from some very particular actions.[11] They include:

1. *Enhance your situational awareness:* Focus on your strategic intent and purpose, develop deeper customer insights, and enhance your peripheral vision of boundary conditions by probing the environment to detect early trends.
2. *Empower a culture of rapid learning:* Lower the center of gravity for decisions, enable experimentation, and incubate innovation.
3. *Accelerate dynamic resourcing:* Reallocate capital and talent, share knowledge, and strengthen the core.

Figure 6.1 shows some of the key characteristics of agility that we'll discover together. Note the balance and integration of external and

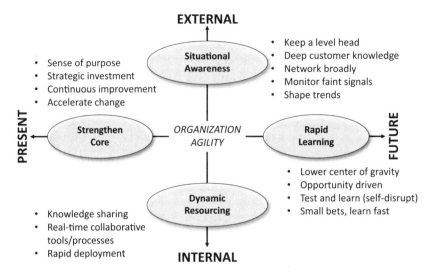

FIGURE 6.1. Cultivate Organizational Agility

internal factors, as well as the ambidexterity to address the present while creating the future.

## STEP 1: ENHANCE YOUR SITUATIONAL AWARENESS

Agility depends on situational awareness; that is, detecting and inter-preting changes in your broader surroundings to improve your capacity to respond and make decisions. Often it involves paying close attention to the things that matter most, including events that directly drive in-dustry change. Other times, it involves sensing small, nonobvious, or unexpected events that indirectly impact the future.

Mayo Clinic's Gianrico Farrugia describes the challenge this way:

> You have to learn how to anticipate change, and that's different from the past, where perhaps health care leaders were able to better understand where things were going to go and then adapt to them. Now change comes quickly, as you very well know. It comes from places we wouldn't have imagined: technology, data, consumerism. I truly believe leaders cannot just respond to what's happen-ing. They have to anticipate where things are, where things are going, and then they have to chart a course for their organization to get them there. Of course, gut-checking everything with their organization's value.[12]

When the future is not like the past, agile response is both more difficult and more important. Situational awareness is a meta-capability that transcends other aspects of transformation. Ask yourself these questions:

- Do we get distracted by unexpected events, or do we remain focused on our purpose and strategic intent?
- How thoroughly do we learn about our customers to foster deeper relationships?
- How many points of contact have we created with external stakeholders to ensure relevance and responsiveness?
- How do we detect faint signals to stay ahead of emerging trends?[13]

## Keep a Level Head

Executives consistently offer a word of caution about agility. It does not change the first immutable rule of transformation—that is, it must improve the connection between your capabilities and your customer value. In this regard, agility is NOT—as some would suggest—constantly reinventing yourself.

My advice is to keep a level head. Stay focused on your mission, purpose, and strategic intent *while* you simultaneously flex and adapt to the environment.

By way of analogy, consider cats. Have you ever noticed their uncanny ability to always land on their feet? Have you ever wondered why? (Do you care?) I checked with my friends at Purina, and the company has a whole website dedicated to the answer. I guess they get this question a lot.[14]

Cats have an innate reflex called the "righting reflex." Inside a cat's ear is something called a vestibular apparatus, a unique structure that helps them to quickly determine which direction is up and which is down. Once they do this, they can more quickly orient and balance themselves.

Unique aspects of cat anatomy help them flip over to the "right-side up" posture. A cat has a flexible backbone with thirty vertebrae and no collarbone. This makes arching its back, turning, and gyrating easier.

Cats also have a low size-to-weight ratio, which reduces air speed when falling. When they hit the ground, their angled muscular legs and torso absorb the impact reducing its force.

What does this have to do with strategic transformation? Good question. Like a cat, you must always know which way is up. Keep a level head and build a flexible anatomy to respond.

Mayo Clinic during the pandemic provides an exemplary case. As Mayo's new CEO, Farrugia emphasized the importance of staying focused during times of disruptive change. He said this regarding Mayo's response to COVID-19:

> I'd say that every Mayo Clinic CEO experiences a significant event in their tenure. Be it an economic crisis, a war, national events like 911. So, I already knew. I knew something would come my way ... I'd say there was a lot of uncertainty, except for one certainty that Mayo Clinic was going to live up to our mission and to our values. We're going to look after our staff and our patients. And that kept us going. ...
>
> [B]ecause we have invested in preparations for a crisis long before this particular crisis, because we looked after our patients, we looked to our values for guidance, because we worked so well together with our partners, and really because we seized opportunities to develop solutions for the pandemic and for our patients, both nationally and globally, we actually find ourselves in a position we did not expect to be in April last year. We felt empowered to lead, and in fact, we led, and our 2030 Bold.Forward. strategy has enabled us to transform healthcare even during the pandemic.[15]

Rather than default to a mad scramble, Mayo Clinic responded quickly with a strategic focus. Farrugia continued:

> I think we all kind of expected that with the COVID-19 extended crisis ... all our attention would divert away from anything else, we stopped making progress in our strategic plan, everything would be put on hold. But what surprised me, and I think a lot of us, is just the opposite happened. The pandemic served to reinforce that our Mayo Clinic 2030 Bold.Forward. strategy ... was indeed the right strategy.[16]

Mayo's unwavering focus on its purpose and values helped stabilize the firm during disruptive change. To paraphrase a famous poem by

Rudyard Kipling, your success depends in part on "if you can keep your head while all about you are losing theirs."[17]

## Develop Deep Market Intelligence to Stay Out Front

Your organization's ability to rapidly respond and adapt is predicated on what you can see and what you are able to understand. Wesley Cohen and Daniel Levinthal's research on firm-level "absorptive capacity" hits on exactly this issue. When an organization can recognize and evaluate external information, interpret patterns that evade others, assimilate that knowledge, and act on it, it is in a much better position to respond quickly and build its adaptive capability. Perhaps intuitively, the depth and breadth of your firm's prior related experience influences its ability to process new information and knowledge, and because of that, it is a prerequisite to further organizational learning.[18]

Customer data—and more precisely, customer insights from that data—provide a catalyst for rapid response. Recall from chapter 3 that your customers are the focal point of your firm's operating model and the primary arbiter of value creation. That's true universally, and it is especially important when your goal is to embed change agility in the organization.

Patrick Chalhoub understood that his group's prospects of omnichannel transformation were limited—unless it could generate deeper and more personalized customer insights. The pace of change and growth of new buying channels required exactly that.[19]

To improve responsiveness and customization, the Chalhoub Group created a specialized "intelligence team" to track relevant market data and build predictive forecasts of the future. The intelligence team was positioned to spot new trends and points of disruption in the industry, in order to equip retail teams with timely information they could use to make more informed decisions, thereby enabling better organizational agility.[20]

The Group's chief experience officer, Bernadette Geagea, put it this way: "Companies are now forced to look at customer experience in its new reality ... You will not be able to draw the customer journey map the same way we used to in the recent past. The CX [customer experience] wheel is moving at a high velocity ... it has changed a lot recently which makes it very difficult to predict how it will be in the future." To adapt, Geagea's team gathers key insights around how the customer interacts with products, what they think of the experience, and how and where they get their information.[21]

These customer insights serve both as a focal point for agility and a catalyst for rapid response. They can sound an alarm for rapid change and signal in which direction the action needs to occur. But agility is not only about improving your firm's ability to predict behavior or understand the wants and needs of customers. It is also about information: Good data also helps to promote innovation and cultivate better relationships with your customers over time.

### Expand Your Peripheral Vision

And of course, customers are not your only stakeholders. Recall that a central point in chapters 3 and 4 was that firms often don't have a full understanding of their business ecosystems, or of the dynamic interdependencies among related stakeholders. Consequently, they are often surprised by events that, in retrospect, they might have anticipated. The job of leaders, in part, is to make certain that potential opportunities and threats are identified and evaluated in light of the firm's transformation.

Enhancing your peripheral vision is an important requirement of agility in VUCA environments; that is, detecting those sometimes faint or ambiguous signals that portend significant future events. This means being aware of what's happening on the margins. For example, the government monitored cell phone data during the COVID-19 pandemic, and when the results suggested an uptick in population mobility in 2021, it was a signal that people were no longer hunkering down. Faint signals such as this can be leading indicators of change.[22]

One of the most famous examples of peripheral signal detection—and how difficult it can be—is the surprise attack on Pearl Harbor. Repeatedly, U.S. officials failed to recognize Japanese forces' preparations for war and overlooked signs of the impending attack. On December 6, 1941, they ignored a Japanese message inquiring about mooring positions at Pearl Harbor. Later that day, a destroyer identified—and sank—a small Japanese submarine at the mouth of the harbor, but officers dismissed the episode. Early in the morning of December 7, a radar unit sighted a large group of airplanes flying toward Oahu but misinterpreted it as a squadron of B-17s inbound from the West Coast. Each instance, on its own, might be a rookie mistake, but the pattern of data should have revealed something more substantive.

Examples like this abound at pivotal turning points in industry as well. Disruption typically occurs at the margins of industries, orthogonal to the focused attention of organizations. Paradigmatically, innovation often occurs similarly, at the boundaries within and between organizations. Leading indicators of both innovation and disruption are easy to miss. Agility thus involves building capacity for *lateral thinking*— addressing potential situations from a point of view that is not linear or a direct extrapolation from the past.

Research by George Day and Paul Schoemaker found that less than 20 percent of firms develop the acuity to stay continually attentive. In their book *Peripheral Vision*, they offer five key things organizations can do to widen their aperture of attention, effectively creating an early warning system for opportunities and threats that begin as weak signals from boundary areas: (1) scope the environment widely enough to ask the right questions, (2) actively scan in the right places, (3) interpret what the signals mean, (4) probe and shape future developments, and (5) act wisely on signals before others do.[23]

How do these factors help organizations cultivate better change agility? Let's look at a few examples. You'll recall that Paul Polman established a wide-angle lens for his transformation of Unilever by basing its Sustainable Living Plan (USLP) on input from a broad range of stakeholders, partners, government agencies, NGOs, philanthropies, and societal groups. Bill Bratton transformed the NYPD by engaging a diverse set of stakeholders, community groups, politicians, and news media. He also held periodic forums with his constituencies because he wanted to detect concerns before they grew into large issues. Mayo Clinic's 2020 Initiative was explicitly designed to identify emerging trends in the medical field that would presage future challenges and opportunities for the firm. Some of the most important factors were not obvious, and their effects were initially indirect. Microsoft, of course, has worked assiduously to develop a better understanding of a rapidly evolving tech sector. More broadly, its peripheral vision extends to social, economic, and climate-related concerns, as indicated most famously by its central role in the World Economic Forum.

### Probe the Environment to Shape the Future

Not all situational awareness is based on reactive response to the environment. Peter Drucker is often quoted as saying "The best way to predict the future is to create it." Easier said than done, of course, but to shape the future, firms often probe the environment, investigate emerging trends and technologies, influence events and innovation, and nudge the direction of change. In many cases, firms take a measured financial stake in potential disruptors to get out in front and stay apprised of those trends.

Chalhoub Group, for example, created what it refers to as "the Greenhouse," an external retail tech accelerator focused on carrying out pilots and case studies with brands other than Chalhoub. The idea is to shape events, not merely react to them.[24]

According to Patrick Chalhoub,

> We launched the Greenhouse being aware that we have not only big competitors, but also startups that we feel threatened by. So, we decided to consider those startups as our allies. For that reason, the Greenhouse is open to any entrepreneur in the tech retail space. We offer a working space, mentorship, and so on, but what we have noticed that startups need most is not money but a ground to test their proof of concept. And through our more than 600 retail stores or 10 websites they can do that—test their technologies. If it works, we scale it up with them throughout the group. So, the message for entrepreneurs and our team is that if you have an idea, make it happen, and we'll support you.[25]

The Greenhouse was set up to run three-month programs for post-MVP (minimum viable product) start-ups, enabling them to work closely with Chalhoub Group's brand managers and corporate partners. The program gave priority to start-ups, from anywhere in the world, working in areas having to do with customer experience online and in-store, supply chain, and customer data analytics.

In a similar initiative, the Group partnered with L'Occitane to support the development of retail technology. In this program, selected start-ups received grants, market access, and retail advice through the firm's many partnerships and wide geographic reach.[26]

After their Greenhouse experience, many of the start-ups not only found success but also signed agreements with Chalhoub Group brands. The initiative thus enables Chalhoub to shape its industry while exchanging ideas with innovators.

More generally, Chalhoub Group supports small local entrepreneurs, helping them grow and thrive. In 2022, the Group partnered with the Fashion Commission of Saudi Arabia's Ministry of Culture and launched a "fashion lab" to help bolster regional designers and small-scale businesses. Why? Because even if Chalhoub Group doesn't benefit directly, these investments create a healthier business environment in which Chalhoub Group can flourish.

Strategically, these kinds of investments help Chalhoub identify the key drivers of change, enabling the company to keep a finger on the pulse of potential disruption. Chief executive of the Fashion Commission Burak Cakmak observed, "Strategic collaborations with authoritative private sector entities will play a pivotal role in supporting us with intelligence and insights on the fashion industry. Such collaborations will ultimately benefit the regional fashion industry, nurture local talents, and support the growth of retail."[27]

Mayo Clinic also has a strong tradition of partnering to shape industry change. Its founding more than 100 years ago was predicated on the idea that no one person or entity could master the universe of medical knowledge on their own. The Mayo brothers' original business model was to canvass the world—and partner broadly—to shape the vanguard of health care. That tradition continues today.

To not only keep pace with industry changes but also to stay ahead of the curve, the Clinic seeks out and invests in a broad array of external experts, clinicians, scientists, and entrepreneurs around the world, "paving the way for increased economic development opportunities in the process."[28]

For example, Mayo set up the Innovation Exchange, a membership-based platform created to advance industry collaboration, accelerate commercialization, and provide internal innovators and external entrepreneurs with premier medical and business insights. The Innovation Exchange is designed to serve as a marketplace that provides connections to the "right people, places, and resources" to accelerate breakthrough advances in health care.[29]

As it identifies trailblazers and thought leaders, Mayo also provides much-needed seed funding and sponsorship. Its corporate venture capital arm, Mayo Clinic Ventures, invests in medical technology, medical devices, biopharmaceuticals, diagnostics, and other health care sectors. Its aim is to help advance promising technologies from early-stage concepts toward clinical testing and commercialization. It allocates seed money and venture funding to support early-stage companies, which then work together with Mayo Clinic to advance promising ideas and discoveries.

"Our team serves as a catalyst for improving health outcomes by tirelessly encouraging innovation and empowering inventors to bring transformational interventions to market for the benefit of patients," said James Rogers, Mayo Clinic's chief business development officer.[30]

As shown in Figure 6.2, the payoff to medical science is an acceleration of innovation, and reciprocally, Mayo Clinic can shape the future of health care and stay abreast of emerging technologies. Equally impressive is the scope of Mayo Clinic Ventures' contributions to economic growth locally, regionally, nationally, and globally.

These examples give you a better sense of the ways organizations build an informed foundation for agility. Before moving on, summarize in your own mind the keys to developing better situational awareness in your organization. How do you anticipate where change might occur, where possibilities exist, and how your organization can respond? First, how do you use customer data—and insights derived from that—to help you focus on what customers want today, and what they might value in the future? Second, how do you ascertain changes in your business ecosystem to respond or shape the dynamics of interrelated parties? Finally, how are you

**THE OUPUT**

- 10,528 Disclosures Filed
- 9,109 Patents Filed
- 3,540 Patents Issued
- 312 Companies Formed Using Mayo Clinic Technology

**THE IMPACT**

- 600+ Ideas Disclosed Each Year
- Millions of Lives Touched by Mayo Clinic Innovations
- Mayo Clinic Licensed Technology on Every Continent in the World
- 4,297 Technologies Licensed Since Inception

Stats represent inception to 2022

FIGURE 6.2. Mayo Clinic Ventures

expanding peripheral vision to detect early signs of outlying events and developments that may affect your business? Addressing all these issues will give you a more "heads-up" approach to agile execution with a wider field of vision, more acuity, and a better ability to see what's coming.[31]

## STEP 2: EMPOWER A CULTURE OF RAPID LEARNING

Cultivating change agility in organizations involves placing a premium on rapid learning and translating that learning into action. Research by Dorothy Leonard-Barton suggests that organizational learning involves four key characteristics: (1) being open to the outside world, (2) empowering employees to own and solve problems, (3) experimentation and small tests, and (4) sharing knowledge throughout the organization.[32]

Consider the following questions as you gauge your own organization's potential:

- How well do we empower members of the organization to own and solve problems, to distribute decision-making lower in the organization, and to gain from their collective knowledge?

- In what ways have we established a culture that accepts reasonable risk as a function of trying new things, testing, and learning?
- How well do we cultivate innovation, growth, and new avenues of value creation?[33]

## Lower the Center of Gravity

Recall the CEO in chapter 4 who cautioned, "It is very difficult to lead strategic change entirely from the C-suite—the organization is too complex, and you are too far away from the action." That advice is relevant for any transformation and is crucial for cultivating change agility. To build dynamic capability in the organization, it is necessary to lower the center of gravity of decision-making, action, and energy.

In their book *The Agility Factor*, Christopher Worley, Thomas Williams, and Ed Lawler argue that empowered decision-making leads to faster response and more points of contact with the environment, thereby providing more useful information. They refer to this as maximizing the "surface area" of the organization.[34]

Bill Bratton did this within the NYPD. He empowered his precinct commanders to drive transformation and held biweekly meetings to raise their accountability for results. He also expected them to convene regular community meetings so that citizens within each precinct could come together and share their concerns. By empowering commanders in the NYPD—lowering the center of gravity for decisions and action—the commanders began to see the situation differently, take ownership for making improvements, and share data and best practice with their colleagues. The changes spread quickly through this peer network, and the results were impressive, rapidly changing the culture of engagement.

If viewed in its entirety, the scale and scope of complete transformation might have been overwhelming to the precinct commanders. To give commanders agency and support their empowerment, Bratton framed the process as a sequence of manageable goals. He described it as NYPD improving safety "block by block, precinct by precinct, and borough by borough."[35]

Chalhoub Group also saw the value of empowering employees, delegating authority, and decentralizing decisions to increase agility. Recall that it had set up its "SHIFT team" to work alongside business units to ensure they were "agile, quick and use the best possible technology," as Patrick Chalhoub described it.[36] But while the SHIFT team was instrumental, it was only a catalyst for agility. To embed agility more deeply, Chalhoub fostered a culture change that encouraged employee initiative and bottom-up innovation. The effort was anchored by seven guiding principles that empowered people to make bold moves, start small, fail fast or scale fast, celebrate and learn from successes and failures—all while keeping the customer front and center (see Figure 6.3).[37]

The approach located decision-making "much closer to the market and the customer," said Patrick Chalhoub. This made the business nimbler and able to respond more quickly. Employees had greater autonomy and were better equipped to serve customers locally; company leaders focused more on coaching and mentoring than on supervising. The changes resulted in a significant shift in company culture. From the beginning, Chalhoub saw the potential in such an approach: "If we could crack it and get people not only to be trusted but to trust themselves and move forward, this by itself would be really transformative. As soon as people discover what we mean by empowerment we will see a huge change."[38]

### Seven Guiding Principles –from now on….

## CHALHOUB
## Group

- The **CUSTOMER** is at the heart.
- We empower **EMPLOYEES**: Let them be **BOLD** and **MAKE IT HAPPEN**.
- We start **SMALL**, we **FAIL FAST** or **SCALE FAST**.
- Failure and success are **LEARNING & SHARING** moments.
- We think **HYBRID & GLOBAL** from the start.
- Startups will be **OUR ALLIES**.
- We play on the **OFFENSE**.

FIGURE 6.3. Chalhoub Group: Seven Guiding Principles (Adapted from "Digitalization," Chalhoub Group, Sustainability Report, 2018.)

To help encourage this culture change, the Group adopted an innovative, experimental mindset that welcomed new ideas and allowed failures in the service of trying things out. "We will become totally customer centric ... with teams that are totally empowered to take their own decisions. It will be a radically different organization, but much more relevant for the client of today."[39]

The parallels to Mayo Clinic are unmistakable. "The future calls for staff who are innovative, who are empowered, who are adaptable to the changes we all know are coming," said Farrugia. "We as leaders now have a responsibility to empower and energize our teams to create solutions for our patients and even for each other. And our staff cannot do it, nobody can do it if you're bogged down in all sorts of administrative work."[40]

As a first step in that direction, Mayo Clinic streamlined bureaucracy, alleviating the staff's administrative burden. Farrugia believed that one part of empowerment was limiting the number of committees needed to get approvals, and to instead place more trust in employees. By taking a hard look at "administrivia," Mayo was able to chip away at lower-value activities and focus on tasks that truly mattered.

Digitalization is obviously a potential way to declutter work, freeing up more employee time and thereby enabling empowerment. As Farrugia observed, "I'm a human-focused person, but I very much know that technology will play an even bigger part. I see AI as further reducing clerical burden so that our staff can tackle complex, interesting, and innovative projects. It's better for them, it's better for us, and it's certainly better for our patients."[41]

### Test and Learn at Higher Velocity

Empowerment is one element of organizational learning—but only one. Empowered employees are more likely to take responsibility, engage with customers and partners, identify opportunities, and embrace personal initiative. They are also likely to learn more quickly in the process, upgrading their knowledge and skills. That's a good thing, because as Richard Teerlink, former CEO of Harley-Davidson, observed, "The only thing you get when you empower dummies is bad decisions faster."

So, a good question is: How do you create an environment that continually upgrades employee learning? One of the truisms of the agile movement is that organizations need to experiment, test and learn quickly, reallocate, and chalk up the inevitable mistakes as investments in learning. Fail small, fail fast, scale fast. These small experiments are often opportunity driven—quick responses empowered on the front line to invent a better way.

Ironically, your efforts to cultivate change agility often derive from taking smaller steps rather than giant leaps. We know from research that firms adapt better—especially under conditions of uncertainty—when they make incremental moves, continually questioning and learning as they go, iterating quickly with repeated data tests, and validating their progress. This approach sits in contrast to the image of an agile beast that lurches rapidly at a new object.

Microsoft, under Satya Nadella's leadership, has emphasized more rapid testing and learning particularly in how it approaches new product launches. For many years, Microsoft had a reputation for what some critics referred to as "launch and leave." Product and software developers adopted an internal-facing approach, emphasizing their own ideas and expertise, perhaps ignoring external feedback, launching to the market with a big splash, and then returning to their labs to work on the next big thing. The measure of success was product sales, and while there is nothing wrong with that, it created a very long feedback cycle for improvement. Frequently, Microsoft had a dearth of good market data, particularly on how customers applied the product. This made it difficult to learn quickly.

Scott Guthrie, EVP of Cloud and AI, described how Microsoft has changed to embed agile principles: "One thing that we have tried to change is how to get a minimum viable product or a strategy that we think is right, use data, and then course correct." Microsoft now uses customer usage, rather than revenue, as the key metric. "Revenue's a trailing indicator," Guthrie continued. "Let's be agile, and let's be data driven. The first thing I do in the morning isn't check my revenue. I check the usage for each of my core businesses."[42]

With these changes, Microsoft has shorter customer feedback loops, allowing faster analysis with more accurate data, which makes product updates much more effective. And now that its business is run on the cloud, updates are almost immediate.

Microsoft's approach frames each iteration as a hypothesis, using data to test it. "[If] something isn't working, what are the hypotheses for how we fix it? And then every time we try one of these hypotheses, did it actually move the needle?" Learning in that sense is both systematic and incremental. As Guthrie observed, "It's infinitely easier to move one degree at a time, 365 days of the year, than it is to do one fell swoop."[43]

Recall this agile approach was all part of Microsoft's culture change to drive transformation. Nadella emphasized the importance of a growth mindset to support agility. As Chief HR Officer Kathleen Hogan observed, "This notion of constantly being curious and learning and open to feedback, and you don't have all the answers, breeds agility. If you have that fixed mindset, where you feel you need to be the smartest person in the room, you have to have it all figured out."[44]

Nadella was fond of saying that learning was more important than knowing. "If you take two people, one of them is a learn-it-all and the other one is a know-it-all, the learn-it-all will always trump the know-it-all in the long run, even if they start with less innate capability," Nadella explained. "A growth mindset emphasizes execution as learning, asking not telling, not being afraid to make mistakes but recognizing that learning fast requires some risk. It embraces the idea of the uncertainty and ambiguity, giving people a foundation for resilience in the face of change."[45]

To encourage a learning culture, Nadella instituted an annual Microsoft Hackathon, which the company calls the "largest private hackathon in the world." Among tech workers, hacks are a popular and effective way of working around constraints and developing creative innovations. Microsoft Hackathon was a great way to reinforce a growth mindset, and in the first year, 12,000 employees in 83 countries contributed more than 3,000 hacks. But it wasn't just the innovative solutions that mattered; it was creating a tangible manifestation of the new culture of innovating together.[46]

The approach also reduces the prevalence of threat rigidity, mentioned at the opening of this chapter. A growth mindset accepts occasional mistakes as an investment in learning. But because learning is occurring faster—and mistakes are corrected faster—the costs of an error are typically smaller, and performance improves more rapidly.[47]

In reality, of course, you might wonder how open Microsoft is to people actually making mistakes. Chuck Edward, CVP of Human Resources, said, "I think this alone was probably the biggest shift in our company. We had a lot of smart, passionate people, but when you remove this fear of judgment or fear of mistake and you allow people to try things, it was just cathartic." In the end, Guthrie observed that agility and "growth mindset isn't about being right. There's no absolute, and if you think you're right, and you think you're perfect, that's a really dangerous place to be because the world's constantly changing."[48]

Like Microsoft, Mayo Clinic has become a world-class learning organization. One example of rapid experimentation leading to agile adaptation occurred during the pandemic. In July 2020, Mayo Clinic piloted Advanced Care at Home, a new delivery model that used a tech platform to provide comprehensive and complex care to patients in the comfort of their homes, equivalent to what they'd receive in a hospital. The program worked because Mayo physicians conducted daily "video visits" and were on call 24/7; physician assistants and nurse practitioners visited homes periodically, and the Clinic's partners took care of corollary tasks such as laundry, meals, and the like.

The program was tested on over 400 patients and was shown to be safe and effective. Farrugia observed, "We learned that with this home hospital model, we're able to cut readmissions in half because we can rescue patients before they normally need to come to the emergency room. And of course, that means patients can spend less time with us, and more time with their families enjoying life." Patient satisfaction was very high, scoring 4.9/5.0.[49]

In an example of "reverse innovation," once patients learned they could connect with physicians 24/7, they asked, "Why can't we do the same when were actually in our hospital room?" As a result, Mayo Clinic is transferring the same technology into its hospital rooms.[50]

There are several notable aspects to this kind of experimentation at Mayo Clinic. First, the pilot was done on a limited scale, but with rapid feedback from the patients. That feedback loop is critical. Proof of concept occurs quickly, and then, with good data, it can scale broadly. Ultimately, not only was Mayo Clinic able to transfer the knowledge globally, but it also adapted the virtual system to other (in-person hospital) applications.

And from the standpoint of agility, experimentation provides optionality. In Mayo Clinic's case, Advanced Care at Home, digital visits, and remote monitoring didn't simply replace in-person visits. These innovations enabled Mayo Clinic to care for patients at a distance, in settings where patients have more control.

To be sure, not all experiments work out as well as Advanced Care at Home. Experimentation inevitably involves risk of failure. The key is to manage acceptable risk. As Farrugia said, "You can take measured risk, which is very different from being risky, taking risky behavior ... If you're going to effect change, you need to be authentic; you need to be transparent about it. When you think about a better way, you better have the data and the information to back it up, and then ... be willing to assume some risk."[51]

These examples underline how a culture of continuous learning fuels agile transformation. This works in two ways. First, experimentation, testing, and learning enable continuous improvement, eliminating inferior approaches and replacing them with more effective solutions. Every idea is a hypothesis to be tested. The key is to learn quickly from these small bets, collect data, test assumptions—in other words, iterate quickly—and relearn what you think or thought you knew about the markets.

Second, experimentation and learning generate new ideas, new discoveries, different approaches in different contexts, and alternative solutions for a variety of situations. More alternatives equate to more optionality. When you have access to more options and alternatives, you can increase the repertoire and versatility of your organization. The more you implement and encourage these kinds of experiments, the more your organization begins to develop a repository of choices for different situations.[52]

## Incubate Innovation to Cultivate Breakthroughs

To turbocharge idea generation, Chalhoub Group established an internal business incubator and innovation lab called Ibtikar. "We have decided to empower our team so that if their idea succeeds, we will scale it quickly, but we wouldn't fire people who failed, but learn with them," said Patrick Chalhoub.[53]

Designed to foster innovation within the Group, Ibtikar provided a unique opportunity for any employee across fourteen countries to experiment and test ideas with dedicated time, funding, and mentorship. The program sponsors up to three big business ideas per cohort, twice a year. The Group also encouraged everyday entrepreneurship, empowering employees to take initiative in small ways, creating significant impact.[54] Patrick Chalhoub said this of Ibtikar:

> Both failures and successes have become sharing moments. We invited our employees to work on their ideas and develop a proof of concept with our support, giving them three months to move away from their day-to-day work but remaining on the same salary and with the job being secured after this period in the case that the idea fails. When we launched Ibtikar, we had 150 employees coming up with the ideas, three were chosen and they got three months to work on them. One has been retained and we will invest in it, one [woman] got three more months to develop hers, and one has been rejected.[55]

Private equity firms, venture funds, and other organizations often operate in an analogous way: The expected return from any single investment may be low, but the expected return of the overall portfolio is high.

Mayo Clinic extends this logic. You've already learned about how it partners externally to shape the health care environment. But Farrugia is resolute in his belief that Mayo Clinic needs to continuously shoulder responsibility for innovation internally as well:

> The one thing that pandemic has taught us is that innovation in healthcare is not going to come from outside of healthcare. Yes, it can come [from outside], but we shouldn't expect it to only come from outside of healthcare. So now, we disrupt ourselves right when we set up digital healthcare. And we know now that disruption within healthcare with the right partners is the right way to

transform in a scalable way. So, this is a fundamental shift. It's a shift where others will not do it for us. Mayo Clinic has to do it.[56]

In addition to Mayo Clinic Ventures discussed earlier, the Clinic also created a Department of Business Development to collaborate internally and externally to bring "strategic, innovative and mission-advancing" technologies and therapies to market. More than just funding the organizations, Mayo Clinic's multidisciplinary team of experts works with established inventors and even the "new entrepreneur on the block" to accelerate and scale disruptive technologies that meet unmet patient needs. The team navigates the "twists and turns of the paradigm shift" in health care, and Mayo's intellectual property has been central to the success of myriad collaborations, exclusive agreements, start-up businesses, and new ventures.[57]

## STEP 3: ACCELERATE DYNAMIC RESOURCING

So far in this chapter, we've discussed two of the three major steps involved in cultivating change agility: (1) enhancing situational awareness, and (2) empowering a culture of rapid learning. The third step is building what we often call "dynamic resourcing," that is, the ability to reconfigure your organization's resources—money, people, information, and technology—to orchestrate and mobilize rapid change.

In truth, dynamic resourcing is not independent from situational awareness and organizational learning; in fact, it relies on them. Without good situational awareness and the capacity for organizational learning, it is impossible to effectively reshape the organization's resources in ways that improve responsiveness. In that regard, the capacity to bring about change is itself a capability. And in agile environments, it is a core capability.[58]

What is often missed in this pithy narrative of agile learning is the discipline required for dynamic resourcing. As noted in chapter 5, letting a "thousand flowers bloom" through boundless experimentation is not a viable transformation strategy on its own. Your management team needs to be ready to kill unpromising projects and reallocate resources to more auspicious alternatives. As one leader put it, "We need to practice addition *and* subtraction." Decisiveness is critical. Gianrico Farrugia explained its importance at Mayo Clinic: "When we needed to make quick decisions, we made them, moving our workforce online, or moving into new research on COVID-19, or creating new medical plans for COVID patients or even rotating our staff to wherever COVID was surging."[59]

How dynamic is your organization? Gauge yourself with the following questions:

- Do we have a flexible budgeting process that enables us to reallocate resources to where they are needed most?
- Is our talent management process adaptive and responsive to redeploy people to new assignments quickly?
- How well do we share what we've learned in one part of the organization with those in other parts?[60]

### Rapidly Reallocate Money and Talent

At its heart, agility is about reallocation. A recent McKinsey study found that dynamic resource reallocation—shifting money, talent, and management attention to where they will deliver the most value—was the strongest predictor of total returns to shareholders.[61] Intuitively, we already know that getting the necessary resources in place, and in a timely manner, can either make the organization nimble and productive or leave it lumbering and ineffectual. This is the essence of dynamic capability.

**Develop a flexible budgeting process.** Companies in the McKinsey study weren't very good at dynamic reallocation, despite its strong effect on shareholder returns. On average, firms reallocated only 8 percent of capital from one year to the next; a third reallocated only 1 percent. Meanwhile, a full 83 percent of senior executives identified dynamic resourcing as the top management lever for spurring performance.[62]

Other research by Don Sull and colleagues found similar trends. Only one-third of managers in their study believed that their organizations reallocated funds to the right places quickly enough to be effective.[63]

At Microsoft, Nadella worked to address these dynamic resourcing challenges. Like all organizations undergoing transformation, Microsoft wrestled with the challenges of strategic ambidexterity; that is, making certain to continuously improve current products and services that drive today's performance, while also investing more in innovation and technologies that will drive future potential. Nadella implemented several touch points, at different intervals, with his executive team and others in the organization. One change he made was to combine the annual fiscal year planning process—which was not likely to go away—with quarterly and monthly forecast updates evaluating how the company was doing against the plan, just like any other company would do and as its shareholders would expect.

Nadella also instituted weekly alignment meetings with his top team. Reflecting the principles of "One Microsoft," these meetings were used to do strategy reviews, product reviews, and execution reviews, all together as a group. It was a very simple tool that had an outsize impact. As one of his team members told me, "We've been able to build agility into the system because we never go more than six days from identifying an issue to figuring what we're going to do about it."[64]

Nadella's approach to decision-making was based on the premise that agility depends first on alignment, and then on affording some discretion to the business leads. Guthrie explained, "We've got the areas that are aligned together, organized together, and execute with a great deal of autonomy while at the same time contributing to the overall Microsoft strategy. But we try to make sure that not every decision has to go through the Microsoft senior leadership team because just for the number of businesses we're in, there's just no way we can scale."[65]

A. G. Lafley, Procter & Gamble's former CEO, advised senior leaders to build flexibility into the budgeting process by establishing a rolling forecast with fixed short-term and adaptable long-term goals. In his view, the most important aspect of budgeting is to align it with the rhythm of the business, using a three-point approach: (a) deliver in the short term, (b) invest in and plan for the midterm, and (c) place experimental bets for the long term.[66]

Mayo Clinic has instituted several mechanisms to enable flexible budgeting and discretionary financing. For example, its President's Strategic Initiative Fund was designed to be a powerful tool for Mayo Clinic's president and CEO, giving discretion to respond quickly and flexibly to the institution's greatest needs and highest priorities.[67]

**Develop a flexible talent model.** Although the dynamic resourcing of finances often proves problematic, the challenge of reallocating talent is even tougher. Sull and colleagues found that only 20 percent of managers say their organizations move people effectively across units to support strategic priorities. As a result, resources are often stuck in unproductive places.[68]

Part of the challenge is that talent is hoarded. Rapid reallocation depends on freeing up talent from prior placement, and then repositioning—and potentially reskilling—to new ones.

Microsoft took on the challenge of dynamic talent resourcing by using smaller teams. As Guthrie described it, "Historically at Microsoft we often had teams that were very big that would own many, many different businesses. That works really well when you're in a mature business and your goal is to grow by some small percentage." But Nadella understood that embedding agility required a different architecture. "After we got alignment, we moved from very big teams managed by senior people to much smaller teams." Nadella flattened out the structure and went from a handful of direct reports to more than twenty-five at one point. Guthrie said, "Let's create some single threaded teams, laser focused on a critical objective, and put the best people—in some cases the most senior people—in some of the most strategic, important positions."[69]

In addition to reassigning senior leaders to teams, Microsoft took steps to ensure its agility in deploying other human capital as well. One method for doing this was to combine talent reviews with business reviews. With this approach, the reassignment process was more logical and driven by business necessity; employee development also improved as a biproduct. As Chuck Edward, Microsoft's CVP of HR said, "We see the pace of technology changing and we know we have to continue to evolve our technical skills and our technical talent. We recognize that when you're adding AI, robotics, sensors, quantum computing, those are just all happening so much faster."[70]

All these efforts have helped Microsoft improve its dynamic resourcing and organizational ambidexterity. The upshot was a clearer connection between, on the one hand, managing performance in its traditional businesses, and, on the other, quickly redeploying resources to create a more responsive organization for the future. Its approach to financials, decision-making, structure, leadership, and talent all help to achieve these goals.[71]

### Transfer Knowledge to Leverage What You Learn

In addition to rapidly reallocating financial and human resources, cultivating agility involves getting knowledge and information to the right places and the right people. Agile transformation is stopped in its tracks when knowledge gets cut off, trapped in one location and unavailable to others around the organization. Knowledge is power, as they say, and too often the lack of information sharing or knowledge transfer is rooted in power struggles. The effect is severely debilitating to strategic transformation.

As Carla O'Dell and C. Jackson Grayson note in their book, *If Only We Knew What We Know*, companies invest significantly in developing new knowledge and then often fall short in leveraging it around the organization.[72] As one executive said, "We have no problem generating new ideas, but they don't get shared, and they soon recede, and we're no better off." In turbulent environments where agility is paramount, no amount of knowledge or insight can keep a company moving ahead if it is not distributed where it's needed. When companies don't know what they know, they hamstring their own ability to be agile.

Research by Gary Neilson and colleagues found that information flow is both a chief enabler of agility and its main obstacle. In the best cases, important information about the environment gets to headquarters and senior leaders quickly, information flows freely across organizational boundaries, and line employees have the information they need to understand the bottom-line impact of their day-to-day activities. As the researchers observed, "When information does not flow horizontally across different parts of the company, units behave like silos forfeiting economies of scale and the transfer of best practice."[73]

Recall from chapter 5 that firms increasingly leverage their collaborative networks and relational technologies to share best practices around the enterprise. Digital platforms and shared databases speed the exchange of knowledge much faster—and more broadly—than traditional centralized processes do. The payoff is that although the costs of acquiring knowledge (and making inevitable mistakes along the way) are paid once, the benefits are multiplied by rapidly sharing and leveraging it across the entire enterprise.

## Strengthen Your Core to Accelerate Faster

One last point about dynamic resourcing. Embedding change agility typically implies strengthening your core so that you can accelerate faster. Even though many strategic transformations involve—and indeed are premised on—augmenting the core capabilities of the firm, the change is typically not a complete reincarnation. Although some firms do completely start over from scratch to reinvent themselves, that's not the story of the firms in this book, nor of most firms, in my experience. Microsoft remains in software; Mayo Clinic remains in health care; Chalhoub Group remains in luxury retailing; Unilever remains in packaged consumer goods; and NYPD remains in law enforcement. Their transformations—bold as they were—helped them get better at what they do best, and by strengthening that core, they now accelerate change faster.

Remember, the dynamic capability of your firm hinges on "the capacity of an organization to purposefully create, extend, or modify its resource base" to integrate, build, and reconfigure those core capabilities to drive value in a rapidly changing environment.[74]

In his book *Antifragile*, Nassim Nicholas Taleb contrasts "fragile systems" that shatter under stress and "antifragile" (agile) systems that become better with stress. Agile systems become stronger because they respond to stress, disruption, and disorder by transforming themselves, improving functionality and adaptability to the environment. Along the continuum from fragile to agile are two other types of systems: robust (systems that are strong and stand like a wall under stress) and resilient (those that absorb the shock and then bounce back to their original shape).[75]

Mayo Clinic works to make certain that it is creating a more "antifragile" (agile) system. Its transformation leverages its strengths, innovates in response to disruption, and then makes certain that it doesn't drift back to the status quo. Farrugia described it this way:

> From a healthcare standpoint, we absolutely need to make sure there are lasting changes ... I've many times said that healthcare is like a stiff rubber band, it snaps back if you let go. And if you look at it like that, then you sort of realize why it's so hard to transform healthcare. It takes efforts to stretch, but also once you transform, it's really hard to stay there. And so, that has been part of what I've been pushing Mayo Clinic to do in the past year. Purposely create barriers that prevent us from going back. And a good example is of course, establishing benchmarks for virtual and digital care, instead of just letting them return the way they were.[76]

## REALITY CHECK

Let's pause for reflection. The main points of this chapter have been that strategic agility involves continual responsiveness, empowered experimentation to learn new ways of creating value, and the discipline to dynamically redeploy key resources. Organization agility involves generating new knowledge and capabilities (creating and acquiring new ways of doing things), sharing and transferring knowledge to others, and embedding knowledge and insights into the existing systems and processes of the organization.

As with the prior chapters, the checklist in Figure 6.4 summarizes the key takeaways of the chapter related to: (a) improving situational awareness, (b) empowering a culture of rapid learning, and (c) ensuring dynamic resourcing to accelerate change. Each of these is a subcapability of agile transformation and needs to be developed over time. Consider how they play out in your organization, where barriers might exist, and what actions you can take to improve.

| CULTIVATING CHANGE AGILITY | |
|---|---|
| Situational Awareness | ☑ We work to develop deep customer insights to determine their changing interests and needs. |
| | ☑ We monitor peripheral events and faint signals in the remote environment to look for emerging opportunities and threats. |
| | ☑ When we see promising developments outside our business, we look for ways to probe and/or shape them. |
| Rapid Learning | ☑ We encourage experimentation, testing, and learning, in order to quickly generate innovation and new ways of working. |
| | ☑ We embrace manageable risk and see mistakes as an inevitable by-product of our investment in learning. |
| | ☑ We work hard to make sure that what we learn in one part of the organization is shared, transferred, and applied to other parts. |
| Dynamic Resourcing | ☑ Our budgeting process allows for exceptions in order to reallocate capital for arising opportunities. |
| | ☑ We have a flexible staffing model to quickly redeploy talent and resources where and when they are needed. |
| | ☑ Our information systems provide timely and accurate data to those who need it so they can make better decisions. |

FIGURE 6.4. Checklist for Cultivating Change Agility

## Enhance Your Situational Awareness

Situational awareness helps you recognize how events around you are changing. The admonition to "keep a level head" reinforces the idea that your agility does not mean constant reorientation or reinvention. Organizations that achieve agile transformation tend to stay focused on their purpose, strategic intent, and value as they respond to changing exigencies. Situational awareness requires that you develop deeper insights into your customers, a better sense of the dynamic business ecosystem, and a wider view of peripheral concerns and opportunities. Better situational awareness helps prepare the organization and mitigate blind spots. In what ways has your organization built in this capacity?[77]

## Empower a Culture of Rapid Learning

Organizational learning helps you to generate, share, and apply new knowledge and ways of working that give your organization more options, more alternatives, and a better repertoire for adapting quickly to the environment. In that regard, a culture that empowers organizational learning helps increase the versatility of the organization. Both are important for strategic transformation. Would you say that your organization is a learning organization? What could be done to improve this capability?

### Dynamic Resourcing

If your firm is going to cultivate change agility, you'll need more than "agile people." You'll also need to build an agile organization. That means that key resources—financial, information, and people—need to be reallocated quickly to arising opportunities. Most organizations have not developed provisions for this, so resources get trapped. How does your organization free up key resources to support agile transformation?

## PLAYBOOK TOOLS

As you did at the end of other chapters, take time with your team to flesh out a playbook for cultivating agility. What are the most powerful—and immediate—possibilities for enhancing situational awareness, rapid learning, and dynamic resourcing? How could these help you build better capabilities to drive transformation in a world of continuous change?

**Directions for Building a Playbook:** Work through the following actions as a team. Use Playbook Template 6.1 at the end of the chapter to get consensus on the following:

- *Strategic Importance of Agility.* Review why and where organizational agility is strategically important in your organization. Are your reasons related to the requirements of market responsiveness and/or innovation? Make clear how these connect to your firm's core capabilities and value proposition.
- *Enhance Situational Awareness.* Agility depends on your level of acuity to outside occurrences that are often not easily recognized.
  - Enablers: How do you engage with customers and key stakeholders, giving you deeper understanding as well as broader peripheral vision of the environment?
  - Inhibitors: What deters your ability to discern external events, occurrences, and surprises?
  - Required Action: What changes would improve situational awareness in your organization?

- *Empower Rapid Learning.* Cultivating agility depends on learning quickly and turning that learning into action.
    - Enablers: How is your organization empowering decision-making at lower levels, enabling small experiments, rapid testing and learning, and the generation of new possibilities? How do you share knowledge and best practice widely?
    - Inhibitors: What are the primary obstacles to rapid learning and empowerment?
    - Required Action: Where in the organization could changes be instituted to enable empowered learning? What would be the payoff in doing so?
- *Accelerate Dynamic Resourcing.* Agility depends on getting resources "unstuck" and reallocated quickly to where they are needed most.
    - Enablers: Are decision structures sufficiently flexible to enable rapid resource (re)allocation? Is your budgeting process sufficiently flexible? Is your talent management system responsive? Does information get shared quickly?
    - Inhibitors: What gets in the way of dynamic resourcing? Why do these inhibitors persist?
    - Required Action: What changes does your organization need in order to reallocate resources more effectively and efficiently in a dynamic environment?
- *Strengthen the Core.* Agile organizations use rapid learning and innovation to strengthen their core capabilities in order to accelerate transformation.
    - Enablers: How are you using new knowledge and learning to improve decision-making and enhance your core processes and capabilities? How does improving your core accelerate change agility?
    - Inhibitors: What stands in the way of applying new innovations and knowledge to improve core capabilities? Are these related to organization design, culture, etc.? What is the effect?
    - Required Action: What changes are needed to overcome these inhibiting conditions? What would be the impact?

## WHAT'S NEXT: DEVELOP A GAME PLAN

In the next chapter, think about how you would incorporate the four-factor framework into your game plan for change. I'll summarize some of the key watchpoints at early phases of transformation as well as when things gain momentum, scale, and renew.

PLAYBOOK TEMPLATE 6.1. Cultivate Change Agility

| | Enablers | Inhibitors | Required Action |
|---|---|---|---|
| ENHANCE SITUATIONAL AWARENESS: How do you engage with customers and key stakeholders, giving you deeper understanding, as well as a broader vision of the environment? | | | |
| EMPOWER RAPID LEARNING: How is the organization empowering small experiments, testing and learning, and generating new possibilities? How do you share knowledge widely? | | | |
| ACCELERATE DYNAMIC RESOURCING: Are decision structures sufficiently flexible to enable rapid resource (re)allocation? How do you "un-stick" critical resources? | | | |
| STRENGTHEN THE CORE: How are you using new knowledge and learning to improve decision-making and enhance your core processes and capabilities? How does improving your core accelerate change? | | | |

# 7 DEVELOP A GAME PLAN: KEY PHASES AND WATCHPOINTS

NOW THAT YOU'VE gone through the four factors of strategic transformation, you likely have better insight into challenges and requirements involved in establishing the strategic context, engaging stakeholders, orchestrating mobilization, and cultivating change agility. You can appreciate how each of these factors plays a unique role in transformation, as well as how they combine in a mutually reinforcing system.

That's all good. But a common question I get at this point is, "What do I do now—how do I use this information?"

Let's pull together some key ideas for application. My goal in this last chapter is to lay the groundwork to help you create a game plan for transformation. It is organized around three critical junctures in transformation. These are inflection points where problems surface and there is a higher risk of failure. Although the phases can be considered as temporal stages—early, middle, later—they are also qualitatively distinct. Each has its own unique objectives and challenges that need tailored solutions.

The first phase is about the launch—or rather the challenges in preparing for the launch. The second phase is about building momentum and normalizing efforts. And the third phase is about scaling the transformation beyond projects and pilots to full-blown organizational renewal.

| | Phase 1:<br>Prepare to Launch | Phase 2:<br>Build Momentum | Phase 3:<br>Scale and Renew |
|---|---|---|---|
| Purpose | Build readiness and align the organization for change | Build momentum and normalize transformation | Scale portfolio of initiatives and sustain performance |
| Problems | 1. Endless analysis<br>2. Lack of alignment<br>3. Lack of ownership<br>4. Resistance | 1. Change doesn't normalize<br>2. No change in routines<br>3. No leader transition<br>4. No capability upgrade | 1. Leadership wanes<br>2. Discipline is lost<br>3. Complexity of portfolio<br>4. Failure to adapt |
| Watchpoint | 1. Assess readiness<br>2. Build capacity<br>3. Energize the team | 1. Foster strategic dialogue<br>2. Use data to course correct<br>3. Guide the conversion | 1. Evolve the system<br>2. Adapt AARs<br>3. Sustain progress |

FIGURE 7.1. Develop a Game Plan

In the following sections, we'll cover the primary purpose and objectives of each phase, as well as associated *watchpoints*. Watchpoints are areas where extra vigilance is necessary, and where further intervention may be neeeded. We'll discuss what often goes wrong, what to be careful of, and recommended actions to keep things moving forwad. A quick summary is shown in Figure 7.1.

## PHASE 1: PREPARE TO LAUNCH

In his classic novel *Don Quixote*, Miguel de Cervantes wrote, "Forewarned, forearmed; to be prepared is half the victory."[1] Doing the groundwork and preparation *before* strategic transformation is critical to its success.

Prior to embarking on a transformation journey, it is important to prepare the organization by aligning and energizing the senior team, convening a likely change coalition, and then assessing where you stand regarding each of the four factors. At the end of the day, strategic transformation is a meta-capability of the organization, and some are frankly not ready.

It may be obvious, but you cannot easily do this when you're already headlong into the process of transformation. To improve your chances of success, you need to prepare in advance. Many executives admit they didn't allocate the time or commit the resources to the four factors before initiating the transformation. Consequently, they did not develop the *capacities for change*: the capabilities or readiness for bringing it about.

As a result, a large percentage of transformations never get off the ground. Research suggests that executive teams sometimes spin, caught in seemingly endless debates and analysis, "admiring the problem" as they say, unable to align around a path forward or even to define a target strategy signaling in which direction they should go. Not surprisingly, if your senior executive team isn't aligned, other managers won't ante up, won't be accountable, and will never make the conversion from "bystander to buy-in." Logically, others in the organization will keep their heads down as well, resisting change if only because of confusion. You get the idea of the pernicious cycle.[2]

In chapter 3, I shared some perspective on the imperative to establish the strategic context for transformation. Its three subcomponents—analyzing disruption in your business ecosystem, evaluating the potential for business model innovation, and communicating strategic intent—are key actions you'll need to do to prepare for transformation. Much of the advice in chapter 3 applies here. But there is more to pre-launch preparation than establishing the context.

## Watchpoint: Assess Readiness

A key watchpoint at this phase is assessing readiness. Prior to launch, it is advisable to conduct a realistic self-evaluation of your organization's readiness and capacity for change. More specifically, determine for yourself where the organization stands regarding the four factors of transformation. For example, how often—and how well—does your organization conduct a thorough analysis of the strategic context? How routinely does your organization systematically engage different stakeholders? Does your firm do a good job of resourcing strategic initiatives across the enterprise to achieve key objectives? Do you explicitly cultivate the requirements of agility and innovation? If the answer to these questions is yes, you're in a much better position to kick-start your

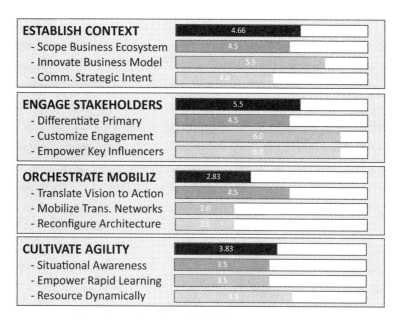

FIGURE 7.2. Transformation Capability Diagnostic

transformation. If the answer is no, you'll need to do some remedial work prior to launch.

To help you and your colleagues make this assessment, I've included a diagnostic survey that focuses on the most important enablers of readiness and helps the leadership team make improvements before they undertake transformation in earnest. In the appendix, you'll find the thirty-six-item *Transformation Capability Diagnostic Survey.*

To visualize the results of the self-assessment, I present sample data graphically. Figure 7.2 shows both an overall assessment for each of the four factors as well as scores for the underlying dimensions of each.

The assessment can be conducted at multiple levels in your organization.

First, the CEO and each member of the senior leadership team should complete the diagnostic. Their results will reflect where they see the organization on the four factors. Second, the senior team members should share their assessments with one another, to discover where they agree and disagree.

Two types of discussions emerge from this. Where leaders agree, their collective assessment of the organization's strengths and weaknesses regarding the four factors gives them a baseline for preparing to launch. For example, they might agree that the organization does a good job engaging stakeholders (factor 2) but has problems cultivating change agility (factor 4). Their agreement on low ratings is especially important, as it sets the stage for developing an improvement plan to build better readiness.

Where the team members disagree is important too. They'll need to reconcile those differences before moving forward. In my experience, divergent ratings on this diagnostic are eye-opening and lead to robust debate. The differences are typically due to where each executive sits in the organization. Their perspectives are based on their unique experiences and responsibilities. The goal is not to debate who's right or wrong but to uncover new information and build alignment around a path forward. More importantly, as shown in Table 7.1, it helps you identify where preparatory work is most needed.

Beyond the senior team, it is also good to invite others in the organization to complete the assessment, perhaps collecting data across different business units, around different functions, and more deeply through multiple levels of the organization. This is a more comprehensive undertaking. The rationale is that the terrain changes just a few levels below the CEO. Many leaders overestimate the level of organizational preparedness at the senior echelons and throughout the organization. While people lower in the organization may not see the entire enterprise from the vantage point of the senior leaders, they do see things the CEO does not. For this reason, I recommend that in addition to the senior team, a sample of other senior and midlevel managers take the survey. Inviting participation in the diagnostic has the added benefit of helping those other individuals begin to mentally prepare for change as well, leading to more buy-in.

## Watchpoint: Build Capacity

Another key watchpoint in phase 1 is to make sure you develop capacity. Sometimes low diagnostic ratings serve as a wake-up call to the

TABLE 7.1. Diagnostic Assessment: Aggregated Results

| | Executive | Director | Sr. Producer | Digital Producer | Sr. Coordinating Producer | Average | Range |
|---|---|---|---|---|---|---|---|
| **Establish Context** | 3.55 | 3.22 | 3.55 | 1.77 | 2.33 | 2.884 | 1.78 |
| Business Ecosystem | 3 | 3.33 | 2.66 | 1 | 1.66 | 2.33 | 2.33 |
| Bus. Model Innovation | 4 | 3.66 | 4 | 3.33 | 2.66 | 3.53 | 1.34 |
| Comm. Strategic Intent | 3.66 | 2.66 | 4 | 1 | 2.66 | 2.796 | 3 |
| | | | | | | | |
| **Engage Stakeholders** | 3.22 | 3.33 | 2.88 | 2.44 | 2.22 | 2.818 | 1.11 |
| Differentiate Primary | 2.66 | 4 | 3.33 | 3.33 | 3 | 3.264 | 1.34 |
| Customize Engagement | 3.33 | 3.33 | 3 | 2 | 1.66 | 2.664 | 1.67 |
| Empower Influencers | 3.66 | 2.66 | 2.33 | 2 | 2 | 2.53 | 1.66 |
| | | | | | | | |
| **Orchestrate Mobilization** | 3.33 | 3.88 | 4.11 | 2.11 | 3 | 3.286 | 2 |
| Translate Vision to Action | 3.66 | 3.66 | 4.33 | 2 | 3.33 | 3.396 | 2.33 |
| Collaborative Network | 2.33 | 3.66 | 4 | 1 | 3 | 2.798 | 3 |
| Organization Architecture | 4 | 4.33 | 4 | 3.33 | 2.66 | 3.664 | 1.67 |
| | | | | | | | |
| **Cultivate Agility** | 3.33 | 3.55 | 3 | 2.66 | 3.11 | 3.13 | 0.89 |
| Situational Awareness | 3.33 | 4.33 | 3.33 | 2.33 | 3.33 | 3.33 | 2 |
| Empower Rapid Learning | 3 | 3 | 2.66 | 3.66 | 2.66 | 2.996 | 1 |
| Dynamic Resourcing | 3.66 | 3.33 | 3 | 2 | 3.33 | 3.064 | 1.66 |

executive team. Once the results have been aggregated and reconciled, you can have a more targeted discussion of your next steps to build transformation capability prior to launch. For transformation to succeed, your organization will need to develop capabilities for each of the four factors. My advice is to build the capability, as much as possible, before you need it. Take the time and allocate the resources.

To build your playbook for transformation, it is useful to get some granularity around (a) how your organization currently approaches each of the four factors, (b) where there are concerns and risks that would jeopardize transformation, and (c) what required actions would build capacity in those areas. Playbook Template 7.1 at the end of the chapter is useful for summarizing each of these key points.

As you may recall from chapter 2, the four factors function as an interactive system. They are interdependent. For example, establishing the strategic context helps you engage stakeholders, and engaging stakeholders helps to establish the strategic context. A clearly articulated strategic intent makes orchestrating mobilization easier, and so on.

Note that while the system is interactive, it is not compensatory. What I mean by that is exceptional capability in one area cannot make up for deficiencies in another. For example, excellence in establishing strategic context cannot make up for failings in engaging stakeholders. Why is this important? Because it makes the job of preparation more difficult. Successful transformation depends on all four factors.

But let's be pragmatic. Your organization may not have the luxury of time. Given market pressures, you may need to go forward with strategic transformation before you have fully mastered each of the four factors. What then?

If you know that your transformation capability is lower on one of the four factors, you can prioritize that area, devoting additional resources, particularly time, talent, data, and finances, to build capacity. Vigilance is critical, if only to make certain that nothing is taken for granted. Shine a light on this area, and be explicit about high expectations, accountabilities, and support. Keep a watchful eye as you move forward, and take immediate action where needed.

In my experience, your time spent building capacity for transformation will help galvanize efforts around the follow-on work of (a) analyzing your business ecosystem, (b) calibrating stakeholder influences, (c) identifying candidates of the transformation network, and (d) investing in agile capability.

One exercise that I find very useful during the preparation phase is called *hypothesis testing*. The premise is that every strategy can be viewed as a hypothesis: "If you do X, then Y will follow as a result." When things don't work out as you've planned, it is always because reality turned out to be different from your hypothesis. Before taking action, focus on identifying the key elements necessary for success, and collect data to test your underlying assumptions.[3] For example, the following four tests are especially useful:

- *Value:* Will the transformation lead to new or better customer value? What data suggest that this would be the case? What available evidence would refute this assumption?
- *Execution:* Do we have the capabilities to implement the change and deliver value? What evidence suggests that these are in place? What data would refute this assumption?
- *Scale:* Do we have the resources and capacity to sustain and scale the initiative more broadly?
- *Sustainability:* Once we transform the organization, will we be able to maintain and renew it over time, or is the advantage temporary?[4]

Let's assume your answer to each question is yes. Test your assumptions underlying that answer by considering what data would change your mind. Play devil's advocate. Imagine that you knew in advance that this strategic transformation will fail. What is the most likely reason? In some ways, hypothesis testing serves as a "pre-mortem" for your transformation and gives you information to set priorities for building capacity in advance. Typically, working with management teams, we'll use Playbook Template 7.2 at the end of the chapter to record their responses to these questions.

Note: This exercise typically doesn't refute your hypothesis altogether, but it will highlight risks and areas of potential deficiency. In preparation for launch, this helps clarify where to allocate extra time and energy.

### Watchpoint: Energize the Team

Another key watchpoint is team energy. Your objective at this stage—preparing for launch—is to make certain your leadership is energized and aligned prior to announcing your plans. Energized means that they are committed to: (1) the need for change, (2) its purpose and goals, and (3) the path the organization will take. As part of this, each member of the leadership team needs to know their roles and responsibilities, as well as expectations and accountabilities to others.

Because these leaders will serve as change agents themselves, they'll need to start demonstrating the behavior they'll soon ask of others. For example, if the transformation requires a new or different connection to customers, they need to start making those touch points. If the transformation requires cross-functional collaboration (as it will), leaders must begin to model better cooperation and teamwork with each other.

Bill Rogers, CEO of Truist Financial, utilized "accountability partners" among his top leadership team. During transformation, each senior leader had a peer who was tasked with telling the sometimes-hard truths about what their partner had committed to and how (or whether) they had followed up. The system was simple but effective. It led to better accountability, transparency, and teamwork. Other organizations have implemented similar approaches.[5]

There are a few other pieces that need to be in place prior to launch. As noted in chapter 5, many organizations appoint a chief transformation officer (CTO) and establish a program or project management office (PMO). In the near term, the CTO will be involved in devising the plans for change and may be the implicit *chief strategy officer* during this period. Especially when they report directly to the CEO, the CTO and PMO will be highly visible, and they will be the sources of valuable information—answers to questions, updates on progress, and clearinghouses for best practice. These roles and responsibilities need to be established in advance.[6]

The CTO and senior team will begin to lay out the rubric and portfolio of strategic initiatives to achieve key priorities and strategic intent. All the granularity and detail of these initiatives need not be defined before the launch; some specifics manifest with the input of others as change initiatives get underway. But the framework of key actions, owners, and investments need to be made clear in advance so that others in the organization understand not just the *why* of transformation, but also the *how*. The key is to focus on the outcomes desired, not just the activities themselves.

## PHASE 2: BUILD MOMENTUM

Once your leadership team announces the transformation—which necessarily includes articulating the rationale for change and strategic vision—the next phase can get a little tricky. There is often a great deal of energy and excitement (and a little apprehension) at the launch phase. The goal in phase 2 is to convert that launch energy into building and growing momentum.

Unfortunately, many heralded transformations never gain momentum and soon dissipate. Research suggests the predominant reasons for this all come back to the failure of leaders to normalize the new ways of working. The lesson to be learned is that if a transformation initiative remains a distinct and separate entity from the organization—set apart and seen as a collection of special projects or unique circumstances—the shift in momentum will not occur, and the transformation is unlikely to succeed.

The biggest momentum killer is when the transformation initiatives don't result in any lasting change in day-to-day behavior. Employees don't pick up the ball and run, and they don't incorporate new ways of working into their daily routines. Often this is because change agents and consultants, rather than line managers, lead the initiatives. Specialists are often necessary components of strategic transformation, because their expertise is needed in unfamiliar domains. But at some point, there must be leadership sharing, transitions, and hand-offs. Recall in chapter 5 on orchestrating mobilization, my advice was that the CTO/ PMO build a network with line managers from the outset and involve them in the development of strategic initiatives. Their ownership of the work is important from the beginning.

Without dedicated efforts to normalize your initiatives, they are very unlikely to result in lasting capability upgrades in the business. And re-member: The whole point of strategic transformation is to create new capabilities and new business models to deliver superior value. Even if new ways of working prove valuable, old structures, processes, and legacy systems often remain in place, perpetuating the distinction. If strategic initiatives remain separate projects, they will likely compete unsuccessfully for resources. Special projects and pilots may demon-strate proof of concept and initial operating capability, but improve-ments don't get baked into budgets. Resource allocations are sticky, and most companies have a difficult time reallocating capital, as you know.[7]

### Watchpoint: Foster a Strategic Dialogue

So, what can be done to normalize transformation and build momentum? A key watchpoint is whether—and in what way—the transformation is being discussed within the organization. That narrative begins with how the leadership team communicates the transformation in the first place. The goal should be to inspire a compelling vision of the future, but also to begin a strategic conversation. At times this may include a challenge to the organization, a realistic diagnosis of the present situation, and an in-vitation to consider the risks of the status quo. As Satya Nadella, Paul Pol-man, and others did, the message combines both a rationale for change and an ambitious vision. But ultimately, it needs to shake up how people see the old organization. At the same time, the dialogue needs to encour-age transparency and trust that generates buy-in and shared commitment.

At Microsoft, Nadella developed a series of communication oppor-tunities to engage with others down into the organization. For example, he established regular forums to assess and reinforce alignment around his vision and discuss how people were working together to achieve

Microsoft's three key ambitions. Those efforts cascaded through the organization, translating key messages and helping everyone develop a deeper understanding of Microsoft's transformation.

Cascading meetings can also enable issues to percolate upward to senior leaders, opening a two-way dialogue. It is an unfortunate fact of life in many organizations that rank-and-file employees often don't understand much about the company strategy. Consequently, transformation happens to them rather than comes from them.

Some executives have adapted cascading meetings to translate the strategy into more operational terms that have more meaning and urgency to employees. UPS, for example, developed a straightforward process called "Eyes on the Enterprise" to translate strategy and help employees see their role in the change initiatives. After defining the strategic purpose and key business priorities, the leadership team worked with the communications team to design visual maps to use as discussion starters in lower levels of the organization. At each subsequent level, and fanning out to other business units, the mapping process helped employees understand how they contributed to the strategy, owned it, and could invest in it.[8]

Others use town halls, social media, and other forums to continue the dialogue. The options are many. But the value of these meetings and workshops is that they encourage leaders to have open, honest conversations with others about the opportunities and impediments to change.

### Watchpoint: Use Data to Course Correct

As your initiatives pick up momentum, a key watchpoint is data gathering and analysis. During phase 2, data becomes the lifeblood of transformation. Big interventions are risky, and for some the decision to commit to the journey is a leap of faith. Nothing will mollify their fears and increase buy-in—which propels performance—like data-based evidence of progress. W. Edwards Deming, the father of modern quality management, is reputed to have said, "In God we trust. All others must bring data."[9]

Your organization is likely generating a lot of data during this phase of transformation. If not, get it. Use that data to evaluate key metrics that communicate progress and milestones. For example, your portfolio of initiatives can be subdivided by strategic priority, owners, actions, and investment dollars. Keeping track of your progress, monitoring performance, providing status reports—not just on what has been done, but on what has been accomplished—helps build energy in the organization. When the data shows early impact and results, it reinforces why transformation was undertaken in the first place. These achievements can feed the pipeline of new initiatives, phased over time. This is especially valuable in building continuity during the first year of the transformation.

Data also obviously enables better decision-making when things aren't going so well. It enables you to surface problems, diagnose causes, and document solutions. Recall that this is one of the primary roles the CTO and PMO play during transformation. They serve as problem-solvers and sources for data-driven decision-making.

As initiatives gain traction and momentum, each at their own pace, they develop their own energy and focus, taking on their own identity. They may drift a little bit from their original purpose, resulting in "mission creep." This is a gradual or incremental expansion of the projects and programs beyond their original scope or objectives, often exacerbated by initial successes. When multiplied by the number of strategic initiatives you have in your transformation portfolio, mission creep can be a major challenge in terms of managing complexity and divergence in the overall process. By using a data-driven approach, it is easier to course correct and return the initiatives to their original purpose and approach, reinforcing progress along the way.

## Watchpoint: Guide the Conversion

As the transformation builds momentum, the portfolio of initiatives will begin to systematize as learning curves develop. Ideally, repeatable processes and procedures begin to form, and your operating protocols will become better defined and shared. When the initiatives convert from being ad hoc efforts of a team of individuals to more normalized organizational routines, you will have reached a critical inflection point.

To keep things on track and enable the conversion from initial viability to full operational capability, leaders and line managers need to pay close attention, convening regularly with one another to calibrate where things stand. As one executive put it, "These initiatives have a lot of my fingerprints on them at this stage." Key metrics and milestones (e.g., KPIs) are critical at this phase to help ground the performance reviews and progress reports. But equally important are informal sessions for listening, learning, and sharing best practices. In this regard, your program-management toolkit should also include frequent touch points to ensure better collaboration and communication.

The essence of capability development is that new knowledge from these strategic initiatives becomes codified in your people, processes, and systems. Informal becomes formal—and this doesn't happen automatically. Your leaders and frontline managers play important roles in implementing these changes.

For example, if one of your initiatives involves developing a new platform or channel to market, managers need to formalize and incentivize the new approach. Employees may need training and other inducements to change their day-to-day behavior. Other stakeholders, such as customers, may need development as well. Otherwise, despite their progress, the initiatives will never become normalized, and momentum will die.

Tracking progress and conversion across the entire portfolio of initiatives is important as well. Your CTO and PMO have eyes on this, and so should the leadership team. Remember, it is that portfolio—the overall strategic framework—and not just the individual initiatives that underpins the transformation. Your strategic transformation to new capabilities and a new business model is the net result of the complete set of initiatives.

## PHASE 3: SCALE AND RENEW

Once the transformation initiatives have gained momentum and begun to normalize, it is time to begin scaling the programs, which will expand their impact and build sustained performance. This is when the transformation stops looking like a set of strategic initiatives and starts looking like the new organization.

Oddly enough, this is also a time when failure can occur. As Sohil Kalra and colleagues put it, many companies have difficulty "breaching the great wall to scale." Incredibly, leaders often become distracted or diverted to other priorities at this point, sometimes making the mistake of declaring victory too early and not giving the transformation the continued attention and support it requires.[10]

Sometimes these leaders simply lose interest as their sense of urgency and energy wanes, and discipline fades. They are likely still committed to the transformation, but they are less involved in the initiatives themselves. Transformation takes time and effort, and some leaders experience change fatigue and convince themselves—perhaps rationalizing—that it is time to get back to their regular day jobs. Consequently, the transformation doesn't get the sustained human and financial resources it sorely needs.[11]

Ironically, even leaders who remain very energized can hit the wall if they try to scale too quickly, attempting to do "everything, everywhere, all at once." Success at earlier phases may lead them to be overly optimistic and ambitious with the rollout. As noted previously, too many separate initiatives all moving in their own direction and at their own speed can become untenable. And that level of complexity can prove unmanageable. Inevitably, it is difficult to sustain performance. In those cases, transformation to scale can falter under its own weight.

## Watchpoint: Evolve the System

The solution to these challenges is to continually renew your perspective on the transformation, recognizing that it needs to evolve over time. As you have learned, an underlying premise of this book is that in today's world, transformation has no fixed ending.

In the discussion of phase 2, building momentum, I noted the importance of making course corrections to get your initiatives back on track if they drift. Well, there's another type of course correction you'll likely need to make: when you discover that the path you're on isn't going to get you to your destination.

Frequently, you may find that initiatives as first conceived prove inadequate to achieve your strategic intent. You'll need to adapt them.

That's why pilot programs are so useful: They enable you to learn in advance of scaling. Evolving the system means changing the programs and/or changing your objectives. In that regard, transformation is, in part, a discovery process. Strategic initiatives may help you discover other outcomes that are more worthy.

Recall, for example, from chapter 5 that Microsoft adapted its transformation plan when it finally concluded that the Nokia deal was not going to pay off. After that, Microsoft wrote off $7.6 billion and laid off 7,800 employees. Hard lesson learned, but in the process Microsoft went from a "devices and services company" to a software and services company. It was a critical shift. Importantly, Microsoft stayed focused on its mission and strategic priorities, even as it adjusted its portfolio of initiatives. Revisions helped Microsoft evolve the system in its transformation journey.

Chris Argyris, eminent organizational psychologist, described the distinction between two types of learning—single-loop and double-loop—with the following analogy:

> [A] thermostat that automatically turns on the heat whenever the temperature in a room drops below 69°F is a good example of single-loop learning. A thermostat that could ask, "why am I set to 69°F?" and then explore whether or not some other temperature might more economically achieve the goal of heating the room would be engaged in double-loop learning.[12]

During transformation, it is vital that you get feedback and course correct to put you back on track. That's single-loop learning. But it is also important to reconsider what you were trying to accomplish strategically and question your assumptions about achieving that. That's double-loop learning and the key to evolving your transformation.

Sometimes this is referred to as *learning to learn*. As you go through your transformation, the process of renewal means adapting to new information. To achieve continuity and sustained performance, the process will need to iterate as conditions change. In today's business environment, the ambiguity of change means there are fewer fixed rules and prescriptions, and therefore, you'll need more ongoing touch points that offer opportunities to recalibrate.

The leadership team needs to periodically reconvene key players, celebrate progress, and reaffirm or readjust. As one leader told me, "When we embark on change, we don't always know exactly what we'll encounter. So, I tell my team, 'This is truth as I know it today. Let's continuously adjust accordingly, keeping a steady gaze on the horizon and toward our destination, our goal.'" The transparency and honesty of this approach can pay big dividends in establishing a posture of continual learning.

### Watchpoint: Adapt After-Action Reviews

One approach, originally developed by the military and adapted to other organizations, is the after-action review (AAR). You've likely heard of AARs, and perhaps even participated in one. Their purpose is not only to review performance, but to *understand* performance by comparing intended outcomes to actual outcomes. By analyzing the reasons for performance gaps—if they exist—the organization can establish a forward-looking approach that makes it possible to discern which actions should be continued and which can be modified, thereby creating learning points for the next iteration of the review.[13]

The AAR process is essentially built around four sets of questions:

- *Intent:* What results did we aspire to achieve? What did we intend to do? What were our goals, mission, and expectations? (Sometimes we refer to this as "commander's intent.")
- *Reality:* What actually transpired? What did we do? What were the results?
- *Learn:* What worked well? What went wrong? What can be improved next time? (Note: The focus is explicitly *not* about blame.)
- *Adapt:* What are we going to do differently next time?

For each strategic initiative, the AAR can be adapted as an interim learning tool, providing a way for the leadership team to identify adjustments and areas for improvement, and establishing action plans for what needs to be modified, who is responsible, and the timeframe (as well as resource allocation).

Sometimes I'll use a shorthand version of the AAR with management teams called "Keep, Lose, Create." I'll ask them to identify three short lists: things that the organization is doing well and should *Keep* doing; things in place that are not effective that they should stop doing or *Lose*; and finally, things they should be doing but are not, and thus should *Create*. The team synthesizes the Keep-Lose-Create lists to build an action plan going forward.

AARs are useful, not just at the end of an initiative, but as intermediate checkpoints as well. As the environment continues to change, the initiatives will likely need to evolve. As they do, AARs help leadership teams reinforce the intent of their plans and adjust the parameters over time. As a result, they continually reinvest and reallocate resources in their portfolio of initiatives. That process of renewal often proves instrumental for sustaining strategic transformation.

### Watchpoint: Sustain Progress

The surest way to sustain progress as your transformation matures is to continue working the four factors: (1) Establish the Strategic Context, (2) Engage Stakeholders, (3) Orchestrate Mobilization, and (4) Cultivate Change Agility.

**(Re)Establish the Strategic Context.** As a matter of practice, it is valuable to analyze how your business ecosystem is evolving, both in terms of the external forces of disruption and the internal capabilities. Are things developing in ways that you did not anticipate? As a routine part of your strategic planning cycle, it is important to assess the prospects of business model innovation, adaptation, and reinvention.

**(Re)Engage Stakeholders.** Similarly, continuing to engage stakeholders is the best way to learn how their interests and priorities are changing and how their influence is shifting. Just as your ecosystem continues to adapt, the relative positioning of your key stakeholders is dynamic as well. Your transformation likely changed that positioning with them, and you'll need to keep them abreast of developments going forward, in part to influence and preserve valuable relationships over time.

**(Re)Orchestrate Mobilization.** The difficult work of mobilizing your organization during transformation reaffirms that it should be kept alive. In addition to your strategic initiatives, which continue to drive performance, the architecture of your organization is alive and changing. Structures, processes, and systems are not just static diagrams on paper: They are dynamic interdependencies that continue to channel information and resources. Are there new organizational constraints or emerging allegiances that facilitate or inhibit your progress? Too many executives neglect these concerns or treat them as fixed. They are not and need to be continually fine-tuned.

**(Re)Cultivate Change Agility.** Cultivating change agility implies continuous flexing and responsiveness. Strategic transformation depends on organizational agility, and at the same time, it builds that agility. The best leadership teams are constantly vigilant to evolving customer needs, peripheral events, opportunities to invest in innovation via dynamic resourcing, sharing new information, and so on. They build their organization culture around these principles, and it helps them sustain progress and dynamic capability.

## CONCLUSION

At the end of the day, organizations that master the four factors of strategic transformation dramatically increase their odds of success. Although there are pitfalls along the way, there are some fundamental things you can do to take your organization through to conversion. The framework, principles, and practices in this book help leadership teams focus more precisely on what matters most and guide their interventions to build an organization capable of strategic transformation.

This approach is transportable to your organization as well. The success stories you read about are replicable in your firm. My purpose in writing this book was to share a comprehensive approach—but one that is digestible and usable—to help you and your leadership team better frame the challenges and priorities of transformation, provide you with a set of relevant guides for action, and offer concrete recommendations to shape your path forward. If you develop a discipline around this approach and embed it in the way your organization operates, you can not only drive transformation but also sustain momentum and renewal over time. In my experience, the potential benefits are considerable.

The world keeps changing, and the complex challenges you'll face require astute leadership. While other organizations may falter or fail, your strategy is ultimately about adapting and improving to create more value in the face of disruptive change. Your success will come not so much from safely avoiding these challenges as from embracing them. Ironically, turbulent times provide great opportunities if you approach them with discernment. When you do, you'll learn more and learn faster, and you'll develop a repository of lessons from experience. That will help you build a dynamic organization that can endure the pressures and adapt over time.

What's your next step? My hope is that you'll share these ideas with others in your organization and work together to apply them. Ideally, it will help you strengthen your collaboration and give you insights into the possibilities for your organization.

Good luck in your journey, and in all your future endeavors.

PLAYBOOK TEMPLATE 7.1. Build Transformation Capacity

| Four Factors: | Current Approach | Concerns and Risks | Required Action |
|---|---|---|---|
| ESTABLISH CONTEXT<br>- Scope Business Ecosystem<br>- Business Model Innovation<br>- Communicate Strategic Intent | | | |
| ENGAGE STAKEHOLDERS<br>- Differentiate Primary Stakeholders<br>- Customize Engagement Strategies<br>- Empower Key Influencers | | | |
| ORCHESTRATE MOBILIZATION<br>- Translate Vision to Action<br>- Mobilize Collaborative Networks<br>- Align Organization Architecture | | | |
| CULTIVATE AGILITY<br>- Situational Awareness<br>- Empower Rapid Learning<br>- Dynamic Resourcing | | | |

PLAYBOOK TEMPLATE 7.2. Hypothesis Testing

| Hypothesis Testing: | Evidence to Support | Evidence to Refute | Overall Assessment |
|---|---|---|---|
| VALUE: Will the transformation lead to new or better customer value? What data suggests this is the case? What evidence refutes this assumption? | | | |
| EXECUTION: Do we have capabilities to implement the change and deliver value? What data supports this? What evidence refutes this assumption? | | | |
| SCALE: Do we have the resources and capacity to sustain and scale the initiative more broadly? Does evidence support or refute this assumption? | | | |
| SUSTAINABILITY: Once we transform the organization, will we be able to maintain and renew it over time, or is the advantage temporary? | | | |

# APPENDIX: TRANSFORMATION CAPABILITY DIAGNOSTIC SURVEY

TABLE A.1. Transformation Capability Diagnostic Survey

**Directions: Rate each item below from 1 (strongly agree) to 5 (strongly disagree)**

| | ESTABLISH CONTEXT |
|---|---|
| **Scope your business ecosystem** | 1. We clearly understand our business ecosystem, including the complex relationships among suppliers, partners, customers, competitors, etc. |
| | 2. We continuously analyze the dynamic nature of our industry, sources of change, innovation, and potential disruption. |
| | 3. We regularly evaluate our business model, our standing in the industry, and how we create value. |
| **Innovate your business model** | 4. We work closely with our customers to understand and anticipate what they might need or expect in the future. |
| | 5. We strive to lead the market, seeking new opportunities and new channels, new products and/or services. |
| | 6. We thoroughly assess capabilities needed for the future and make investments to build these ahead of the curve. |
| **Communicate strategic intent and rationale** | 7. Our leaders create a compelling vision of the future that inspires new possibilities and a higher purpose. |
| | 8. Our leaders clearly communicate the key factors needed to propel our success and breakthrough performance. |
| | 9. We understand how by working together, we can all achieve great things. |
| | ENGAGE STAKEHOLDERS |
| **Differentiate primary stakeholders** | 10. We analyze our various stakeholders to determine their influence and identify the role they play in our business. |

(*continued*)

TABLE A.1. (*continued*)

| ENGAGE STAKEHOLDERS | |
|---|---|
| | 11. We spend time with our stakeholders to better understand their interests, motivations, and expectations of us. |
| | 12. We prioritize our relationship with a core subset of primary stakeholders who are most important to our success. |
| Customer your engagement strategy | 13. We are quite strategic in how we engage advocates as well as critics to bring about the best possible outcomes. This is not left to chance. |
| | 14. We actively partner with stakeholders who have complementary resources, skills, and interests. |
| | 15. We work to align the interests of shareholders, customers, employees, and others to achieve long-term mutual gains for all. |
| Empower key influencers | 16. We build coalitions with key influencers in the organization to be catalysts and champions of change. |
| | 17. Our leaders routinely empower teams to bring about positive change. |
| | 18. In our organization, empowerment and accountability go hand in hand. |

| ORCHESTRATE MOBILIZATION | |
|---|---|
| Translate vision into action | 19. We have articulated clear priorities that operationalize our strategic intent and focus the organization on what matters most. |
| | 20. We have established a coherent set of initiatives and performance metrics that guide our strategic investment and action. |
| | 21. Our strategic initiatives all tie together in order to help us build new capabilities for the future. |
| Mobilize your transformation network | 22. We have strong alignment at the top of the organization, and this energizes the entire enterprise. |
| | 23. We routinely work in cross-functional and cross-business teams to build collaboration across the enterprise. |
| | 24. We coordinate with external partners to leverage complementary skills, knowledge, and resources. |

| ORCHESTRATE MOBILIZATION | |
|---|---|
| **Reconfigure architecture** | 25. We have streamlined our organization structures and processes to improve workflow, decision-making, and collaboration. |
| | 26. We have a clearly defined process to prioritize technology deployment toward the most strategically important efforts. |
| | 27. Our culture supports the values, expectations, and behaviors necessary to drive our business forward. |

| CULTIVATE CHANGE AGILITY | |
|---|---|
| **Situational awareness** | 28. We work to develop deep customer insights to determine their changing interests and needs. |
| | 29. We monitor peripheral events and faint signals in the remote environment to look for emerging opportunities and threats. |
| | 30. When we see promising developments outside our business, we look for ways to probe and/or shape them. |
| **Rapid learning** | 31. We encourage experimentation, testing, and learning, in order to quickly generate innovation and new ways of working. |
| | 32. We embrace manageable risk and see mistakes as an inevitable by-product of our investment in learning. |
| | 33. We work hard to make sure that what we learn in one part of the organization is shared, transferred, and applied to other parts. |
| **Dynamic resourcing** | 34. Our budgeting process allows for exceptions in order to reallocate capital for arising opportunities. |
| | 35. We have a flexible staffing model to quickly redeploy talent and resources where and when they are needed. |
| | 36. Our information systems provide timely and accurate data to those who need it so they can make better decisions. |

© Scott A. Snell

NOTE: An online version of this diagnostic survey can be found on the Stanford University Press portal at http://bit.ly/transformationsurvey. The online diagnostic will provide you with customized feedback similar to Figure 7.2.

# NOTES

*Chapter 1*

1.  Steve Denning, "Why Did IBM Survive?," *Forbes*, July 10, 2011.

2.  "Gartner Forecasts Worldwide IT Spending to Reach $4 Trillion in 2021," press release, April 7, 2021, https://www.gartner.com/en/newsroom/press-releases/2021 -04-07-gartner-forecasts-worldwide-it-spending-to-reach-4-trillion-in-2021; Behnam Tabrizi et al., "Digital Transformation Is Not about Technology," *Harvard Business Review*, March 13, 2019.

3.  Jeff Boss, "This Study Reveals Why Leaders Derail," *Forbes*, May 16, 2018, https://www.forbes.com/sites/jeffboss/2018/05/16/this-study-reveals -why-leaders-derail/?sh=7c1e3c1d7295.

4.  Lars Fæste et al., "Transformation: The Imperative to Change," Boston Consulting Group, November 3, 2014; Scott Keller and Colin Price, *Beyond Performance: How Great Organizations Build Ultimate Competitive Advantage* (Hoboken, NJ: John Wiley & Sons, 2011).

5.  Fæste et al., "Transformation: The Imperative to Change."

6.  Thanks to my friend and colleague Shad Morris for reinforcing this point.

7.  Alan D. Meyer, Geoffrey R. Brooks, and James B. Goes, "Environmental Jolts and Industry Revolutions: Organizational Responses to Discontinuous Change," in "Corporate Entrepreneurship," special issue, *Strategic Management Journal* 11 (Summer 1990): 93–110.

8.  Michael F. Kipp, "Strategic Leadership in Permanent Whitewater," *Handbook of Business Strategy* 6, no. 1 (December 2005): 163–70.

9.  Warren Bennis and Burt Nanus, *Leaders: Strategies for Taking Charge* (New York: HarperCollins, 1985).

10.  Peter F. Drucker, *Management Challenges for the 21st Century* (London: Routledge, 2007).

11. Here is a short list of some contemporary books that are very instructive: Julian Birkinshaw and Jonas Ridderstråle, *Fast/Forward: Make Your Company Fit for the Future* (Stanford University Press, 2017); Stephen Denning, *The Age of Agile: How Smart Companies Are Transforming the Way Work Gets Done* (AMACOM, 2018); John P. Kotter, Vanessa Akhtar, and Gaurav Gupta, *Change: How Organizations Achieve Hard-to-Imagine Results in Uncertain and Volatile Times* (Wiley, 2021); Nigel Vaz, *Digital Business Transformation: How Established Companies Sustain Competitive Advantage from Now to Next* (Wiley, 2021); Michael Wade et al., *Orchestrating Transformation: How to Deliver Winning Performance with a Connected Approach to Change* (Lausanne, Switzerland: IMD—International Institute for Management Development, 2019); Christopher G. Worley, Thomas Williams, and Edward E. Lawler III, *The Agility Factor: Building Adaptable Organizations for Superior Performance* (Jossey-Bass, 2014).

12. This is the same approach I used in my earlier book with Kenneth J. Carrig, *Strategic Execution: Driving Breakthrough Performance in Business* (Stanford University Press, 2019).

13. "Living Well," Mayo Clinic, accessed April 25, 2023, https://mcpress.mayoclinic.org/living-well/.

14. "History Presentation," Mayo Clinic History and Heritage, accessed April 25, 2023, https://history.mayoclinic.org/toolkit/grab-and-go-history-presentation/; "Mayo Clinic Healthy Living Program," Mayo Clinic, accessed April 25, 2023, https://healthyliving.mayoclinic.org/the-mayo-clinic-difference.php.

15. "Meet the Coalition," Veteran Jobs Mission: Unilever, accessed April 25, 2023, https://veteranjobsmission.com/meet-the-coalition/unilever.

16. Christopher A. Bartlett, "Unilever's New Global Strategy: Competing through Sustainability," Harvard Business School Case 916–414 (Boston, MA: Harvard Business Press, 2016).

17. William Bratton and Peter Knobler, *Turnaround: How America's Top Cop Reversed the Crime Epidemic* (Penguin Random House, 2009); W. Chan Kim and Renée Mauborgne, "Tipping Point Leadership," *Harvard Business Review*, April 2003.

18. Much of this approach is similar to my approach with Carrig in *Strategic Execution*.

*Chapter 2*
1. Michael E. Porter, "What Is Strategy?," *Harvard Business Review,* November–December 1996; Rainer.

2. Also quoted in Kenneth J. Carrig and Scott A. Snell, *Strategic Execution: Driving Breakthrough Performance in Business* (Stanford University Press, 2019).

3. Letter to Lady Pollock, October 24, 1902, in *Holmes-Pollock Letters: The Correspondence of Mr. Justice Holmes and Sir Frederick Pollock, 1874–1932*, 2nd ed., ed. Mark DeWolfe Howe (Cambridge, MA: Belknap Press, 1961).

4. Alvin Ward Gouldner, "Industry and Bureaucracy" (PhD diss., Columbia University, 1954).

5. Richard Rumelt, *Good Strategy, Bad Strategy* (Profile Books, 2017).

6. Andrew White et al., "Six Key Levers of a Successful Organizational Transformation," *Harvard Business Review,* May 10, 2023; Andrew Pettigrew, Ewan Ferlie, and Lorna McKee, "Shaping Strategic Change—The Case of the NHS in the 1980s," *Public Money & Management* 12, no. 3 (July 1992): 27–31.

7. Bob Johansen, *Leaders Make the Future: Ten New Leadership Skills for an Uncertain World* (Berrett-Koehler Publishers, 2012).

8. R. Edward Freeman, *Strategic Management: A Stakeholder Approach* (Boston: Pitman, 1984).

9. George W. Casey, "Leading in a VUCA World" (lecture, Cornell University, Samuel Curtis Johnson Graduate School of Management, Executive Education, 2019), accessed May 5, 2023, https://www.johnson.cornell.edu/wp-content/uploads/sites/3/2019/04/Cornell-Executive-Education-VUCA-Leadership-February-2017.pdf, 6.

10. "Merge Ahead: Electric Vehicles and the Impact on the Automotive Supply Chain," PwC, accessed May 5, 2023, https://www.pwc.com/us/en/industries/industrial-products/library/electric-vehicles-supply-chain.html.

11. "An Electric Vehicle–Only Approach Would Lead to the Loss of Half a Million Jobs in the EU, Study Finds," CLEPA, European Association of Automotive Suppliers, June 12, 2021, https://clepa.eu/mediaroom/an-electric-vehicle-only-approach-would-lead-to-the-loss-of-half-a-million-jobs-in-the-eu-study-finds/.

12. Leo Geddes, Robin Nuttall, and Ellora-Julie Parekh, "The Pivotal Factors for Effective External Engagement," McKinsey & Company, May 2020, https://www.mckinsey.com/~/media/McKinsey/Business%20Functions/Strategy%20and%20Corporate%20Finance/Our%20Insights/The%20pivotal%20factors%20for%20effective%20external%20engagement/The-pivotal-factors-for-effective-external-engagement.pdf.

13. Jeb Blount, *Fanatical Prospecting* (Wiley, 2015), chap. 7.

14. Kevin Laczkowski, Tao Tan, and Matthias Winter, "The Numbers behind Successful Transformation," *McKinsey Quarterly,* October 7, 2019.

15. Alejandro Sandoval et al., "Transform the Whole Business, Not Just Parts," McKinsey & Company, October 10, 2019, https://www.mckinsey.com/capabilities/operations/our-insights/transform-the-whole-business-not-just-the-parts.

16. Michael Wade et al., *Orchestrating Transformation: How to Deliver Winning Performance with a Connected Approach to Change* (Global Center for Digital Business Transformation, 2019).

17. Rumelt, *Good Strategy, Bad Strategy.*

18. Edward E. Lawler III and Christopher G. Worley, *Built to Change: How to Achieve Sustained Organizational Effectiveness* (Jossey-Bass, 2005).

19. Dan Pinkney, "Digital Transformation Leaders Deliver Higher Profitability; Comprehensive and Systematic Orchestration Is Essential to Driving Full Potential Digital Acceleration," Bain & Company, January 22, 2018.

20. "Jack Welch's Passing Leaves a Management Legacy That Still Resonates," *Forbes,* March 3, 2020, https://www.forbes.com/sites/forrester/2020/03/03/jack-welchs-passing-leaves-a-management-legacy-that-still-resonates/?sh=1e54ae7834a0.

21. "The Elusive Agile Enterprise: How the Right Leadership Mindset, Workforce and Culture Can Transform Your Organization," Forbes Insights, 2018, https://www .scrumalliance.org/ScrumRedesignDEVSite/media/Forbes-Media/ScrumAlliance _REPORT_FINAL-WEB.pdf.

22. Aleksandra Zhbajnova-Mircheska and Ljupcho Antovski, "Transitioning of IT Companies from Waterfall to Agile Methodologies," ICT Innovations Conference Web Proceedings, 2020, accessed May 5, 2023, https://proceedings.ictinnovations .org/attachment/paper/534/transitioning-of-it-companies-from-waterfall-to-agile --methodologies.pdf.

23. Gary L. Neilson, Karla L. Martin, and Elizabeth Powers, "The Secrets to Successful Strategy Execution," *Harvard Business Review*, June 2008.

24. Carrig and Snell, *Strategic Execution*.

25. The second law of thermodynamics.

## Chapter 3

1. "Five Disruptive Trends Worth Watching," KPMG, accessed May 11, 2023, https:// www.kpmg.us/growth-strategy/five-disruptive-trends-worth-watching.html.

2. Regina A. Herzlinger, Robert S. Huckman, and Jenny Lesser, "Mayo Clinic: The 2020 Initiative," Harvard Business School Case 615–027 (Cambridge, MA: Harvard Business Publishing, 2014).

3. Bartlett, "Unilever's New Global Strategy."

4. Ali Farhoomand and W. H. Lo, "Microsoft: New Wine in an Old Bottle?," Case HK1039 (Asia Case Research Centre, University of Hong Kong, 2014).

5. Scott A. Snell, "Chalhoub Group: Transforming the Luxury Retailer," UVA-S-0319 (Charlottesville, VA: Darden Business Publishing, 2019).

6. "Inside Chalhoub Group's 900-Day Sprint Towards Digital Transformation," *Arabian Business*, August 7, 2018, https://www.arabianbusiness.com/industries/ retail/402045-abe-1928-900-days-counting.

7. Mark Raskino, "Avoid These 9 Corporate Digital Business Transformation Mistakes," *CDO Trends*, February 10, 2020.

8. This notion is originally attributed to Peter Drucker.

9. A. G. Lafley, "What Only the CEO Can Do," *Harvard Business Review,* May 2009.

10. Scott A. Snell et al., "The HR Ecosystem: Emerging Trend and a Future Research Agenda," in "The Ecosystem of Work and Organization: Theoretical Frameworks and Future Directions," special issue, *Human Resource Management* 62, no. 1 (January/February 2023): 5–14.

11. *Interconnected Economies: Benefiting from Global Value Chains* (Paris: OECD Publishing, 2013), https://doi.org/10.1787/9789264189560-en.

12. "Exclusive Q&A: Meet Mayo Clinic's Next CEO, Gianrico Farrugia," *Advisory Board* (blog), August 13, 2018.

13. Herzlinger, Huckman, and Lesser, "Mayo Clinic: The 2020 Initiative."

14. Lawler and Worley, *Built to Change*; Scott Keller, Mary Meaney, and Caroline Pung, "What Successful Transformations Share," McKinsey & Company, 2010; Scott

Keller and Colin Price, *Beyond Performance: How Great Organizations Build Ultimate Competitive Advantage* (Wiley, 2011).

15. Joan Magretta, "Why Business Models Matter," *Harvard Business Review*, May 2002.

16. Mark W. Johnson, Clayton M. Christensen, and Henning Kagermann, "Reinventing Your Business Model," *Harvard Business Review*, December 2008.

17. Alexander Osterwalder, "A Better Way to Think About Your Business Model," *Harvard Business Review,* May 6, 2013.

18. "Committing to Sustainability with Unilever CEO Paul Polman," McKinsey & Company, video, 4:03, May 16, 2014, https://www.youtube.com/watch?v=nShlnBJko5s&t=10s.

19. Andrew Saunders, "The MT Interview: Assuming His New Role in the Midst of a Global Recession," *Management Today*, March 1, 2011; Bartlett, "Unilever's New Global Strategy."

20. Mary Jo Foley, "Windows Phone 8: What's Microsoft's Developer Story?" *ZD-Net*, April 6, 2012.

21. Farhoomand and Lo, "Microsoft: New Wine in an Old Bottle?"

22. Ulrich Pidun, Martin Reeves, and Maximilian Schüssler, "Why Do Most Business Ecosystems Fail?" BCG, June 22, 2020, https://www.bcg.com/en-us/publications/2020/why-do-most-business-ecosystems-fail.

23. Paul Polman, "Captain Planet," interview by Adi Ignatius, *Harvard Business Review*, June 2012, https://hbr.org/2012/06/captain-planet.

24. Bartlett, "Unilever's New Global Strategy."

25. Polman, "Captain Planet."

26. "New, Disruptive Technologies & Trends in Your Industry: Hype or Reality?" Blue Canyon Partners, 2022, accessed May 11, 2023, https://bluecanyonpartners.com/new-disruptive-technologies-trends-in-your-industry-hype-or-reality/.

27. Ernest Hemingway, *The Sun Also Rises* (Scribner's, 1926).

28. Tamara Pupic, "Follow the Leader: Patrick Chalhoub, Co-CEO, Chalhoub Group," *Entrepreneur Middle East*, August 19, 2018.

29. "Inside Chalhoub Group's 900-Day Sprint."

30. "Inside Chalhoub Group's 900-Day Sprint."

31. Snell, "Chalhoub Group: Transforming the Luxury Retailer."

32. Joseph A. Schumpeter, *Capitalism, Socialism and Democracy* (London: Routledge, 1942; 1994), 82–83.

33. Ron Winslow, "Mayo Clinic's Unusual Challenge: Overhaul a Business That's Working," *Wall Street Journal*, June 2, 2017.

34. Carrig and Snell, *Strategic Execution*.

35. Steve Hill, "Five Disruptive Trends Worth Watching," KPMG, 2021, https://info.kpmg.us/news-perspectives/technology-innovation/five-disruptive-trends-worth-watching.html.

36. Jeff Galvin, Laura LaBerge, and Evan Williams, "The New Digital Edge: Rethinking Strategy for the Postpandemic Era," McKinsey Digital, May 26, 2021.

37. "New, Disruptive Technologies & Trends in Your Industry."

38. Clayton M. Christensen, Michael E. Raynor, and Rory McDonald, "What Is Disruptive Innovation?" *Harvard Business Review,* December 2015.

39. Rosabeth Moss Kanter, "Leadership for Change: Enduring Skills for Change Masters," Harvard Business School Case 9-304-062 (Cambridge, MA: Harvard Business Publishing, 2005).

40. Alfonso Natale, Thomas Poppensieker, and Michael Thun, "From Risk Management to Strategic Resilience," McKinsey & Company, March 9, 2022.

41. Herzlinger, Huckman, and Lesser, "Mayo Clinic: The 2020 Initiative."

42. Polman, "Captain Planet."

43. Herzlinger, Huckman, and Lesser, "Mayo Clinic: The 2020 Initiative."

44. Mark W. Johnson, Clayton M. Christensen, and Henning Kagermann, "Reinventing Your Business Model," *Harvard Business Review*, December 2008.

45. Carrig and Snell, *Strategic Transformation.*

46. Robert Coppenhaver, *From Voices to Results—Voice of Customer Questions, Tools and Analysis: Proven Techniques for Understanding and Engaging with Your Customers* (Pakt Publishing, 2018).

47. Snell, "Chalhoub Group: Transforming the Luxury Retailer"; "Chalhoub Group Modernizes the Customer Experience with Oracle Point of Service" (presentation, Chalhoub Group NRF 2018), https://www.oracle.com/webfolder/s/delivery_production/docs/FY16h1/doc31/Chalhoub.pdf.

48. Snell, "Chalhoub Group: Transforming the Luxury Retailer."

49. Herzlinger, Huckman, and Lesser, "Mayo Clinic: The 2020 Initiative."

50. "Quotations from the Doctors Mayo," Mayo Clinic: History & Heritage, accessed May 11, 2023, https://history.mayoclinic.org/toolkit/quotations/the-doctors-mayo.php.

51. Gordon Lubold, "Army Plans Major Cuts to Special-Operations Forces, Including Green Berets," *The Wall Street Journal,* October 5, 2023.

52. "Digitalisation," Chalhoub Group, accessed May 11, 2023, https://sustainabilityreport.chalhoubgroup.com/2018/leadership/digitalisation/;"The Evolving Face of Luxury in the Gulf: On Our Way to a New Norm?" Chalhoub Group White Paper, 2016, https://api.chalhoubgroup.com/content/uploads/Blogs/2016_Chalhoub_White_Paper _ENG-compresse.pdf; Snell, "Chalhoub Group: Transforming the Luxury Retailer."

53. Kevin Laczkowski, Tao Tan, and Matthias Winter, "The Numbers Behind Successful Transformation," *McKinsey Quarterly*, October 7, 2019.

54. Gary Hamel and C. K. Prahalad, *Competing for the Future* (Boston: Harvard Business Review, 1994).

55. Winslow, "Mayo Clinic's Unusual Challenge: Overhaul a Business That's Working."

56. Nadella, letter to employees.

57. Ian Sherr and Connie Guglielmo, "Microsoft's Hackathon Isn't Just about Fixing the World's Problems," *CNET*, August 20, 2018, https://www.cnet.com/culture/internet/microsofts-hackathon-isnt-just-about-fixing-the-worlds-problems/.

58. Francesca Gino, Allison Ciechanover, and Jeff Huizinga, "Culture Transformation at Microsoft: From 'Know it All' to 'Learn it All,'" Harvard Business School Case 921-004 (Cambridge, MA: Harvard Business Publishing, 2022).

59. Unilever annual report, 2014, https://www.slideshare.net/olafusimichael/unilever-annual-report-2014 Bartlett, "Unilever's New Global Strategy."

60. Kanter, "Leadership for Change: Enduring Skills for Change Masters."

61. Farhoomand and Lo, "Microsoft: New Wine in an Old Bottle?"

62. Ian Sherr and Connie Guglielmo, "This Is Not Your Father's Microsoft," *CNET,* August 30, 2018.

63. Carrig and Snell, *Strategic Execution.*

64. "Unlocking Value in Today's Disruptive Trends," KPMG, 2023, https://www.kpmg.us/growth-strategy/five-disruptive-trends-worth-watching.html.

65. David Lancefield and Christian Rangen, "4 Actions Transformational Leaders Take," *Harvard Business Review*, May 5, 2021, https://hbr.org/2021/05/4-actions-transformational-leaders-take.

*Chapter 4*

1. Bartlett, "Unilever's New Global Strategy."

2. Benjamin Landy, "Planet Airbnb: Inside Brian Chesky's Plans to Conquer a Reopened World," *Fast Company,* May 10, 2021; Benjamin C. Esty and Allison M. Ciechanover, "Airbnb during the Covid Pandemic: Stakeholder Capitalism Faces a Critical Test," Harvard Business School Case 9-221-050 (Cambridge, MA: Harvard Business Publishing, 2021); Benjamin C. Esty and Allison M. Ciechanover, "Airbnb Emerges from the Pandemic: Lessons for Stakeholder Governance (B)," Harvard Business School Case 9-222-003 (Cambridge, MA: Harvard Business Publishing, 2021).

3. Kim and Mauborgne, "Tipping Point Leadership."

4. Geddes, Nuttall, and Parekh, "The Pivotal Factors for Effective External Engagement."

5. Rosabeth Moss Kanter and Daniel Fox, "Uber and Stakeholders: Managing a New Way of Riding," Harvard Business School Case 9-315-139 (Cambridge, MA: Harvard Business Publishing, 2015).

6. Adam Lashinsky, "How Uber Is Swerving to Survive Post-Pandemic," *Fortune,* May 18, 2020, https://fortune.com/longform/coronavirus-uber-ipo-business-model-ceo-fortune-500/; M. G. Siegler, "Uber CEO: I Think I've Got 20,000 Years of Jail Time in Front of Me," TechCrunch, May 25, 2011, https://techcrunch.com/2011/05/25/uber-airbnb-jail-time/.

7. Jared Harris and Jenny Mead, "Uber: The Turbulent Rise of 'Everyone's Private Driver,'" UVA-S-0354 (Charlottesville, VA: Darden Business Publishing, 2022).

8. John Boitnott, "7 Fascinating Peter Thiel Quotes from TechCrunch Disrupt 2014," Inc., September 9, 2014, https://www.inc.com/john-boitnott/7-fascinating-peter-thiel-quotes-from-techcrunch-disrupt-2014.html.

9. Josh Constine, "Facebook's S-1 Letter from Zuckerberg Urges Understanding before Investment," TechCrunch, February 1, 2012, https://techcrunch.com/2012/02/01/facebook-ipo-letter/.

10. Preetika Rana, "What Happened When Uber's CEO Started Driving for Uber," *Wall Street Journal,* April 7, 2023.

11. Paul Polman, introduction to "Unilever Sustainable Living Plan: Small Actions, Big Difference," Unilever, 2011, accessed May 12, 2023, https://www.readkong.com/page/unilever-sustainable-living-plan-small-actions-big-8584553, 3.

12. R. Edward Freeman, *Strategic Management: A Stakeholder Approach* (Boston: Pitman, 1984).

13. Lafley, "What Only the CEO Can Do."

14. Tim Koller and Robin Nuttall, "How the E in ESG Creates Business Value," *McKinsey Sustainability*, June 29, 2020, https://www.mckinsey.com/business-functions/sustainability/our-insights/sustainability-blog/how-the-e-in-esg-creates-business-value.

15. Bernard Burnes and David Bargal, "Kurt Lewin: 70 Years On," *Journal of Change Management* 17, no. 2 (March 2017): 91–100.

16. Nora Eckert, "Ford's Talk of New EV-Selling Rules Rattles Some Dealers," *Wall Street Journal*, June 29, 2022.

17. Mike Colias and Nora Eckert, "GM Says Unfinished Cars to Hurt Quarterly Results," *Wall Street Journal*, July 1, 2022.

18. Joe Flint, "Hollywood Actors Join Writers on Strike," *Wall Street Journal*, July 14, 2023.

19. Scott Snell and Shad Morris, *Managing Human Resources* (Boston: Cengage Learning, 2019).

20. "Our Commitment," Business Roundtable, accessed May 12, 2023, https://opportunity.businessroundtable.org/ourcommitment/.

21. Kim and Mauborgne, "Tipping Point Leadership."

22. Bartlett, "Unilever's New Global Strategy."

23. Samuel B. Bacharach, *Get Them on Your Side* (Adams Media Corp, 2005).

24. "Edelman Trust Barometer," Edelman, March 2021, https://www.edelman.com/sites/g/files/aatuss191/files/2021-03/2021%20Edelman%20Trust%20Barometer.pdf.

25. James R. Detert and Amy C. Edmondson, "Implicit Voice Theories: Taken-for-Granted Rules of Self-Censorship at Work," *Academy of Management Journal* 54, no. 3 (2011): 461–88.

26. "Update About Our Extenuating Circumstances Policy," Airbnb, May 15, 2020, https://news.airbnb.com/update-about-our-extenuating-circumstances-policy/.

27. "A Letter to Hosts," Airbnb, March 30, 2020, https://news.airbnb.com/en-in/a-letter-to-hosts.

28. Aubrey Mendelow, "Stakeholder Mapping," *Proceedings of the 2nd International Conference on Information Systems, Cambridge, MA* 5, no. 2 (1991): 91.

29. Carrig and Snell, *Strategic Execution.*

30. Bartlett, "Unilever's New Global Strategy."

31. "CFO Insights: Effective Investor Relations (IR): Lessons from the Trenches," Deloitte, accessed May 12, 2023, https://www2.deloitte.com/us/en/pages/finance/articles/cfo-insights-effective-investor-relations-ir-lessons-activist-shareholders-value-challenges.html.

32. "Committing to Sustainability with Unilever CEO Paul Polman."

33. Kenneth W. Thomas and Ralph H. Kilmann, "Comparison of Four Instruments Measuring Conflict Behavior," *Psychological Reports* 42, no. 3 (1978): 1139–45.

34. "The Superhost Relief Fund," Airbnb, accessed May 12, 2023, https://www.airbnb.com/superhostrelief.

35. Andy Boynton, "Unilever's Paul Polman: CEOs Can't Be 'Slaves' to Shareholders," *Forbes*, July 20, 2015.

36. "15 Strategies for Balancing Competing Stakeholder Priorities," *Forbes,* March 23, 2022.

37. Kim and Mauborgne, "Tipping Point Leadership."

38. Bartlett, "Unilever's New Global Strategy."

39. "Unilever Sustainable Living Plan 2013," Unilever, 2013, accessed May 12, 2023, https://assets.unilever.com/files/92ui5egz/production/910902bc7c415bbb6fdd0d9474ccb10da1e7c671.pdf/slp_unilever-sustainable-living-plan-2013.pdf, 13.

40. "Airbnb Rode the Pandemic Wave, Now It Faces a Potential Recession," *Wall Street Journal,* August 4, 2022.

41. Anthony Fisher, "Why Do We Have a Department of Education? Jimmy Carter's Debt to a Teachers Union," *Reason*, February 7, 2017, https://reason.com/2017/02/07/department-of-education-jimmy-carter.

42. John P. Kotter, *Accelerate: Building Strategic Agility for a Faster-Moving World* (Boston: Harvard Business Review Press, 2014).

43. Kim and Mauborgne, "Tipping Point Leadership."

44. Kim and Mauborgne, "Tipping Point Leadership."

45. "Create Change, Embrace Crisis & Lead with Passion: Former NYPD Police Commissioner William Bratton Talks about What You Have to Do to Really Make an Impact as a Leader," *Inc.,* August 13, 2012.

46. Bob Tita and Austen Hufford, "Consumer Demand Snaps Back. Factories Can't Keep Up," *Wall Street Journal,* February 22, 2021.

## Chapter 5

1. Herzlinger, Huckman, and Lesser, "Mayo Clinic: The 2020 Initiative."

2. Snell, "Chalhoub Group: Transforming the Luxury Retailer."

3. Pinkney, "Digital Transformation Leaders Deliver Higher Profitability."

4. Michael Wade et al., *Orchestrating Transformation: How to Deliver Willing Performance with a Connected Approach to Change* (Global Center for Digital Business Transformation, 2019).

5. Snell, "Chalhoub Group: Transforming the Luxury Retailer."

6. Tamara Pupic, "Follow the Leader: Patrick Chalhoub, Co-CEO, Chalhoub Group," *Entrepreneur Middle East*, August 19, 2018.

7. "13 Industry Experts Share Reasons Companies Fail at Digital Transformation," *Forbes*, June 15, 2021.

8. Rainer Zitelmann, "What Focus Really Means: Learning from Bill Gates, Warren Buffett and Steve Jobs," *Forbes*, October 28, 2019.

9. "Satya Nadella Email to Employees on First Day as CEO," Microsoft News Center February 4, 2014, https://news.microsoft.com/2014/02/04/satya-nadella-email-to-employees-on-first-day-as-ceo/.

10. "Scaling for Impact: Summary of Progress 2014," Unilever, 2014, https://www.unilever.com/files/92ui5egz/production/2563c41835fe326900ec47fcdf9785b9b1aef70b.pdf, 11.

11. For more information, see Microsoft "Annual Report 2022," accessed May 18, 2023, https://www.microsoft.com/investor/reports/ar22/.

12. Herzlinger, Huckman, and Lesser, "Mayo Clinic: The 2020 Initiative."

13. Laurent-Pierre Baculard et al., "Orchestrating a Successful Digital Transformation," Bain & Company, November 22, 2017.

14. Herzlinger, Huckman, and Lesser, "Mayo Clinic: The 2020 Initiative."

15. Charles A. O'Reilly III and Michael L. Tushman, "Organizational Ambidexterity: Past, Present, and Future," *Academy of Management Perspectives* 27, no. 4 (2013): 324–38.

16. Baculard et al., "Orchestrating a Successful Digital Transformation."

17. Jim Collins, *Good to Great: Why Some Companies Make the Leap and Others Don't* (New York: Harper Business, 2001).

18. Carrig and Snell, *Strategic Execution*.

19. "Microsoft CEO Nadella's Memo on Leadership Changes," *The Wall Street Journal*, March 3, 2014.

20. Carrig and Snell, *Strategic Execution*.

21. Carrig and Snell, *Strategic Execution*.

22. Bartlett, "Unilever's New Global Strategy"; Lucia Moses and Nicholas Carlson, "Unilever's Keith Weed Says Business Case for the Company's Sustainable Brands Are Delivering 70% Of Its Growth," *Business Insider*, January 24, 2019.

23. Bartlett, "Unilever's New Global Strategy."

24. "Digitalization and Transformation," 2019 Sustainability Report, Chalhoub Group.

25. Rania Masri El Khatib, "Shift—Chalhoub Group: 900-Day Transformation," 2021, https://www.raniamasrielkhatib.com/shift---chalhoub-group; "Inside Chalhoub Group's 900-Day Sprint Towards Digital Transformation."

26. Stanley McChrystal, *Team of Teams: New Rules of Engagement for a Complex World* (New York: Portfolio, 2015).

27. Baculard et al., "Orchestrating a Successful Digital Transformation."

28. Kevin Laczkowski, Tao Tan, and Matthias Winter, "The Numbers behind Successful Transformation," *McKinsey Quarterly*, October 7, 2019.

29. Snell, "Chalhoub Group: Transforming the Luxury Retailer"; "Farfetch and Chalhoub Group Enter Joint Venture Partnership," Sandbridge Capital, February 1, 2018.

30. Snell, "Chalhoub Group: Transforming the Luxury Retailer"; "Farfetch and Chalhoub Group Enter Joint Venture Partnership."

31. Herzlinger, Huckman, and Lesser, "Mayo Clinic: The 2020 Initiative."

32. Andrew C. Inkpen and Eric W. K. Tsang, "Learning and Strategic Alliances," *Academy of Management Annals* 1, no. 1 (2007): 479–511.

33. Clayton M. Christensen et al., "The Big Idea: The New M&A Playbook," *Harvard Business Review*, March 2011.

34. Colin Wittmer and John D. Potter, "Transformational M&A," PwC, https://www.pwc.com/us/en/services/consulting/deals/library/transformational-mergers-and-acquisitions.html.

35. Clayton M. Christensen et al., "The New M&A Playbook," *Harvard Business Review*, March 2011.

36. Herzlinger, Huckman, and Lesser, "Mayo Clinic: The 2020 Initiative."

37. Jay R. Galbraith, *Designing the Customer-Centric Organization: A Guide to Strategy, Structure, and Process* (Jossey-Bass, 2005).

38. Carrig and Snell, *Strategic Execution*.

39. Carrig and Snell, *Strategic Execution*.

40. Steve Ballmer, memo to all Microsoft employees, July 11, 2013.

41. Ballmer, memo to all Microsoft employees.

42. Carrig and Snell, *Strategic Execution*.

43. Paul R. Lawrence and Jay W. Lorsch, "Differentiation and Integration in Complex Organizations," *Administrative Science Quarterly* 12, no. 1 (1967): 1–47.

44. "Gartner Forecasts Worldwide IT Spending to Reach $4 Trillion in 2021"; Nathan Furr et al., "The 4 Pillars of Successful Digital Transformation," *Harvard Business Review*, January 2022.

45. Jeff Galvin, Laura LaBerge, and Evan Williams, "The New Digital Edge: Rethinking Strategy for the Postpandemic Era," McKinsey Digital, May 26, 2021; Tabrizi et al., "Digital Transformation Is Not about Technology."

46. Snell et al., "The HR Ecosystem."

47. Alexandra Larkin, "How AI Is Already Reshaping White-Collar Work," *Wall Street Journal*, July 6, 2023.

48. Rose Spicer, "Luxury Retailer Chalhoub Modernizes the Customer Experience with Oracle Point of Service," Oracle Retail Blog, January 15, 2018.

49. "Inside Chalhoub Group's 900-Day Sprint Towards Digital Transformation," *Arabian Business*, August 7, 2018.

50. Snell et al., "HR Ecosystem."

51. "Simplify Life at Work with a Single System to Manage Your Business," Aberdeen Group, 2014.

52. Snell, "Chalhoub Group: Transforming the Luxury Retailer."

53. Snell, "Chalhoub Group: Transforming the Luxury Retailer"; "Farfetch and Chalhoub Group Enter Joint Venture Partnership."

54. Nicolaj Siggelkow and Christian Terwiesch, *Connected Strategy: Building Continuous Customer Relationships for Competitive Advantage* (Cambridge, MA: Harvard Business Publishing, 2019).

55. Anusha Dhasarathy et al., "How to Become 'Tech Forward': A Technology-Transformation Approach That Works," McKinsey Digital, November 2, 2020.

56. Tabrizi et al., "Digital Transformation Is Not about Technology."

57. Peter Killing, Thomas Malnight, and Tracey Keys, *Must-Win Battles* (Financial Times Prentice Hall, 2005).

*Chapter 6*

1. Tamara Pupic, "Follow the Leader: Patrick Chalhoub, Co-CEO, Chalhoub Group," *Entrepreneur Middle East*, August 19, 2018.

2. Carrig and Snell, *Strategic Execution*.

3. Gianrico Farrugia and Halena Gazelka, "New Final Mayo Clinic Podcast," April 9, 2021, 27:21.

4. Kenneth Burke, *Permanence and Change* (New York: New Republic, 1935), 70.

5. Carrig and Snell, *Strategic Execution*; Donald Sull, Rebecca Homkes, and Charles Sull, "Why Strategy Execution Unravels—and What to Do about It," *Harvard Business Review*, March 2015.

6. On a personal note, Dr. Baldwin passed away this past year. I miss his uncanny brilliance.

7. Dorothy A. Leonard, "Core Capability and Core Rigidities: A Paradox in Managing New Product Development," *Strategic Management Journal* 13, no. 1 (June 1992): 111–25.

8. Dennis Carey et al., "The CEO's Playbook for a Successful Digital Transformation," *Harvard Business Review,* December 20, 2021.

9. Ben Cohen, "What the NFL Playoffs and Tech Layoffs Have in Common," *Wall Street Journal*, January 26, 2023.

10. Carrig and Snell, *Strategic Execution*.

11. Thanks to Johnny C. Taylor for his advice and insights on this book. See also Johnny C. Taylor, *Reset: A Leader's Guide to Work in an Age of Upheaval* (New York: Hachette Book Group, 2021).

12. Gianrico Farrugia and Thomas H. Lee, "Cure, Connect, Transform: Three Mayo Clinic Strategy Components for Servant Leaders," *New England Journal of Medicine* (*NEJM*) Catalyst, July 9, 2020.

13. Carrig and Snell, *Strategic Execution*.

14. "Do Cats Always Land on Their Feet?," Purina, accessed May 18, 2023, https://www.purina.ca/articles/cat/behaviour/why-do-cats-land-on-their-feet.

15. Farrugia and Gazelka, "New Final Mayo Clinic Podcast."

16. Farrugia and Gazelka, "New Final Mayo Clinic Podcast."

17. From the poem "If—," by Rudyard Kipling.

18. Wesley M. Cohen and Daniel A. Levinthal, "Absorptive Capacity: A New Perspective on Learning and Innovation," in "Technology, Organizations, and Innovation," special issue, *Administrative Science Quarterly* 35, no. 1 (1990): 128–52.

19. "Inside Chalhoub Group's 900-Day Sprint Towards Digital Transformation," *Arabian Business*, August 7, 2018.

20. Rose Spicer, "Luxury Retailer Chalhoub Modernizes the Customer Experience with Oracle Point of Service," *Oracle Retail Blog*, February 9, 2020, https://blogs.oracle.com/retail/post/luxury-retailer-chalhoub-modernizes-the -customer-experience-with-oracle-point-of-service; "Chalhoub Group—Rooted in Luxury," *Retail and Leisure International*, May 10, 2022, https://www.rli.uk.com/ chalhoub-group-rooted-in-luxury/.

21. "Businesses Are Now More Educated about CX, Says Chalhoub Group Official," *Khaleej Times*, July 29, 2022, https://www.khaleejtimes.com/business/ businesses-are-now-more-educated-about-cx-says-chalhoub-group-official.

22. Phillip Reese, "Cell Phone Data Reveals How COVID-19 Made Us Hunker Down, and Start Moving Again," *Los Angeles Times*, March 16, 2021.

23. George S. Day and Paul J. H. Schoemaker, *Peripheral Vision: Detecting the Weak Signals That Will Make or Break Your Company* (Boston, MA: Harvard Business School Press, 2006).

24. "Dubai-Based Chalhoub Group's Retail Tech Accelerator Greenhouse Is Now Accepting Applications for the Second Cohort," *menabytes*, February 12, 2019, https:// www.menabytes.com/greenhouse-second-cohort-applications/.

25. Tamara Pupic, "Follow the Leader: Patrick Chalhoub, Co-CEO, Chalhoub Group," *Entrepreneur Middle East*, August 19, 2018.

26. Mita Srinivasan, "L'Occitane MENA and Chalhoub Group Launch Retail-Tech Accelerator," SME10x.com, August 30, 2022.

27. Rashid Hassan Reem Walid, "GCC Luxury Market to Hit $11bn by 2023: Chalhoub Group," *Arab News*, March 27, 2022.

28. "Economic Development," Mayo Clinic, accessed May 18, 2023, https:// businessdevelopment.mayoclinic.org/economic-development/.

29. Mayo Clinic Innovation Exchange, accessed May 18, 2023, https://innovation exchange.mayoclinic.org/.

30. "About Us," accessed May 18, 2023, https://businessdevelopment.mayoclinic .org/about/#our-story.

31. Carrig and Snell, *Strategic Execution*.

32. Dorothy Leonard-Barton, "The Factory as a Learning Laboratory," *Sloan Management Review*, October 15, 1992.

33. Carrig and Snell, *Strategic Execution*.

34. Christopher G. Worley, Thomas Williams, and Edward E. Lawler III, *The Agility Factor: Building Adaptable Organizations for Superior Performance* (Jossey-Bass, 2014).

35. Kim and Mauborgne, "Tipping Point Leadership."

36. "Inside Chalhoub Group's 900-Day Sprint Towards Digital Transformation."

37. "Digitalisation," 2018 Sustainability Report, Chalhoub Group, accessed October 24, 2019, https://www.sustainabilityreport.chalhoubgroup.com/2018/leadership/ digitalisation/.

38. "Inside Chalhoub Group's 900-Day Sprint Towards Digital Transformation."

39. "Inside Chalhoub Group's 900-Day Sprint Towards Digital Transformation."

40. Farrugia and Lee, "Cure, Connect, Transform: Three Mayo Clinic Strategy Components for Servant Leaders."

41. Farrugia and Lee, "Cure, Connect, Transform: Three Mayo Clinic Strategy Components for Servant Leaders."

42. Carrig and Snell, *Strategic Execution.*

43. Carrig and Snell, *Strategic Execution.*

44. Carrig and Snell, *Strategic Execution.*

45. Dina Bass, "Satya Nadella Talks Microsoft at Middle Age," *Bloomberg Businessweek,* August 4, 2016.

46. Sherr and Guglielmo, "This Is Not Your Father's Microsoft"; Satya Nadella, *Hit Refresh: The Quest to Rediscover Microsoft's Soul and Imagine a Better Future for Everyone* (Harper Business, 2017).

47. Rebecca Zucker and Darin Rowell, "Six Strategies for Leading Through Uncertainty," *Harvard Business Review*, April 26, 2021.

48. Carrig and Snell, *Strategic Execution.*

49. Farrugia and Gazelka, "New Final Mayo Clinic Podcast."

50. Farrugia and Gazelka, "New Final Mayo Clinic Podcast."

51. Farrugia and Lee, "Cure, Connect, Transform: Three Mayo Clinic Strategy Components for Servant Leaders."

52. Carrig and Snell, *Strategic Execution.*

53. Pupic, "Follow the Leader: Patrick Chalhoub"; "Middle East Luxury Retailer Chalhoub Group Invites Applications for Its Retail Accelerator," *Entrepreneur Middle East*, June 21, 2018.

54. "What Is Ibtikar?" The Greenhouse, Chalhoub Group, accessed October 24, 2019, https://www.chalhoubgreenhouse.com/ibtikar.

55. Pupic, "Follow the Leader: Patrick Chalhoub."

56. Farrugia and Gazelka, "New Final Mayo Clinic Podcast."

57. Mayo Clinic Business Development, accessed May 18, 2023, https://businessdevelopment.mayoclinic.org/about/.

58. Carrig and Snell, *Strategic Execution.*

59. Farrugia and Gazelka, "New Final Mayo Clinic Podcast."

60. Carrig and Snell, *Strategic Execution.*

61. Stephen Hall, Dan Lovallo, and Reinier Musters, "How to Put Your Money Where Your Strategy Is," *McKinsey Quarterly*, March 1, 2012.

62. Hall, Lovallo, and Musters, "How to Put Your Money Where Your Strategy Is."

63. Sull, Homkes, and Sull, "Why Strategy Execution Unravels."

64. Carrig and Snell, *Strategic Execution.*

65. Carrig and Snell, *Strategic Execution.*

66. Lafley, "What Only the CEO Can Do."

67. "President's Strategic Initiative Fund, Mayo Clinic," accessed May 18, 2023, https://www.mayoclinic.org/giving-to-mayo-clinic/our-priorities/presidents-strategic-initiative-fund.

68. Sull, Homkes, and Sull, "Why Strategy Execution Unravels."

69. Carrig and Snell, *Strategic Execution.*

70. Carrig and Snell, *Strategic Execution.*

71. Carrig and Snell, *Strategic Execution.*

72. Carla O'Dell and C. Jackson Grayson, *If Only We Knew What We Know* (Free Press: 1998).

73. Gary Neilson, Karla Martin, and Elizabeth Powers, "The Secrets to Successful Strategy Execution," *Harvard Business Review*, June 2008.

74. Constance E. Helfat et al., *Dynamic Capabilities: Understanding Strategic Change in Organizations* (Malden, MA: Blackwell, 2007); David J. Teece, Gary Pisano, and Amy Shuen, "Dynamic Capabilities and Strategic Management," *Strategic Management Journal* 18, no. 7 (August 1997): 509–33.

75. Nassim Nicholas Taleb, *Antifragile: Things That Gain from Disorder* (Random House, 2012).

76. Farrugia and Gazelka, "New Final Mayo Clinic Podcast."

77. This and the following paragraph rely on Carrig and Snell, *Strategic Execution.*

## Chapter 7

1. Miguel De Cervantes Saavedra, *Don Quixote* (Penguin Classics, 2003).

2. Gauthier Van Eetvelde, James Stanford, and Josh Sens, "70% of Strategic Initiatives at Hospitals Fail—How to Make Yours Succeed," *Objective Health* (webinar), September 19, 2012; Scott Keller and Colin Price, *Beyond Performance: How Great Organizations Build Ultimate Competitive Advantage* (Wiley, 2011); Sohil Kalra et al., "Breaching the Great Wall to Scale," McKinsey & Company, December 11, 2020.

3. Jared D. Harris and Michael J. Lenox, *The Strategist's Toolkit* (Charlottesville, VA: Darden Business Publishing, 2013); Jeanne Liedtka and Tim Ogilvie, *Designing for Growth: A Design Thinking Tool Kit for Managers* (New York: Columbia Business School Publishing, 2011).

4. Harris and Lenox, *The Strategist's Toolkit*; Liedtka and Ogilvie, *Designing for Growth.*

5. Carrig and Snell, *Strategic Execution.*

6. Jens Jahn et al., "Are You Ready to Transform?" Boston Consulting Group, January 6, 2020.

7. Van Eetvelde, Stanford, and Sens, "70% of Strategic Initiatives at Hospitals Fail"; Keller and Price, *Beyond Performance*; Kalra et al., "Breaching the Great Wall to Scale."

8. Carrig and Snell, *Strategic Execution.*

9. Mary Walton, *The Deming Management Method* (New York: Dodd, Mead & Company, 1986).

10. Kalra et al., "Breaching the Great Wall to Scale."

11. Kalra et al., "Breaching the Great Wall to Scale."

12. Chris Argyris, "Teaching Smart People How to Learn," *Harvard Business Review* 69, no. 3 (May–June 1991): 99–109.

13. Marilyn Darling, Charles Parry, and Joseph Moore, "Learning in the Thick of It," *Harvard Business Review*, July–August 2005; John E. Morrison and Larry L. Meliza, "Foundations of the After-Action Review Process," Defense Technical Information Center, July 1, 1997; Angus Fletcher, Preston B. Cline, and Matthew Hoffman, "A Better Approach to After-Action Reviews," *Harvard Business Review*, January 12, 2023.

# INDEX